AF182744

CONSTITUTIONAL EFFECTIVENESS

This book presents a unique account of the social and political impacts of the German Basic Law on the German Republic from 1949 to the present day. It considers the way in which the history of the Federal Republic of Germany has been decisively influenced by its Constitution, the Basic Law of 1949, and by the jurisprudence of the Federal Constitutional Court.

The book argues that the historiography of the Federal Republic does little to reflect this influence. The Basic Law is mentioned and so occasionally are rulings of the Federal Constitutional Court. But the reader does not get the impression that they were of specific importance in Germany before and after reunification.

Legal scholars, on the other hand, are concerned about the legal consequences of the Basic Law, but do not analyse its impact in the real world. There is, thus, a gap between the two disciplines – one not being familiar with social reality, the other not familiar with the normativity of the law. The history of the effectiveness of the constitution falls into this gap.

In this book, Dieter Grimm, himself a Justice of the Federal Constitutional Court from 1987 to 1999 and an expert on interdisciplinary research in law, history and political science, guides the reader through important developments and events that were determined or influenced by the constitution and its judicial interpretation.

Constitutional Effectiveness

The Case of Germany's Basic Law

Dieter Grimm

•HART•

OXFORD • LONDON • NEW YORK • NEW DELHI • SYDNEY

HART PUBLISHING

Bloomsbury Publishing Plc

Kemp House, Chawley Park, Cumnor Hill, Oxford, OX2 9PH, UK

1385 Broadway, New York, NY 10018, USA

Bloomsbury Publishing Ireland Limited, 29 Earlsfort Terrace, Dublin 2, D02 AY28, Ireland

HART PUBLISHING, the Hart/Stag logo, BLOOMSBURY and the Diana logo are trademarks of Bloomsbury Publishing Plc

First published in Great Britain 2026

1

Copyright © Dieter Grimm, 2026

Dieter Grimm has asserted his right under the Copyright, Designs and Patents Act 1988 to be identified as Author of this work.

All rights reserved. No part of this publication may be: i) reproduced or transmitted in any form, electronic or mechanical, including photocopying, recording or by means of any information storage or retrieval system without prior permission in writing from the publishers; or ii) used or reproduced in any way for the training, development or operation of artificial intelligence (AI) technologies, including generative AI technologies. The rights holders expressly reserve this publication from the text and data mining exception as per Article 4(3) of the Digital Single Market Directive (EU) 2019/790.

While every care has been taken to ensure the accuracy of this work, no responsibility for loss or damage occasioned to any person acting or refraining from action as a result of any statement in it can be accepted by the authors, editors or publishers.

All UK Government legislation and other public sector information used in the work is Crown Copyright ©. All House of Lords and House of Commons information used in the work is Parliamentary Copyright ©. This information is reused under the terms of the Open Government Licence v3.0 (http://www.nationalarchives.gov.uk/doc/open-government-licence/version/3) except where otherwise stated.

All Eur-lex material used in the work is © European Union, http://eur-lex.europa.eu/, 1998–2026.

A catalogue record for this book is available from the British Library.

A catalogue record for this book is available from the Library of Congress.

Library of Congress Control Number: 2025951321

ISBN: HB: 978-1-50998-889-1
ePDF: 978-1-50998-887-7
ePub: 978-1-50998-888-4

Typeset by Compuscript Ltd, Shannon
Printed and bound in Great Britain by TJ Books, Padstow, Cornwall

MIX
Paper | Supporting responsible forestry
FSC® C013056

For product safety related questions contact productsafety@bloomsbury.com

To find out more about our authors and books visit www.hartpublishing.co.uk. Here you will find extracts, author information, details of forthcoming events and the option to sign up for our newsletters.

Originally published in German as *Die Historiker und die Verfassung*
(Munich: Beck, 2022).

Translated for the present volume by Raymond Kerr.

The translation was made possible by a generous grant from the
Carl Friedrich von Siemens-Stiftung, Munich.

PREFACE

The origin of this book is a lecture that I delivered a few years ago at the Carl Friedrich von Siemens Foundation in Munich, entitled '*Kann man die Geschichte der Bundesrepublik ohne ihre Verfassungsgeschichte schreiben?*' ('Can the history of the Federal Republic be written without the history of its constitution?'). The reason for the title is that this was precisely what had been done in various general histories of the Federal Republic that I had read. The Basic Law and its interpretation and application, chiefly by the Federal Constitutional Court (FCC), played a comparatively insignificant role in those histories. A different view is taken by the general public, not to mention scholars of constitutional law. I wanted to explore the reasons for that discrepancy.

Heinrich Meier, Managing Director of the Siemens Foundation, who had invited me, suggested that I publish the lecture. Wolfgang Beck, who was in the audience, urged me to expand it into a book. Wolfgang Beck and Heinrich Meier are thus, as it were, the 'fathers' of the work. The role of midwife was played by the pandemic. Despite all the restrictions and losses that it entailed, it also gave me an entirely unexpected amount of time, which helped with the plan for the book. The manuscript, or parts of it, had been read through at various stages in its development by five critical readers from various countries, disciplines and research fields, namely Aurore Gaillet, Ingrid Gilcher-Holtey, Jürgen Kocka, Barbara Stollberg-Rilinger and Rainer Wahl. I also regard them as key members of the obstetrics team and owe them a great debt of gratitude.

The book is not intended as a constitutional history of the Federal Republic, nor is it a substitute for such a work. It has a more modest aim, namely to show where the history of the Federal Republic cannot be adequately understood without its constitutional history. By the back door, however, it has become a contribution on the history of the reception and impact of the Basic Law and of its interpretation and application by the FCC, a history which, as such, has never yet been written and can only emerge from a combined review of legal, politological and historical research. Perhaps this book will serve as an inspiration in that respect.

Dieter Grimm
Berlin, April 2022

PRELIMINARY REMARK ON THE SELECTION OF HISTORICAL LITERATURE FOR EXAMINATION

The literature under examination comprises comprehensive presentations of the history of the Federal Republic which have appeared since the *caesura* of reunification. Older works on the history of the Federal Republic, notably the five-volume *Geschichte der Bundesrepublik Deutschland* edited by Karl Dieter Bracher, Theodor Eschenburg, Joachim C Fest and Eberhard Jäckel, which covers the period up to 1982, have not been taken into consideration. Nor does the examination include newer books that deal only with one phase of that history, such as Andreas Wirsching's *Abschied vom Provisorium* or Christoph Kleßmann's history of Germany from 1944 to 1955 (*Die doppelte Staatsgründung*) and from 1955 to 1970 (*Zwei Staaten, eine Nation*). It does, however, cover the two part-volumes 19 and 19A of the *Oldenbourg Grundriss der Geschichte* series, although they were written by different authors. Two works in which the history of the Federal Republic is presented by political scientists (Dietrich Thränhardt's *Geschichte der Bundesrepublik Deutschland* (Suhrkamp, 1996) and Peter Graf Kielmansegg's *Nach der Katastrophe. Eine Geschichte des geteilten Deutschland* (Siedler, 2000)) have not been taken into account either, although it would have been interesting to see whether, in terms of the focus of the present work – the role of the Basic Law and constitutional adjudication – they differ from the historians' portrayals. I have also chosen not to include *Die Geschichte der Bundesrepublik Deutschland* by Guido Thiemeyer, because its title is misleading, as it is really a history of the internationalisation and Europeanisation of the Federal Republic. I have likewise disregarded the short version of Manfred Görtemaker's vast work (*Kleine Geschichte der Bundesrepublik Deutschland*) as well as Bernd Stöver's book *Die Bundesrepublik Deutschland* (Wissenschaftliche Buchgesellschaft, 2002) from the *Kontroversen um die Geschichte* series, because its declared purpose is to treat only a selection of 'interpretation controversies'. In particular, the monographs and essays of history scholars have been passed over, even though examples of a sharper focus on constitutional history are to be found there. This restriction seems warranted, however, because the general public's conception is determined by comprehensive presentations, not by specialised works, and because students of history, for whom modern history is, of course, only a small part of their field of study, will resort primarily to didactic literature.

The analysed works can be divided into the large comprehensive treatments dedicated to the history of the Federal Republic; the large comprehensive treatments which are part of a chronologically broader work, study literature – in which I have included, despite some hesitation, Christian Henrich-Franke's book, because it resembles a lecture script – and, finally, the three short histories from the *CH Beck Wissen* series.

Large Comprehensive Treatments of the History of the Federal Republic

1. Manfred Görtemaker, *Geschichte der Bundesrepublik Deutschland. Von der Gründung bis zur Gegenwart* (CH Beck, 1999) 915 pages.
2. Edgar Wolfrum, *Die geglückte Demokratie. Geschichte der Bundesrepublik von ihren Anfängen bis zur Gegenwart* (Klett-Cotta, 2006) 694 pages.
3. Eckart Conze, *Die Suche nach Sicherheit. Eine Geschichte der Bundesrepublik Deutschland von 1949 bis zur Gegenwart* (Siedler, 2009) 1071 pages.

Large Comprehensive Treatments in more Extensive Works

4. Heinrich August Winkler, *Der lange Weg nach Westen*, Vol 2 of *Deutsche Geschichte vom 'Dritten Reich' bis zur Wiedervereinigung* (CH Beck, 2000) from ch 2, 626 pages; English: *Germany: The Long Road West. 1933–1990* (Oxford University Press, 2007) 704 pages.
5. Hans-Ulrich Wehler, *Deutsche Gesellschaftsgeschichte*, Vol 5, *Bundesrepublik und DDR 1949–1990* (CH Beck, 2008) 529 pages.
6. Ulrich Herbert, *Geschichte Deutschlands im 20. Jahrhundert*, parts IV and V (CH Beck, 2014) 905 pages; English: *A History of 20th-Century Germany* (Oxford University Press, 2019) 1264 pages.

Study Literature

7.
   (a) Adolf M Birke, *Die Bundesrepublik Deutschland. Verfassung, Parlament und Parteien* (Oldenbourg, 1997) 153 pages.
   (b) New edition, edited by Udo Wengst (Oldenbourg, 2010) 195 pages.
8.
   (a) Rudolf Morsey, *Die Bundesrepublik Deutschland 1949 bis 1969*, 5th edn (Oldenbourg, 2007) 343 pages.
   (b) Andreas Rödder, *Die Bundesrepublik Deutschland 1969 bis 1990* (Oldenbourg, 2004) 330 pages.
9. Christian Henrich-Franke, *Geschichte der Bundesrepublik Deutschland. Von der Gründung 1949 bis zur Gegenwart* (marix verlag, 2019) 220 pages.

Short Treatments

10. Maria-Luise Recker, *Geschichte der Bundesrepublik Deutschland*, 3rd edn (CH Beck, 2009) 128 pages.
11. Andreas Wirsching, *Deutsche Geschichte im 20. Jahrhundert*, 3rd edn (CH Beck, 2011) chs IV–VI, 42 pages.
12. Dominik Geppert, *Geschichte der Bundesrepublik Deutschland* (CH Beck, 2021) 128 pages.

CONTENTS

TABLE OF CASES

1

Constitutional History and General History

I. The Basic Law as a Source for the Historiography of the Federal Republic

The Basic Law enjoys the reputation of being a successful and effective constitution. Scholars of constitutional law confirm that assessment time and again. And public opinion is similarly convinced. As can be heard and read at every jubilee of the constitution, the Basic Law has been a stroke of fortune for the country, especially when measured against the fate of the Weimar Constitution. According to that view, the generally successful way in which the Federal Republic has developed, by contrast with the Weimar Republic, is not least due to its constitution, the best one that Germany has ever had, as is frequently said. It has steadily grown in public esteem. Ultimately, what has emerged is something as unusual as a 'constitutional patriotism', in other words a sense of pride and social cohesion rooted specifically in the constitution rather than, for example, in the nation or in the heroic phases of its history.

If, on the other hand, one examines the general histories of the Federal Republic that have appeared in considerable numbers since the *caesura* of reunification, they do not confirm the great significance of the Basic Law. They do not contest it either, certainly, but largely manage without it. This does not mean that the Basic Law is entirely disregarded. Its genesis and the main elements of its content have their place in those histories. It is not evident from their portrayals, however, that the Basic Law, once it had entered into force, played a significant role in the subsequent development of the Federal Republic. Only occasionally does a constitutional provision or a Constitutional Court ruling flash across the historians' pages, but it quickly dies away without any significant follow-up. It does not appear to belong to the key factors in the development of the Federal Republic.

How does that contrast come about? Is the importance of the constitution overestimated by the public, the media and legal scholars? Or are historians overlooking an essential aspect of their subject? There are limits, it is true, to what is possible. General history is not total history, even though individual schools of thought have made that claim. It is predominantly understood as political history. There is also room, in varying degrees, for other major fields, such as social, economic and cultural history. Specialised branches – the histories of art, medicine, philosophy, etc – also feature, though their exponents are mostly representatives of those other disciplines rather than historians. Given the futility of any quest for total history and the need to prioritise and filter, no one will accuse a historian of having disregarded, say, the history of architecture or of hygiene.

But does the same apply to constitutional history? Is the history of architecture dispensable, but that of the constitution indispensable? To rephrase the question, do constitutional and legal history rank alongside social, economic and cultural history as aspects that general historians today can no longer bypass? Or do they belong to the long list of special branches of history which are given space in the general portrayal of an era, depending on the historian's aims and the scope of his or her work, but which general historians may also choose to disregard without running the risk of failing in their task?[1] The answer requires clarification of the relationship between the constitution and politics. If the latter cannot be adequately understood without the former, its neglect would be a flaw. Otherwise there would be no compelling reason to include it in a general history of the Federal Republic.

Nothing of general applicability can be said on this point. Constitutions in the sense in which we normally understand them today have not always existed, nor do they exist everywhere. Although every political entity *is* constituted, not every one of them *has* a constitution. If political entities – normally states – have constitutions, that does not mean that equal importance attaches to those constitutions everywhere. There are many possible distinctions and classifications.[2] One of the main distinctions is between effective and ineffective constitutions. Numerous gradations are conceivable between those two poles. One and the same constitution may slide from one notch to another. The significance of constitutions can alter when the context changes. There is little for historians to say about ineffective constitutions other than, perhaps, why they are ineffective and what it means in turn for a country to have an insignificant constitution.

The term 'constitution', when used in connection with the history of the Federal Republic, refers to the kind of modern state constitution that emerged from the two great revolutions of the late eighteenth century.[3] This differs from the

[1] Hans-Ulrich Wehler, who, with his concept of social history, seeks to depict the totality of society but is aware at the same time of the impossibility of achieving that goal, deals in the introduction to his work with this question – see *Deutsche Gesellschaftsgeschichte*, vol 1 (CH Beck, 1987) 6–30 – but without considering the realm of law. On this point, see my opinion in Paul Nolte et al (eds), *Perspektiven der Gesellschaftsgeschichte* (CH Beck, 2000) 47, reproduced in the appendix to the present book. Wehler's response to my opinion is set out in the preface to vol IV of *Deutsche Gesellschaftsgeschichte* (CH Beck, 2003) XVII f.

[2] See Dieter Grimm, 'Types of Constitutions' in Michel Rosenfeld and András Sajó (eds), *The Oxford Handbook of Comparative Constitutional Law* (Oxford University Press, 2012) 98.

[3] See Dieter Grimm, 'Entstehungs- und Wirkungsbedingungen des modernen Konstitutionalismus' in idem, *Die Zukunft der Verfassung*, 3rd edn (Suhrkamp, 2002) 31; English: 'Conditions for the Emergence and Effectiveness of Modern Constitutionalism' in *Constitutionalism: Past, Present, and Future* (Oxford University Press, 2016) 41; idem, *Deutsche Verfassungsgeschichte*, 4th edn (Suhrkamp, 2015) 10 ff; 'Ursprung und Wandel der Verfassung' in idem, *Die Zukunft der Verfassung II* (Suhrkamp, 2012) 11; English: 'The Origins and Transformation of the Concept of the Constitution' in *Constitutionalism: Past, Present, and Future* (Oxford University Press, 2016) 3.

pre-modern instruments governing political rule in that the latter presuppose the existence of legitimate public power and only limit its exercise in certain respects. On the contrary, it constitutes legitimate rule in the first place and regulates its establishment and exercise systematically and comprehensively, not just in a piecemeal fashion and for the benefit of a few privileged individuals in the manner of the older social contracts, electoral capitulations, etc. However, since a constitution cannot fulfil its purpose unless rulers and their acts are subject to it, the modern constitution must enjoy primacy. Political rule is legitimate only if it is exercised on the basis and within the limits of the constitution.

There are, it is true, state constitutions which only partly meet these criteria, such as the German constitutions of the nineteenth century, which did not establish political rule but merely modified it. Such constitutions, however, have always been regarded as inferior forms of modern constitutionalism. The Basic Law is not one of those. Although it does not bear the name 'constitution' and was intended only as a temporary arrangement for a transitional period that would end with reunification, it is a constitution in the full modern sense of the term. It gave the historiography of the Federal Republic its object. The Federal Republic of Germany came into being with the entry into force of the Basic Law. Before 23 May 1949 there was no Federal Republic, and from then on it existed in the form prescribed by the Basic Law, which served henceforth as the mandatory yardstick for all political activity.

Yet the modern constitution is itself a product of politics. It stems from a political decision which, for its part, is not subject to binding legal provisions but which brings forth, in the first place, the entity endowed with the capacity and mandate to legislate. That is the paradox of the constituent power, a paradox which legal scholars just cannot resolve and which they circumvent either by fictionalising (Hans Kelsen's hypothetical basic norm) or by externalising (Georg Jellinek's normative force of the factual). From the historians' perspective, this is of no consequence. What counts for them is the value of the constituent act and of the constitution generated by it as sources of information and explanation regarding the conditions, developments and events with which historians deal.

This value attaches first of all to the legal rules themselves, to the extent that they formulate the structural and substantive conditions for future political activity. It is then no longer a matter of what politicians want and are able to do but also what they are permitted or obliged to do. But the value is not confined to the legal substance of the constitution. As products of a political decision, all constitutions are also a reflection of the balance of power in a politically organised society and of the concept of governance of those who call the tune within that society. These are mirrored – in a particularly condensed and authentic way – in constitutions. This makes the constitution a highly informative source for historians.

The same applies to the Basic Law. It permits conclusions to be drawn concerning the values and the concepts of governance that prevailed at the time when the Federal Republic was founded and, in particular, maps the path that the authors of the Basic Law sought to pursue in the wake of the demise of the first democracy, the period of totalitarian rule and the disastrous defeat of 1945, and the ways in which their ideas were to be put into practice. The Basic Law gathers together the aspirations of West German society in a situation of profound upheaval and the principles by which it wanted the actions of its political representatives to be guided. While regarded primarily as a break with the past and a new beginning, the Basic Law also reveals which elements of the traditional German understanding of politics, the state and the constitution still held sway or were reinstated.

Furthermore, the Basic Law affords insight into the political and social power balances at the time when the state was founded. The composition of the Parliamentary Council reveals who, with what ideas and what clientele, was able to influence the constitution and who was excluded from that process. The deliberations and decisions, in their turn, indicate who managed to gain acceptance for which points of view and whose ideas left no mark on the constitution. The issues that were controversial and how conflicts were handled says something about the breadth of consensus and the participants' willingness to compromise. The scope for action of the founding fathers and mothers under the supervision of the occupying powers can also be measured in particular by examining the constituent process, for that was a question which needed clarification in that process.

Regardless of its legal independence, however, the constituent power does not by any means act in complete freedom in practice but has always been conditioned by history. Most constitutions follow a profound upheaval in the history of their country – a triumphal revolution or a catastrophic collapse. Constitutions not preceded by such a break with the past are considerably rarer. They occur when rulers find it expedient to limit their political power by means of a constitution, as in the post-1815 wave of constitutionalism in Germany, or to give their absolute rule a cloak of constitutionality, a frequent historical phenomenon that began with Napoleon. They also occur when existing states combine to form a new overarching confederation, as was the case with the founding of the German Empire in 1871. New constitutions which are merely the result of a need to bring existing constitutions up to date, on the other hand, are very rare. These tend to be presented as total revisions which are enacted in the form of an amendment, as in Switzerland in 1999.

The period leading up to the adoption of a constitution, however, always involves laying down basic principles that can no longer be called into question in the constituent process. Even before the constituent power takes up its duties, some options are already non-starters, while others are firm fixtures in the draft. Even if the former are mooted again in the constituent assembly, as the two Communist delegates did in the Parliamentary Council, their prospects remain non-existent. That is the valid core of Carl Schmitt's distinction between a constitution and a constitutional law.[4] However, the conclusion which Schmitt drew from that distinction and which he proposed as a solution amid the terminal

[4] Carl Schmitt, *Verfassungslehre* (Duncker & Humblot, 1928) 20 ff; English: *Constitutional Theory* (Duke University Press, 2008) 75 ff.

crisis of the Weimar Republic, namely the watering down of the constitutional law in favour of the constitution which had never been either formally decided or set down anywhere in writing and was therefore inconclusive,[5] does not necessarily follow.

The Basic Law is one of those constitutions that followed a catastrophic collapse, which was so extreme that there was no German state authority after 8 May 1945 and the slow restoration of that authority took place under the supervision of the victorious powers. The three Western allies also prescribed principles for the Basic Law, which the Parliamentary Council was unable to challenge but would not even have wanted to, namely democracy, federalism and fundamental rights. Yet besides those extremely abstract stipulations, which had to be turned into concrete provisions, there were predetermined features which arose from the continuities and discontinuities of the social structure, from the distribution of power between the newly formed political forces and from post-National Socialist value systems and which were non-negotiable in the constituent process.

Regardless of the absence of legal restrictions on the constituent power, constitutions are therefore, in empirical terms, a product of the conditions in which they materialise. If they were nothing more than that, they could be incorporated into the historical narrative and used as a medium through which historians perceived their subject matter. Their use would not be essential. Constitutions, however, are not completely explained by the prevailing conditions, as they neither result directly from those conditions nor merely serve to perpetuate them. The modern constitution is not a description of reality, which is a definition that befits the older concept of a constitution.[6] On the contrary, it lays down requirements for reality and makes their fulfilment obligatory. What is in the constitution is no longer opinion or theory but enforceable prescript. Its enforcement is made possible by the medium of law. Constitution-making is the transformation of power structures and regulatory ideals into law. The feature that is specific to modern constitutions is their normativity.

The transformation requires selections from a wide diversity of structuring options as well as concrete arrangements for the realisation of regulatory ideals. These are not predetermined by the prevailing conditions but require separate decisions. The constitution must provide for institutions that are empowered to take and implement collectively binding decisions, to prescribe procedures which must be observed and to set substantive objectives and limits for actors. This rules out any automatic conversion of power into law. The only route to legal validity leads through the channels of constitutional law, and they are not open to just any intentions and substance. By virtue of its legal nature, then, the constitution has its own value as a source and cannot be entirely reduced to other factors.

[5] Carl Schmitt, *Legalität und Legitimität* (Duncker & Humblot, 1932); English: *Legality and Legitimacy* (Duke University Press, 2004).

[6] See Heinz Mohnhaupt and Dieter Grimm, *Verfassung. Zur Geschichte des Begriffs von der Antike bis zur Gegenwart*, 2nd edn (Duncker & Humblot, 2002) esp 100 ff.

It is precisely its legal form which makes the constitution a particularly authentic source for historians. The constitution results from a discursive process that culminates in decisions. These relate to texts which, because they demand observance, must be formulated as precisely as possible. The decisions are taken by means of a vote. It is that vote which creates certainty as to what is applicable. It is also the legal form which ensures that the source is not merely a snapshot. On the contrary, the legal form detaches the constitution from the moment of decision and from the individuals involved in the decision-making process and extends its validity into the future and to all persons within its area of application. The legal form is what ultimately ensures that the constitution is not only determined by the prevailing conditions but influences those conditions in turn once it has entered into force. It is both a result and a determinant.

For the increasingly pluralist societies of the modern era the legal constitution makes contributions that could not be made by any other means. As a basis for consensus among rivals for political power and a set of rules governing their competition, it ensures that the rivals engage as adversaries and not as enemies. That makes it easier to accept defeat and permits peaceful changes of government. The decision-making processes that are open to participation and the substantive limits placed on majority rule make for acquiescence, even to disapproved decisions. The constitutionally guaranteed opportunity for minorities to become majorities reduces the propensity for radicalisation. In cases where a relatively homogeneous population committed to traditional values can no longer be taken for granted, the constitution represents a repository of meaning too, transcending divergences. In all of these respects it is a significant gain for civilisation – provided, however, that it does not only exist on paper.

II. Basic Law and Constitutional Adjudication as Factors in the Historical Development of the Federal Republic

On account of that proviso alone, it is not enough to describe the Basic Law at the time of its entry into force. Another reason why such a description does not suffice is that constitutions are amendable. Not all amendments will be of significance to historians. Many merely remedy weaknesses in the original wording that have come to light in practice or resolve doubts that have arisen. Constitutional amendments, however, may also bring about fundamental systemic changes or add innovative elements or new types of content. If they remain disregarded, there is a danger that historical portrayals will be built on false premises. The Basic Law too, by the time of reunification, where most of the historical works end, was no longer the Basic Law of 1949. Once they reach a certain volume or intensity, constitutional amendments can raise the question of the identity of a constitution.[7]

[7] See Dieter Grimm, 'Identität und Wandel. Das Grundgesetz 1949 und heute' (2009) 37 *Leviathan* 603.

Major amendments in particular indicate social change giving rise to problems that cannot be dealt with politically without an amendment of the constitution. They may also be a sign of change in society's values, a change which is obstructed by existing constitutional law or which requires constitutional recognition. Struggles for constitutional amendments, such as the reform of the right of asylum in the 1990s, may expose shifts in the balance of power or assertions of power. It is even possible that the regulation of the amendment procedure is itself a cause of ossifications, anachronisms and aberrations in the political system. The United States Constitution, with its exceptionally high barriers to amendment that are set in Article V, provides many such examples.

That, however, is not the only reason why historians cannot confine themselves to describing the Basic Law. There is more to the Basic Law, of course, than the once-only process of organising the power of the state, for it also regulates, in more or less detail, the exercise of that power, formally by assigning spheres of competence and laying down procedural provisions and substantively by defining state objectives and fundamental rights – and, not infrequently, by assigning mandates for political action. Future development is not thereby determined. Constitutions are regulatory frameworks, not implementation plans. They are intended to enable, guide and limit political activity, but not to replace it. They rule out some options and prescribe others. Between these poles, a wide space opens up for policymaking, which will depend on voters' preferences as expressed in the election or on the power balances that have evolved within society, but that space is ultimately structured by the constitution.

It cannot be presumed, however, that everything envisaged in the constitution comes to pass and that nothing more need be said about the constitution. After all, the Basic Law is, like any constitution, first and foremost just a text, albeit a text that lays claim to legal validity. It approaches reality with expectations, the fulfilment of which is obligatory. What the Basic Law prescribes is meant to be realised in practice. The text, then, is not an end in itself. It is both designed for and reliant on realisation. No one has reminded constitutional theorists as sharply of that fact as Konrad Hesse.[8] Legal validity and practical impact must be kept separate. To deal with the claim to applicability of the Basic Law and leave it at that would be to overlook the link between constitutions and reality. They would thus be disregarded as a factor in historical processes.

Realisation simply means that the demands which the text makes of its addressees are fulfilled. Between the normative expectation and the empirical reality, in other words, there must be actions that match each to the other. Although the

[8] See Konrad Hesse, *Die normative Kraft der Verfassung* (Mohr, 1959). The change of outlook brought about by that work is described in Rainer Wahl, 'Die normative Kraft der Verfassung. Die Antrittsvorlesung Konrad Hesses in ihrem historischen Kontext' (2019) 58 *Der Staat* 195. A basic treatment of the realisation of the Basic Law up to about 1980 is provided by Brun-Otto Bryde, *Verfassungsentwicklung, Stabilität und Dynamik im Verfassungsrecht der Bundesrepublik Deutschland* (Nomos, 1982).

norm may require such actions, it cannot perform them itself. Legal force and practical implementation lie on different planes. That they will coincide is by no means preordained. On the contrary, in the course of realisation the constitution encounters an exterior reality which may prove resistant because its underlying logic is not that of the law but rather political, economic, religious, etc. From the outset, then, the reliance of the constitution on realisation entails the possibility that it will not be realised, not be fully realised or not be realised in the envisaged manner.

Constitutions, it is said, must prove their worth. Proving their worth takes time. Whether they have done so cannot be definitively determined until they are no longer in force. Being well written does not guarantee the success of a constitution. Although it seems unlikely that a poorly written constitution will prove successful, the reverse conclusion cannot be drawn, for it is entirely possible that a well-written text will not stand the test of time. It was long assumed that the reason for the failure of the Weimar Republic was to be found in the flaws in its constitution. Even the Parliamentary Council, when devising the Basic Law, was not immune to that assumption. In the meantime, the view has taken root that the Weimar Constitution was not a bad constitution but encountered unfavourable conditions which prevented it from fulfilling its potential.[9] Whether a constitution proves its worth is determined by a triad of the constitutional text, the challenges it faces and the responses of its interpreters to those challenges.[10]

In extreme cases, it may happen that a constitution which has entered into force remains completely ineffectual because it was not enacted with any view to implementation but was only intended to create an impression of constitutionality, or because it has subsequently lost its effectiveness, for example when its opponents have come to power and ignored or adulterated the constitution, as happened in Germany in 1933. A constitution is then deemed to have failed. A similar situation arises when actors regard a constitution as binding only to the extent that it does not hinder the pursuit of their overriding aims. These may be religious truths or political ideologies or else, as is not infrequently the case, mere power or property interests of the rulers. Ferdinand Lassalle, in his famous speech of 1862, called this the 'real constitution'.[11]

Even where acceptance of a constitution is not merely a pretence and is not subject to reservations, however, there is a possibility that its realisation will remain patchy. This is not a matter of individual infringements of constitutional

[9] See, as an early contribution, Dieter Grimm, 'Missglückt oder glücklos?' *Frankfurter Allgemene Zeitung* (14 August 1999); reproduced in Heinrich August Wikler (ed), *Weimar im Widerstreit* (Oldenbourg, 2002) 151. See also Christoph Gusy, *100 Jahre Weimarer Verfassung. Eine gute Verfassung in schlechter Zeit* (Mohr Siebeck, 2018), and Horst Dreier and Christian Waldhoff (eds), *Das Wagnis der Demokratie. Eine Anatomie der Weimarer Reichsverfassung* (CH Beck, 2019).

[10] See Dieter Grimm, 'Das Grundgesetz nach 50 Jahren' in Bundesministerium des Innern (ed), *Bewährung und Herausforderung. Die Verfassung vor der Zukunft* (Leske + Budrich, 1999) 39 ff.

[11] See Ferdinand Lassalle, *Über Verfassungswesen*, Eduard Bernstein edn (Berlin Verlag, 1907); English: 'On the Essence of Constitutions' (1942) 3 *Fourth International* 25.

provisions which are overwhelmingly observed. Such infringements can never be ruled out, even in functioning constitutional states. Legal instruments are not laws of nature. On the contrary, realisation of the constitution is not impinged upon until the infringements become habitual or structurally ingrained, or essential parts of the constitution are totally disregarded or systematically distorted, or an institution for which the constitution provides is not established or is shaped in such a way that it remains ineffective, or missions assigned by the constitution are not performed.

In this respect, it must be said, there can be considerable differences in the degree of impingement. The consequences of non-realisation may vary, depending on whether the omission concerns a central or peripheral element of the constitution. The original intention of the Basic Law, for example, has not been lastingly jeopardised by the fact that the Supreme Federal Court, for which Article 95 provided and which was to resolve inconsistencies between rulings of the various federal courts, was never established.[12] A different level of significance, however, attaches to the fact that, by the deadline of 31 March 1953 set by Article 117 of the Basic Law, the provisions of the German Civil Code relating to family law which were inconsistent with the equal rights of men and women proclaimed in Article 3(2) of the Basic Law had not been repealed.[13] Article 3(2) was a hard-won achievement of the Basic Law which enjoyed considerable public goodwill and support.

Attempts are often made to encapsulate the discrepancy between ambitions and reality by means of the twin terms 'constitutional law' and 'constitutional reality'. Historians in the Federal Republic also resort to those terms when they wish to show that the Basic Law does not always deliver what it promises. Yet violation of the constitution and the reality of the constitution are two different things. Constitutional reality is a consequence of the fact that constitutions often lay down conditions for political action without comprehensively or definitively determining the nature of that action, or offer options for action without prescribing how to exercise them. Otherwise politics would consist only in implementing the constitution, and democracy would be superfluous. There are always more permissible means of action than can be adopted. Constitutional reality comes into play when one of the options left open by a constitution establishes itself temporarily or permanently as the norm.

In the area that is left open, customs can then take root, practices develop and balances of power solidify which are permitted by the constitution and which may even stretch it to its limits in some circumstances but do not infringe it. They are conditioned, but not ultimately determined, by constitutional rules. When historians display a predilection for calling the Federal Republic a 'chancellor democracy' (*Kanzlerdemokratie*), that is one such case. The system of political parties is another.

[12] The version of that article governing the Supreme Federal Court was not repealed until 1968.
[13] See ch 11 below.

The freedom to found political parties which is guaranteed in the second sentence of Article 21(1) of the Basic Law also means that the party system is left to political developments. The three-party system in the Federal Republic between 1961 and 1983, for instance, was constitutional reality. The constitution came under pressure, for example, through the practice, which was prevalent in the 1990s and the early years of the new century, of eschewing legislative provisions in favour of informal deals with those who were causing problems, because that practice circumvented the requirements of democracy and the rule of law.[14]

It may also be that an available constitutional option is not exercised, as for example in the scope offered by Article 15 of the Basic Law to socialise land, natural resources and means of production. The option is not rendered obsolete by never having been exercised but can be taken up at any time. Equally, constitutional rules may exist which no one has occasion to apply. The highly vaunted innovation of the constructive vote of no confidence, for example, has never served to prevent a government from being brought down by a hostile majority which was not itself in a position to form a new government. The mechanism, however, has been applied in a situation that had nothing to do with the originally envisaged scenario when it was used to engineer a dissolution of the Bundestag even though the Chancellor had not lost his majority.[15]

It is unlikely that the union of norm and reality postulated by the constitution could ever be achieved. Such a state of quiescence is already precluded by constant social change, which necessitates continual updating of the constitution. That union remains present as an ideal for reality and as a yardstick for its assessment. Reality is always measured by the constitution, and new realisation deficits are always being identified, giving rise to new demands. Constitutions can act as driving forces. In the political process, one side tries to lend legitimacy to its demands and undermine the arguments of those who oppose them by invoking the constitution, while the other side invokes the constitution to reject such demands. The realisation postulate of the constitution is a constant demand.

If the constitution has entered into force, its history becomes that of its realisation. Even in functioning states where the rule of law prevails, successful realisation cannot be taken for granted. Although the purpose of constitutions lies not only in restricting political action but also in enabling and legitimising it, constitutional norms are frequently perceived as restrictions in the given situation. Constitutions, of course, require no less of politicians than subjection of the inherent logic of the political system to the systemically alien logic of the legal system. In a constitutional state, it is not enough to be convinced that a political measure is necessary, expedient and beneficial; it must also be constitutional, and the two features do not automatically go hand in hand. The history of realisation, therefore, is a history not only of *how* but also of *whether*.

[14] For more details, see Dieter Grimm, 'Lässt sich die Verhandlungsdemokratie konstitutionalisieren?' in Claus Offe (ed), *Demokratisierung der Demokratie* (Campus, 2003) 193.

[15] Official Digest of the Federal Constitutional Court (BVerfGE) 62, 1 (1983); 114, 121 (2005).

If private individuals or entities are the source of infringements of statutory norms, the state can enforce the law by means of its coercive power. Constitutional law is a different matter. In contrast to statutory law, which governs the conduct of private individuals and entities as well as subordinate state bodies, constitutional law is focused on the organs of state power themselves, including the supreme state institutions. In this case, the addressee and the guarantor of the law are one and the same. There is no superior enforcement instance. Accordingly, the early constitutions already contained provisions designed to safeguard the authority or existence of the constitution. In the nineteenth century, these were predominantly penal in nature. Wilful violation of the constitution by government ministers was punishable, and perpetrators were mainly tried before special courts. Convictions, however, were rare, and it was certainly not possible to eradicate the unconstitutional act by punishing its author.

Today, constitutional adjudication has largely established itself as a means of enforcing the constitution, even against the supreme organs of state power. Be that as it may, constitutional courts can only alleviate the problem, not eradicate it. Although they are empowered to declare invalid any legal act which infringes the constitution, they are not able to remedy the practical consequences of its application when it was in force. In specific cases, they may require the political organs to undertake or refrain from particular actions, as prescribed by the constitution, but they cannot enforce compliance in the real sense of the term. Coercive measures remain reserved to the supreme organs of government, and ultimately to the executive. Compared with the executive branch, constitutional courts have limited leverage. Just as there are relatively ineffective constitutions, there are also relatively ineffective constitutional courts. Where they have the chance to perform their function and take that opportunity, however, that has considerable consequences.

If the relationship between law and politics changed radically with the transition from absolutism to constitutionalism,[16] another fundamental transformation occurred with the introduction of constitutional adjudication. That is seen with particular clarity in the history of the Federal Republic. The existence of the Federal Constitutional Court (FCC) increases the relevance of the question of what the Basic Law requires, permits or forbids. It took constitutional adjudication to make the constitution, which had hitherto existed only 'as a purely normative order' (*Sollensordnung*), 'into "proper" firm law with judicial teeth', says Rainer Wahl; it brought the constitution, he posits, to a 'new stage of development'.[17] Since, moreover, the right to lodge a complaint with the FCC is open to anyone and is amply exercised, the Basic Law is omnipresent, and the question whether political projects are constitutional or unconstitutional is a perennial feature of the public debate.

[16] See Dieter Grimm, 'Politik und Recht' in idem, *Die Verfassung und die Politik* (CH Beck, 2001) 13.

[17] See Rainer Wahl, 'Die praktische Wirksamkeit von Verfassungen. Der Fall des Grundgesetzes' in *Der grundrechtsgeprägte Verfassungsstaat, Festschrift für Klaus Stern* (Duncker & Humblot, 2012) 243 (with fn 31) and 233.

However easy it may be to ask that question, it is often very difficult to answer it. That has to do with the function of the constitution. As the legal basis of the political and social order, the Basic Law is, in many parts, more of a catalogue of principles than a regulatory instrument. Its provisions are therefore considerably more abstractly and vaguely formulated than those of ordinary statutes. In particular, provisions governing the aims and structure of the state, such as democracy, the rule of law and the welfare state, are extremely indefinite. The same is true of the fundamental rights, whose scope of protection the Basic Law often defines with a single word, such as dignity, religion, arts or occupation, and then declares to be free or inviolable, adding what is usually a very generalised authorisation to limit the exercise of the right. What this means in the context of real cases can rarely be directly inferred from the wording. These provisions need a great deal of fleshing out before they can be applied to pending cases.

The basic experience of anyone dealing with constitutional norms, then, is that reading them leaves doubts as to their implications for the adjudication of specific cases. What does the guarantee of human dignity in Article 1 of the Basic Law mean for a statute that permits the Air Force to shoot down a passenger aircraft hijacked by terrorists? What does the right to free development of one's personality guaranteed by Article 2(1) of the Basic Law mean for a statute ordering that a census be conducted, in which individuals are to be asked questions about their home lives, training establishments or workplaces? What does freedom of faith under Article 4(1) of the Basic Law mean when it comes to the question whether a legal trainee who is a Muslim can wear a headscarf in court? What implications does the freedom of reporting by means of broadcasts and films under the second sentence of Article 5(1) of the Basic Law have for the cost of the radio and television users' fee? What is the significance of the fact that no limitation clause has been added to the provisions guaranteeing freedom of the arts and freedom of religion? Is everything allowed if those provisions are invoked?

These are actual examples from cases heard by the FCC, and the compendium of its decisions, which now runs to 170 volumes, is full of such questions where the wording of a particular fundamental right, though providing a starting point for its interpretation, does not hold the key to its application. This does not mean, of course, that the constitution yields no answers to such questions and that the Constitutional Court must decline jurisdiction. On the contrary, it only means that long chains of deduction may be needed before the gap can be bridged between the indefinite norm and the pending case. Cases in which only one single interpretation appears possible are the exception in constitutional law. Even among the eight justices in each of the two Senates, consensus does not always prevail either, which need not mean that anyone has erred.

The FCC, it must be said, does not have a monopoly on interpretation of the constitution. That takes place in any situation where the requirements of the constitution must be met, hence primarily in state institutions and administrative bodies exercising their constitutional powers, but also among citizens or social organisations defending the rights they enjoy under the Basic Law and in the work of the legal affairs directorates and solicitors who advise and represent them, etc. However, in political systems with constitutional adjudication, such as that of the Federal Republic, the Constitutional Court towers above the 'open society of constitutional interpreters',[18] because it has the final say in constitutional conflicts, which means that the other interpreters must take their lead from it. It may therefore be said that the Basic Law ultimately applies in the way that the FCC understands it.

Constitutional adjudication would thus be underestimated if it were merely perceived as *la bouche de la loi*, as adjudication of specific cases on the sole basis of prior decisions reached by the authors of the constitution without any input from the adjudicating body itself. Application of the constitution is not merely the discovery of a meaning with which a norm has always been invested. On the contrary, the meaning of the norm is constituted to a greater or lesser degree in the process of its application. What is at issue here is not the legitimisation problem confronting constitutional adjudicators that arises from the relatively indeterminate nature of the constitutional text but the fact that constitutional adjudication, as a process which, though bound by constitutional law, is not entirely preordained, is a separate factor in the realisation of the constitution, a factor which does not boil down to compliance with an order given by the authors of the constitution and which, in its effect, does not remain confined to the case at hand.

If statutes are subject to judicial review, the said effect already follows from the fact that an unconstitutional statute must not merely be disregarded in a given case but must be set aside and thus no longer be applicable to future cases either. But regardless of the question of the nullity or continuing validity of a statute, the impact of Constitutional Court judgments often goes far beyond the case at hand and determines the structures of entire areas of social life (for example, the media sector), requires effort (for example, in terms of climate action), changes practices (for example, in dealing with public protests), and dictates the adoption of large-scale protective strategies (for example, in the realm of data privacy). These remote effects often derive not from the delivered verdict – the operative part of the judgment – but from the grounds, which, provided they are imperative and not obiter dicta, also possess binding effect. Accordingly, they must not be overlooked in any examination of the repercussions of Constitutional Court rulings.

Anyone, for instance, who assessed the order of the FCC on the Treaty on the Basis of Relations with the German Democratic Republic,[19] which features in most of the historical works under examination, on the sole basis of the operative part – in which the Treaty is found to be compatible with the Basic Law – would have

[18] '*Die offene Gesellschaft der Verfassungsinterpreten*', the well-known title of Peter Häberle's essay which appeared in the *Juristenzeitung* (Mohr, 1975) 297, and was reproduced in idem, *Verfassung als öffentlicher Prozeß* (Duncker & Humblot, 1998) 155.

[19] BVerfGE 36, 1 (1973).

missed a fundamental point, for the whole reasoning is founded on the need to keep public policy focused on the goal of reunification. That was possible only if the preamble of the Basic Law, which the prevailing opinion had hitherto regarded as not sharing the legal substance of the constitution proper, were raised to the status of applicable law. At a time when people were starting to become resigned to the prospect of permanent German partition, that was so important to the Court that it decided to take the extraordinary step of declaring that the complete reasoning was imperative. The long-range effects of that judgment extended to the decision on the method of reunification.[20]

Constitutional adjudication, finally, is not without impact on the balance of power between the organs of the state. Whenever the FCC enriches the meaning of the Basic Law by interpreting any of its provisions, it increases its own radius of action at the expense of Parliament's margin for manoeuvre. That is not the intention, but it is certainly the effect of rulings designed to maximise the enshrinement of values or objectives in constitutional law. That is particularly noticeable in the Court's jurisprudence relating to fundamental rights. Because of rulings from Karlsruhe, the legislature is allowed to do less, on the one hand, than the text of the constitution seems to permit; on the other hand, it is compelled to do more than it would wish to do on its own initiative. That is why arguments about democracy always feature in the discussion of constitutional adjudication.[21]

Once the constitution has entered into force, therefore, its interpretation and application, particularly the rulings of the FCC, become a key source of information. The consequence for historians is that, when dealing with the effects of the Basic Law, they must take into account the distinct role of constitutional interpretation and jurisprudence. The importance of the constitution as a factor in historical developments is decisively increased by constitutional adjudication. The path taken by the Court in its adjudication is rarely the only option, being based as a rule on one possible understanding of the constitution among others. It is therefore important for historians to be aware that different outcomes were possible, with all of the implications they would have had for the subsequent course of developments.[22] From chapter seven, the main focus of this book will be on the extent of the coverage devoted to that aspect in the historians' portrayals.

Without the dominant role of constitutional adjudication in the Federal Republic, which has made the general public keenly aware of the relevance of the constitution on an everyday basis, it would be hard to imagine the Basic Law having become so deeply etched into the popular consciousness as has happened in the

[20] See ch 6 below.

[21] See Dieter Grimm, *Verfassungsgerichtsbarkeit* (Suhrkamp, 2021) 37 f; English: *Constitutional Courts and Judicial Review* (Hart, 2025) 21 f.

[22] See Christian Waldhoff, *Das andere Grundgesetz* (Carl Friedrich von Siemens Foundation, 2019) 9.

course of time. This shows that its significance is not confined to its legal effects but has wider dimensions. The term 'constitutional patriotism' was mentioned above.[23] It implies an affective connection with the Basic Law. The effect of the constitution is not limited to the judicial sphere but has a symbolic dimension too.[24] That is possible if a constitution succeeds in embodying more than its legal content, particularly if the general public see it as reflecting their ideals of a legally and socially just order. The identity of a society is then nourished, at least in part, by its constitution, which becomes an integrating factor.[25]

That effect is not automatically generated by constitutions and was not associated from the outset with the Basic Law. It presupposes the juridical effectiveness of the constitution. That likewise takes time to emerge. Juridically weak constitutions could offer no basis for affective bonds. But not every juridically effective constitution possesses symbolic power by sole virtue of its effectiveness. Constitutions may be irrelevant to the identity and integration of a society or nation. These qualities are then nurtured from other sources. Constitutions may even have the opposite effect, failing to gain or losing general acceptance and then inducing disintegration. Integration by constitution is the exception, not the rule. For a long time, the United States provided the best example of a constitution with an integrative effect. The Federal Republic now provides another.

The basis of this effect of the constitution cannot be elucidated with the instruments of legal scholarship. The symbolic significance can scarcely stem from public familiarity with the provisions of the constitution or with the grounds of judgments delivered by the Constitutional Court but is the product of rather fragmentary perceptions of them, which are essentially conveyed by the media. The symbolic force of a constitution cannot be counted among its functions either, in the sense of its missions, because it cannot be achieved by design, although its development may certainly be fostered or hampered. On the contrary, it quite seldom emerges and, when it does, is the culmination of a lengthy process which is not set in motion systematically. Historians, however, could well have something to say on that point.[26] The culturalist turn, which contributed to an understanding of the constitution as a cultural phenomenon, ought even to have lent momentum

[23] For the origins of the term, see Jan-Werner Müller, *Verfassungspatriotismus* (Suhrkamp, 2010) 21 ff; English: *Constitutional Patriotism* (Princeton University Press, 2007) 15 ff.

[24] See Jürgen Gebhardt, 'Die Idee der Verfassung. Symbol und Instrument, in Adolf Kimmel (ed), *Verfassungen als Fundament und Instrument der Politik* (Nomos, 1995) 9; Hans Vorländer (ed), *Integration durch Verfassung* (VS Verlag für Sozialwissenschaften, 2002); idem, 'Die Verfassung als symbolische Ordnung' in Michael Becker and Ruth Zimmerling (eds), *Politik und Recht, PVS-Sonderheft 36* (VS Verlag für Sozialwissenschaften, 2006) 229; André Brodocz, *Die symbolische Dimension der Verfassung* (Westdeutscher Verlag, 2003).

[25] See Vorländer (n 24); Sandra Obermeyer, *Integrationsfunktion der Verfassung und Verfassungsnormativität* (Duncker & Humblot, 2008); Helge Rossen-Stadtfeld, 'Verfassungsgericht und gesellschaftliche Integration' in Gunnar Folke Schuppert and Christian Bumke (eds), *Bundesverfassungsgericht und gesellschaftlicher Grundkonsens* (Nomos, 2000) 169.

[26] See, for example, Barbara Stollberg-Rilinger, 'Verfassung und Fest. Überlegungen zur festlichen Inszenierung vormoderner und moderner Verfassungen' (2003) *Der Staat, Beiheft 15*, 7.

to historical study of that effect.[27] Yet the integrative power of the Basic Law receives only marginal attention in the historians' works.

III. How much Constitutional Law is Necessary and Possible?

The question whether constitutional history, as the political branch of legal history, belongs to the numerous specialised historical disciplines which may, but need not, be taken into account in general historiography, or whether its relevance to general history, which is primarily treated as political history, is so great that it should not be disregarded, must surely therefore receive the latter answer. It is then no longer a matter of whether the Basic Law has a place in the historiography of the Federal Republic – which none of the authors considered in this volume, if confronted with the question, would be likely to contest – but rather of what that place should be and how much law historians can process. The debate centres on the nature and extent of the inclusion of juridical subject matter in the presentation of history.

The field of study is shared by legal scholars and historians. Law constitutes 'a distinct, partly autonomous sector of historical material as a whole, a sector which, however, would necessarily remain incomprehensible unless presented in the closest possible alignment with events'.[28] The distinctness and partial autonomy derive from its very normativity. Validity is the essence of law. Even past law – in other words law that has lost its force – is still distinguished from other historical phenomena, and thus recognisable as law, by sole virtue of its former applicability. Even provisions that never entered into force, such as rejected constitutional amendments, belong to the sector of law inasmuch as they were intended to become applicable.

Legal scholars and historians, however, approach their common subject from different directions and perspectives. Legal scholars are interested in law for its own sake. Their focus is on the normativity of the law. Law is a normative science. As a doctrinal discipline, it deals with applicable law in terms of its juridically correct interpretation and application. The specifically judicial method of interpreting norms is intended to ensure the 'correctness' of that process. In their doctrinal armoury legal scholars possess a store of tried and tested and largely consensual

[27] On the constitution as a cultural phenomenon, see Peter Häberle, *Verfassungslehre als Kulturwissenschaft*, 2nd edn (Duncker & Humblot, 1998); Rainer Schmidt, 'Verfassungssoziologie als Kulturwissenschaft' in Marcus Llanquel and Daniel Schulz (eds), *Verfassungsidee und Verfassungspolitik* (De Gruyter Oldenbourg, 2015); Hans Vorländer, '"Verfassungskultur" aus politikwissenschaftlicher Perspektive. Prolegomena zu einer Verfassungswissenschaft als Kulturwissenschaft' in Robert C van Ooyen and Martin HW Möllers (eds), *Verfassungs-Kultur* (Nomos, 2016); Waldhoff (n 22).

[28] Michael Stolleis, *Geschichte des öffentlichen Rechts in Deutschland*, vol 1 (CH Beck, 1988) 43, where Stolleis deals with reflection on public law.

approaches and solutions for recurring case constellations, which spare legal practitioners the task of constantly defining the substance afresh or establishing first principles. There is no equivalent to doctrine in historiography.

Historiography is not a normative but an empirical discipline. Where historians engage with legal phenomena, they do so without normative intent. Their interest lies in the law as a product of and factor in social conditions, cultural traditions and political decisions. For them, the law in its various manifestations is a fact that merits consideration whenever it serves to explain a historical state of affairs or a historical event. In that respect, while it is of interest to historians to know how the law is framed and how it is understood and applied, the object of that interest is not the juridically correct application of the law but its conditions and effects. Methodologically, then, historiography is not geared to interpreting norms but to analysing reality. That does include interpreting legal sources, but not with an interest in the application of the law, which is what drives legal scholars.

Legal history and its subcategory, constitutional history, are located between the two disciplines. Their subject matter is the law, while their method is historiographic.[29] Nevertheless, there are differences, which depend on whether constitutional history is written by legal scholars or historians. While both examine past law (or the history of current law), the constitutional historian from the legal field typically considers it from the normativity perspective, focusing primarily on how the law was interpreted and applied in the judicial process when it was in force, whereas the historian's study of constitutional history revolves around the conditions and occurrences of historical interest which are attributable to the constitution and therefore find their explanation in its provisions.

It could therefore be said that what matters to the legal scholar is the validity dimension of constitutional law, whereas the historian is interested in its impact dimension. That must not be taken to mean that the impact of law is of no interest to legal scholars. If the application of law has practical effects that defeat its purpose, there is good reason to check whether it is being correctly interpreted, or to propose amendments. The effects of a law, however, are viewed through the filtering lens of normativity. For that reason, the interest in the effects of a law within the legal system takes precedence for legal scholars, but these lack the tools to measure its external effects.[30] Conversely, the normativity of the law cannot be a matter of indifference to historians, because its political and social effects are due to that very normativity, which historians, however, lack the means to analyse.

[29] See Stolleis (n 28); Christian Waldhoff, 'Verfassungsgeschichte und Theorie der Verfassung' in Otto Depenheuer and Christian Grabenwarter (eds), *Verfassungstheorie* (Mohr Siebeck, 2010) 119; Dieter Grimm, 'Rechtswissenschaft und Geschichte' in idem (ed), *Rechtswissenschaft und Nachbarwissenschaften*, vol 2 (CH Beck, 1976) 9.

[30] An example is provided by a book with the promising title, *Realitätsprägung durch Verfassungsrecht* ('Impact of constitutional law on reality'), edited by Rupert Scholz et al (Duncker & Humblot, 2008), which goes on to deal almost exclusively with legal reality.

The gap that thus emerges is the place where the effects of the law must be studied. It is not an easy subject.[31] The only way to close the gap is by recourse to a degree of interdisciplinarity. For that reason, Reinhart Koselleck argues for 'integral legal history'.[32] That is not necessarily dependent on major cooperation projects. The prerequisites for interdisciplinary research may also be met by individual persons.[33] For the Federal Republic, however, the history of the effects of constitutional law has not yet been written, nor does the present volume purport to fill that gap. It has a more modest aim. It is intended to show, by way of example, where it would have been advisable, and possibly even necessary, for historians to address the constitutional history of the Federal Republic. *It is about the politico-social relevance of law, in this case constitutional law.*

That, however, requires a more detailed clarification of the relevance criteria. Not everything that is relevant to juridical constitutional history also has implications for general history. For historians, constitutional history becomes relevant wherever the Basic Law and its application had a significant impact on circumstances, developments and events which they regard as worthy of narration and explanation. It follows that the relevance of constitutional history to general history is not to be assessed from a juridical but from a historiographic perspective. In such an assessment, the scope and accentuation of the individual works must also be taken into account. Different considerations may then be relevant to Wehler than to Winkler, and Conze will be able to devote more space to the constitution in his 1,000 pages than Recker in her 120.

This raises a second question, namely how to identify the parts of the constitutional history of the Federal Republic which have had significant effects on the course of its general history. The problem is resolved for the purposes of the present volume by taking the selection of material from the examined works as a starting point and considering whether the constitution or constitutional adjudication significantly influenced the subject matter of their portrayals. That, admittedly, is not possible without demonstrating the significance of either factor. The present volume therefore contains a good deal of constitutional history of the Federal Republic, but emanating from historians' portrayals and therefore not comprehensive. The works may indeed fail to offer a cue for the discussion of certain significant constitutional developments. In such cases, there is a need to ask whether those developments would have had to be examined on the basis of the historians' own relevance criteria.

One source of difficulties is that this approach cannot be followed without counterfactual speculation. It is impossible to avoid asking what if the authors of

[31] See, for example, Thomas Gawron and Ralf Rogowski, *Die Wirkung des Bundesverfassungsgerichts* (Nomos, 2007).

[32] Reinhart Koselleck, 'Geschichte, Recht und Gerechtigkeit' in Dieter Simon (ed), *Akten des 26. Rechtshistorikertages* (Klostermann, 1987) 148; English: 'History, Law, and Justice' in idem, *Sediments of Time* (Stanford University Press, 2018) ch 8. See also Wahl (n 17) 248.

[33] A good example is provided by Justin Collings, *Democracy's Guardians. A History of the German Constitutional Court* (Oxford University Press, 2015).

the constitution had omitted this or that norm from the constitution or had framed it differently, if this or that constitutional amendment had not been adopted or if a particular amendment proposal had been successful, or what if there had been no Constitutional Court or if the Constitutional Court had ruled differently on one case or another. Such questions can be answered with some certainty only as far as the immediate consequences are concerned, but the subsequent implications will always remain largely uncertain. Forward extrapolation of causal chains is not possible.[34]

If, for instance, the FCC had ruled against the 2007 Treaty of Lisbon on account of various reservations that it had examined regarding consistency with the Basic Law, the Treaty would have been scuppered – that much is certain – just as the Constitutional Treaty had been thwarted in 2005 by the veto of the French and Dutch people, because EU treaties require the consent of all Member States. That would not have left them without a treaty, however, as the Maastricht Treaty of 1992 would have remained in force. Certain matters that the Treaty of Lisbon brought under the Community umbrella would have remained subject to intergovernmental negotiation, for example, but how that state of affairs would have affected the integration process thereafter ceases to be foreseeable with sufficient certainty.

Yet such what-if questions are unavoidable for anyone seeking to examine the effect of the constitution and its interpretation on the course of general history, as Max Weber demonstrated in his critique of Eduard Meyer,[35] because the significance of a particular factor in the course of history can only be gauged by considering an alternative turn of events. Koselleck therefore poses the following key question: 'What would general history look like if one did not ask to what extent it is legally conditioned and structured?'[36] The constitution or the Constitutional Court judgment will quite rarely be the sole factor. There is also a need to caution against monocausal explanations when it comes to analysing the effects of the constitution.

There remains the problem of how historians can ascertain the significance of constitutional factors for their own purposes. That the materials relating to the constituent process are fertile sources is undeniable. Moreover, they raise no comprehension difficulties, because their focus is not yet on constitutional law but on constitutional politics. Given the paramount importance of constitutional

[34] Examples of counterfactual history can be found in Christoph Nonn and Tobias Winnerling (eds), *Eine andere deutsche Geschichte 1507–2017. Was wäre wenn …* (Brill | Schoeningh, 2017).

[35] See Max Weber, 'Kritische Studien auf dem Gebiet der kulturwissenschaftlichen Logik', particularly part II ('Objektive Möglichkeit und adäquate Verursachung in der historischen Kausalbetrachtung') in *Gesammelte Aufsätze zur Wissenschaftslehre*, 5th edn (Mohr, 1982) 266 ff; English: 'Critical studies in the logic of the cultural sciences', particularly part II ('Objective possibility and adequate causation in the historical causal approach') in Hans Henrik Bruun and Sam Whimster (eds), *Max Weber: Collected methodological writings* (Routledge, 2012) 169 ff. See also Alexander Demandt, *Ungeschehene Geschichte. Ein Traktat über die Frage: Was wäre geschehen, wenn …?*, 3rd edn (Vandenhoeck & Ruprecht, 2001); English: *History that Never Happened: A Treatise on the Question, What Would Have Happened If …?* (McFarland, 1993).

[36] Koselleck (n 32), 148; English: 135.

adjudication, however, historians cannot opt out of reading the text of judgments if they are not content to know the outcome of cases, but seek knowledge of the routing or structuring choices that led there. The difficulties involved in penetrating the world of constitutional doctrine and judicial interpretation methods are evident.[37] Whether they are at all surmountable will be easier to assess once the next chapter is read.

[37] See Wahl (n 17) 248 f.

2

Genesis and Content of the Basic Law

I. Genesis

The Basic Law was not the fruit of a German initiative. The three Western victorious powers required it of the Minister-Presidents of the re-established *Länder* as the basis for a partial state in West Germany. That requirement, however, presented the *Länder* with a dilemma, for while they still thought in terms of Germany in its entirety and sought to avoid anything that was liable to perpetuate its division, the Western allies, for their part, no longer saw any prospect of a pan-German solution to the German Question after the collapse of the foreign ministers' conference of all four victorious powers in December 1947. At the London Six-Power Conference in the spring of 1948, in which the Benelux states had been included, they decided in favour of the creation of a partial state in West Germany.

On 1 July 1948, the military governors of the three Western zones of occupation presented the Minister-Presidents of the *Länder* with the Frankfurt Documents, named after the place of presentation, which had been adopted in London. The first of these documents required the Minister-Presidents to convene a Constituent Assembly. The assembly

> will draft a democratic constitution which will establish for the participating states a governmental structure of federal type which is best adapted to the eventual re-establishment of German unity at present disrupted, and which will protect the rights of the participating states, provide adequate authority, and contain guarantees of individual rights and freedoms.

There followed provisions on the Allied authorisation and German ratification of the draft.

In all of the historians' accounts, the historical background to the founding of the Federal Republic is presented in its context of a widening East–West divide. The Frankfurt Documents are mentioned in each. Only in the shortest book, Andreas Wirsching's *Deutsche Geschichte im 20. Jahrhundert*, are they not given their name, and only Christian Henrich-Franke misrepresents their content, when he portrays as Allied stipulations the concessions which the Minister-Presidents wrung from the Allies to avoid the impression of a definitive partition, namely that the constitution should only be a provisional arrangement and that there should be no referendum (52). In three presentations – those of Adolf Birke (12), Rudolf Morsey (17) and Edgar Wolfrum (39) – the Frankfurt Documents are described as the 'birth certificate' of the Federal Republic.

That, in point of fact, is inaccurate. A birth certificate certifies that a birth has taken place. Anyone who speaks of a birth certificate of the Federal Republic of Germany can only be referring to the Basic Law. To spin out that metaphor, the Frankfurt Documents were actually an invitation to procreate. As the portrayals themselves demonstrate, it could also have been declined, because the Minister-Presidents would rather have avoided responding to the invitation out of concern for the preservation of German unity. In the end, however, they thought it wiser to acquiesce. Later, a miscarriage could well have occurred, because the Parliamentary Council was not prepared to meet Allied demands for a revision of the draft constitution. This time, however, the Allies gave in.

As far as the Parliamentary Council and the drafting of the Basic Law are concerned, on the other hand, the historical portrayals yield more meagre fruit. Mention is made of the efforts of the Minister-Presidents to create only a provisional arrangement for the period up to reunification, which, they imagined, would come fairly soon. For that reason, contrary to the expectations of the victorious powers, they insisted on a Parliamentary Council delegated by the *Länder* parliaments on the basis of relative party strengths rather than a constituent assembly elected by the people. For the same reason, they favoured the designation 'basic law' in place of 'constitution'. When Wolfrum regards that as a substantive difference (39), however, he is mistaken. The Parliamentary Council drafted a full-scale constitution, to which it gave the name 'Basic Law'.

All of the historians also mention the importance of the preparatory work performed by the Constitutional Convention that met at Herrenchiemsee in August 1948. Although its concluding report did not achieve the status of a government bill, it nevertheless paved the way for the Basic Law, especially since some individuals served on both the Parliamentary Council and the Constitutional Convention, including such an influential figure as Carlo Schmid. The Parliamentary Council itself, however, is given rather short shrift. Some of the histories do not even contain information on its party-political composition. Yet the very fact that the CDU and SPD had equally large contingents was certainly significant, for it drew John Rawls's 'veil of ignorance'[1] over the drafting of the constitution as regards the predominant political force of the future and was thus conducive to a fair balance of interests.

Some of the historians point out that the three demands made in the Frankfurt Documents were not contested by their German addressees in any case. Even if the demands had not been made, the result would not have been a different constitution. But those core principles were highly abstract, themselves reflecting disunity between the United States, which thought in terms of global politics and had a role in mind for West Germany in the emerging East–West divide, and France, which was driven by its national interest in a permanent weakening of Germany. So they left a great deal of latitude for the Parliamentary Council to flesh out the bones,

[1] See John Rawls, *A Theory of Justice* (Harvard University Press, 1971) 136 ff.

and how that latitude was to be used certainly stirred up controversy among its members, despite their consensus on the fundamentals.

Of the conflicts that ensued, however, only the one about the federal order of the future state receives closer attention. That was, it is true, the most important issue. Although federalism as such was not in question, there was fierce wrangling in the Parliamentary Council over the distribution of weight between the Federation and the *Länder*. Differences surfaced especially over the financial arrangements and the form of representation of the *Länder* at the federal level. The choice was between a Federal Council (Bundesrat) comprising delegates from the *Länder* parliaments and a Senate elected in the *Länder*. Almost all the authors agree that the Allied influence came to light most clearly in the demand for a more *Länder*-friendly arrangement but that it ultimately missed its mark because the victorious powers did not want that demand to thwart the creation of the Basic Law.

The federal system was not the only point of friction, however. Bitter struggles were also waged over parental rights, the school system, particularly confessional schools, and the relationship between church and state, until a solution was found in the adoption of the church articles from the Weimar Constitution. That is touched upon by Birke (15) and Morsey (20 f), but most of the presentations bypass that issue. Another point which does not feature is the long-running debate on whether the new constitution should enshrine fundamental rights at all. Various authors, such as Ulrich Herbert (610, English 493), express surprise at the minor role played in the deliberations by the economic and social aspects of the constitution. Explanations could have been found in the reference materials. The trade unions severed their links with the Parliamentary Council for that very reason.

On the whole, the histories create the impression of a fairly broad consensus, which was nurtured primarily by experience of the demise of the Weimar Republic. None of them fails to mention the 'lessons of Weimar'. Weimar served, Eckart Conze says, as a 'negative model' (42). Herbert even reduces the work of the Parliamentary Council entirely to a process of coming to terms with the recent past. A constitution emerged, he writes, 'almost every aspect of which was a reaction to the catastrophe of Nazism and war' (607, English 491). It was 'kind of summation of the varying explanations for the downfall of the Weimar Republic' (609, English 492). Wirsching likewise calls it an 'anti-Weimar constitution' (91). Conze's text reads similarly, although his finding is limited to the 'core provisions' (41 f).

Several authors also refer to the 'anti-totalitarian consensus', which could relate to both National Socialism and Communism. Strands of tradition linking the Basic Law with older layers of the German constitution, on the other hand, are scarcely explored. It is seldom mentioned that federalism had been a constant in the political order in Germany for centuries and that the rule of law had also taken shape even before the dawn of constitutionalism. The good starting points offered by the Frankfurt Constitution of 1849 are likewise mentioned by few of the authors. Lastly, as far as the Weimar Constitution is concerned, the history books convey the impression of a complete break in continuity.

II. Content

On 8 May 1949, four years after the end of the war, the work was completed. How is it presented in the history books? That cannot be assessed by focusing solely on the subjects that feature in the works; the question must also be asked whether the portrayals contain gaps and what aspects they accentuate. That is made easier by reference to the usual components of constitutions. It is true that there are no normative stipulations as to what should be in a constitution and what does not belong there. The constituent power, for its part, is not bound by any law. It is nevertheless possible to say what content is dictated by the function of a constitution and what, at least back in those days, could be regarded as belonging to the standard substance of constitutions.

In juridical terms, a constitution is a law the specialised function of which is to regulate the establishment and exercise of public authority. It is therefore imperative to include provisions specifying who is empowered to exercise public authority and by whom, as well as in what ways, and also under what procedural and substantive conditions, it may be exercised. In constitutional states of the liberal democratic type, the central act is the election, and the central principle is the separation of powers, in which public authority is divided functionally into several branches on the horizontal plane and sometimes also territorially, on the vertical plane. In the latter case, the structure is that of a federation, in which the distribution of responsibilities must be regulated, and care must be taken to ensure the mutual compatibility of the tiers of government.

It follows that a constitution must contain specifications about the organs of the state, their formation and composition, their spheres of competence, their forms of action and their procedures. That is the minimum requirement for a constitution which is intended to perform its proper function. Collectively, these provisions are normally described as the organisational part of a constitution. It is the part that enables the state to act. For constitutions which are restricted to provisions of that type, the term 'organisational statute' has taken root. In German constitutional history, the constitution of the German Empire falls into that category. Hans-Ulrich Wehler, however, also regards the Basic Law as a 'carefully thought-out organisational statute for a federalist state with decentralised distribution of power' (5), and Wirsching (91) strikes a similar note.

However, even a constitution confined to organisational provisions does not regulate the structure of the state for the sake of regulation, like a road traffic code, but in the light of particular conceptions of good or just order and particular expectations regarding the compatibility with the common good of decisions taken by those in public office. If a constitution is limited to that purpose, the substantive expectations remain unstated but are guaranteed in practice by the existing balance of power. Indirect safeguards are often in place for that balance, such as limitation of the franchise to particular sections of the population or immunity of particular decision-makers or decision-making procedures from subjection to the will of the electorate.

Besides the organisational part, however, most constitutions have a substantive part. Every constitution is built on a particular legitimisation basis for political rule. That basis is usually emphasised in the introductory provisions of the constitution. Behind the organisation of the state there are also certain supreme principles, provisions defining the aims of the state and provisions defining its structure. These, too, are customarily specified in constitutions. Lastly, fundamental rights, which limit state activity in the interests of individual freedom and social autonomy, are standard components of constitutions. The substantive part of constitutions is often referred to for convenience as the bill of rights.

If these criteria are applied to the works under examination, a motley picture emerges.[2] The legitimisation basis for state rule in the Federal Republic is the sovereignty of the people. 'All state authority is derived from the people', to quote Article 20(2) of the Basic Law. Only three works mention this, perhaps because the question about the legitimisation principle was not asked, perhaps because it was considered self-evident, or perhaps because sovereignty of the people was equated with democracy. Yet it does not appear to be entirely self-evident, for Wehler refers to a 'legitimisation fiction of modern democracy theory, according to which the enfranchised people are recognised as sovereign' (5), by which he apparently means 'without actually possessing sovereignty'. What this implies for the legitimacy of the Federal Republic, for example, goes unsaid.

As far as the supreme principles or the provisions defining the aims of the state and its structure are concerned, the Basic Law, in Articles 20 and 28, calls the Federal Republic a republican, democratic and social federal state governed by the rule of law. Not very many of the works mention those attributes. Only three list them explicitly, and if the republican aspect – which is often disregarded, even in legal literature – is included, only one work actually reproduces Articles 20 and 28 of the Basic Law in full. Rudolf Morsey speaks of 'unequivocal definitions of state aims' (20). Yet what is more equivocal than democracy, the rule of law and, above all, a social state? For the last-named attribute, the Basic Law itself lacks the sort of defining provisions which at least permit some clarification of the concepts of democracy and the rule of law.

If the provisions specifying the aims of the state are distinguished from those concerning its structure, which is not uniformly done in literature on constitutional law, the imperative of reunification and the desire for a united Europe expressed in the preamble may be counted among the provisions specifying state

[2] The descriptions of the Basic Law are to be found on the following pages: in Birke 14–16; Conze 41-43 and various other pages, where the author often takes account of developments and adds his own assessments, such as 57 and 109–13, Geppert 14 f, Görtemaker 65–69, Henrich-Franke 52 f, Herbert 609 f/English 492 f, Morsey 20 f, Recker 19–21 and Wehler 5 f and 236–44, already linked with later developments; Winkler 132–36/English 251–56, Wirsching 91 and Wolfrum 40 f.

aims. The commitment to European integration in the preamble is followed up in Article 24 of the Basic Law by the provision enabling the Federation to transfer sovereign powers to international organisations and to consent to limitations on its own sovereign powers. This also opened the German legal order to the applicability of international law, which was a significant step for its time – some legal commentaries even call it visionary – but that point is addressed in only three of the histories.

The concept of militant democracy, while it was one of the main responses to the supposed oversights in the Weimar Constitution, is not an element that is mentioned by all of the historians. Morsey and Conze omit it, though they subsequently mention the banned political parties. The possibility of forfeiture of basic rights is referred to in Birke (76), Birke/Wengst (88) and Winkler (132, English 251). Closely linked with militant democracy is the eternity clause in Article 79(3) of the Basic Law, which lays down that the fundamental provisions of the constitution cannot be amended, even by a supermajority; this contrasts with the absence of any limits on the amendability of the Weimar Constitution. That important lesson of Weimar features explicitly in Conze (42 f) and Winkler (133, English 252) alone and in substance in Morsey (20).

The histories are at their most expansive when treating the organisational part of the constitution, going into the greatest detail on the federal tier of government, albeit mostly without reference to the underlying principle of the separation of powers. It is also in this context that the 'lessons of Weimar' feature most prominently. Most of the works highlight the purely representative nature of the democracy. About half of the authors expressly emphasise the renunciation of plebiscitary elements. Reference is made to the provisions restricting the head of state to representative functions and reinforcing the position of the federal chancellor by empowering him to form the cabinet, dismiss ministers and determine policy guidelines and, in particular, to the instrument of the constructive vote of no confidence, the provisions reinforcing Parliament by empowering it to elect the federal chancellor and the absence of any norm like the fateful Article 48 of the Weimar Constitution.

Federalism is likewise taken into account by almost all of the historians. Only occasionally, however, does anyone address the high degree of joint decision-making that was characteristic of the West German federal system, even before the reforms of 1967/68. Yet that peculiarity of German federalism should have merited more attention, not least because it is the source of some problems that would later plague the politics of the Federal Republic.[3] Compared with American or Swiss federalism, the German version has, from the outset, been less focused on separation between the tiers of government than on their interdependence. The bulk of legislation is undertaken by the Federation, while the bulk of administration is performed by the *Länder*. The Federation has only a relatively modest

[3] See ch 4 below.

administrative infrastructure. The *Länder* implement not only their own laws but those of the federal legislature too.

This requires, on the one hand, scope for the exertion of federal influence on the *Länder* administrations and, on the other hand, scope for the *Länder* to participate in the federal legislative process. This need is met by the model of the Bundesrat, which, unlike the rejected solution of a Senate comprising elected deputies, consists of delegations from the *Länder* governments, each of which is required to vote *en bloc*. The Bundesrat may lodge an objection to legislative decisions of the Bundestag, but the Bundestag may overrule it. Where federal laws significantly affect the policies and administration of *Länder*, however, their passage depends on the consent of the Bundesrat. As Birke (74) mentions, considerable importance would attach at times to the Mediation Committee, which can be brought in in the event of a stalemate.

The Federal Constitutional Court (FCC) is also dealt with very selectively in the descriptions of the Basic Law. It does not feature at all in Wirsching. In Görtemaker (65) and Morsey (20), its name is mentioned without further explanation. Henrich-Franke chooses a nice photograph of the FCC to introduce his presentation, combining it with a mention of the Lisbon judgment (10 f), but leaves it at that. What role is assigned to the Court in the political system and what powers it has are not explained. That is remarkable, given that judgments delivered by the FCC subsequently feature in these works too, even judgments relating to highly political issues, without the reader having previously been familiarised with the existence and function of that institution.

Birke and Conze mention the FCC, though not in their descriptions of the Basic Law but in later parts of their works. Birke counts it among the 'most important innovations of the Basic Law' (88). In Conze's view, it completed 'the institutional architecture of the Federal Republic and the separation of powers' (120). Other authors likewise stress the innovative nature of the FCC. Wolfrum, for example, calls it 'one of the particularly original bodies in the West German constitutional system' (56), and Herbert terms it an 'innovation in constitutional law' (609, English 493). For Wehler, the FCC, 'modelled on the American Supreme Court', is 'the real innovation in the political system' (6). Wolfrum, too, sees the Supreme Court as a model but also points to roots in the older German legal tradition (57).

However, if references to an American model are warranted, then it is only in the sense that constitutional law became justiciable. Yet that had already been the case under the Weimar Constitution through the creation of a *Staatsgerichtshof*, albeit limited to federal disputes and thus on a far more modest scale than in the Basic Law. Adopting the Supreme Court model, however, was precisely not what the Basic Law did, as the Supreme Court is the highest general instance with jurisdiction for all branches of the law and arrogated the power of judicial review in 1803, whereas the Basic Law followed the model of a specialised constitutional court, which had been established for the first time in Austria in 1920. However, as far as spheres of competence are concerned, the German Court's role went far beyond that of its Austrian precursor.

Dominik Geppert, in his comparison of the Basic Law with the Weimar Constitution, writes that 'In the institutional order of the Federal Republic, it was no longer the President who functioned as the "Guardian of the Constitution" (Carl Schmitt), but the Federal Constitutional Court in Karlsruhe' (15) – as if the President of the Reich had ever been the guardian of the constitution; he only played that role in Carl Schmitt's wishful thinking.[4] Winkler, who makes an earlier reference than Geppert to Carl Schmitt, in connection with the FCC, cannot be accused of that misunderstanding, because he rightly states that the authors of the constitution in Bonn had turned Schmitt's Weimar positions upside down by choosing to make the courts the 'guardian of the constitution', not the president (133, English 251).

Several authors emphasise the wide powers of the FCC, but only Birke lists its core areas of competence (76 f). From the breadth of those powers, however, the authors could have moved on to the political importance of that innovation, but they did not. In the description of the Basic Law, the Court thus appears merely as an addition to the traditional organs of state, namely the head of state, parliament and the government. Yet it is not merely an institution added to the traditional organs of state. On the contrary, it changes the operating conditions for all other organs of state. None of them has the final say any more on matters within the scope of the constitution, and that scope is defined by the Constitutional Court when it interprets constitutional norms.

The fact that this also poses problems is largely drowned out by praise for the Court, but is alluded to when Birke speaks of 'uneasiness about judicial shaping of policies' and calls the FCC a 'substitute legislature' (48), while it appears in Andreas Rödder's history as a 'co-regent' (171) and in Wehler as a 'vetoing actor' (6) and a 'parallel government' (240), while Conze even apportions some blame to it for the fact, as he sees it, that the institutional order of the Federal Republic 'not only stabilises and safeguards democracy but has also made it relatively immobile and reform-proof.' (110). How it is possible that issues of great political import in Germany are ultimately decided by a court and not by the elected politicians who are accountable in turn to the electorate is not evident from the historians' works, however.

In stark contrast to a fairly extensive portrayal of the organisational part of the Basic Law stands the minimal attention devoted to its bill of rights. Even some of the more voluminous works, such as those of Görtemaker and Wehler, omit it entirely. Wehler surely distorted the perception of the fundamental rights from the outset by describing the Basic Law as an organisational statute, thereby attributing no significance to its substantive dimension, although that dimension held particular importance for the Parliamentary Council in its reaction against the positivism and moral relativism that had prevailed in the Weimar

[4] Carl Schmitt, *Der Hüter der Verfassung* (Mohr, 1931); English: 'The Guardian of the Constitution' in Lars Vinx (ed), *The Guardian of the Constitution: Hans Kelsen and Carl Schmitt on the Limits of Constitutional Law* (Cambridge University Press, 2015).

Republic. Herbert confines himself to referring to the existence of the catalogue of fundamental rights, which he relates to the rule of law (609, English 492). Wolfrum regards the fundamental rights as part of the 'nucleus' (*Kernbestand*) of the Basic Law along with the provisions defining the structure of the state (40). Only in Recker do they form the 'centrepiece (*Herzstück*) of the constitutional state that was to be created' (21).

That finds symbolic expression in the fact that the fundamental rights, unlike those in the Weimar Constitution, were given first place in the Basic Law. Hardly ever are readers told, however, what the various fundamental rights are intended to protect. Several authors emphasise the change from the Weimar Constitution, but they see that change primarily in the fact that the fundamental rights enshrined in the Basic Law were to be binding on all state authorities, including the legislature, whereas in the Weimar Republic they had been non-binding, possessing only programmatic significance (Winkler 134, English 253; Wolfrum 19). That reading is correct as regards the fundamental social rights, but otherwise it does a disservice to both the Weimar Constitution and the constitutional doctrine of the Weimar era. What was disputed in the Weimar Republic was not the applicability of the fundamental rights as such but whether the legislature was bound by them.

The Basic Law leaves no room for doubt on that point. Henrich-Franke, however, concludes from this that they cannot be amended (52), while Birke even regards them as natural, 'pre-state' rights (*vorstaatliche Rechte*), which ought to remain outside the reach of ordinary legislation (15). Is this supposed to mean that statutory limitations are inadmissible? That would make the entire Criminal Code – and indeed a considerable part of the whole legal order – unconstitutional. A perusal of the Basic Law, however, would have sufficed to refute such a conclusion. Almost all fundamental rights carry a *Gesetzesvorbehalt* – a provision requiring the specific enactment of a statute for any restriction of the right in question. What is not mentioned, on the other hand, is that the power to restrict fundamental rights by statute is itself subject to limitations. Under Article 19(2) of the Basic Law, such restriction must never affect the essence of a basic right. That certainly differs from the Weimar system.

What is particularly noticeable, however, is that the fundamental rights, which were already familiar from previous German constitutions, were preceded in the Basic Law by a provision that was intended to give them their deeper meaning and purpose, namely human dignity. It was, in actual fact, declared inviolable, in other words immune to any restriction. After the total negation of individual rights under National Socialism, it evidently no longer seemed sufficient to guarantee specific aspects of individual autonomy. On the contrary, the foundation of the fundamental rights, the quality of every individual as a person, was to be put at the top of the constitution. That intention was encapsulated in the term 'dignity'. It soon radiated to many other new constitutions. Only Conze (43) mentions the guarantee of human dignity in Article 1(1) of the Basic Law, but then leaves the other fundamental rights unheeded.

III. Assessments

By undervaluing its substantive components, historians not only misrepresent the Basic Law but also create a false dichotomy between it and the Weimar Constitution.[5] In its substantive parts, it is first and foremost a rejection of National Socialism or of totalitarianism in general. On the other hand, as far as the legitimisation principle, the structural principles and the existence of fundamental rights are concerned, it fully accords with the Weimar Constitution. The applicability and enforcement of the fundamental rights, however, are decisively more robust than in the Weimar Constitution and are underpinned by the guarantee of human dignity, which serves as the central guiding norm. What changes in the light of the 'lessons of Weimar' is the system of government, albeit not fundamentally, for the key principles remain the same, but certainly in its format.

A general impression emerges that the works under examination do not give the Basic Law sufficient coverage. It is taken into account selectively. One general element of selectivity which is more or less characteristic of all the histories is concentration on the organisational part. Then there are the specific selections made by individual authors. The overall result of this approach is a patchwork of fragments of the Basic Law that are not congruent. If the descriptions of content from the various histories were placed side by side without readers being informed of their common subject, they would find it difficult to distinguish that they were all intended to depict the Basic Law. Ultimately, a conception of how to analyse and describe a constitution is lacking. Nowhere is there any focus on the significance of constitutions as such.

The historians' verdict on the Basic Law at the time of its creation is entirely favourable. According to Wolfrum, the fathers and mothers of the Basic Law created 'the framework for the freest democracy that ever existed on German soil' (40). In Conze's view, it is 'the most liberal constitution that Germany has ever had' (42). But the Weimar Constitution received a similar reception at the time of its creation. After the adoption of the Weimar Constitution, Eduard David, Reich Minister of the Interior, praised the Weimar Republic as 'the world's most democratic democracy'. Constantin Fehrenbach, President of the National Assembly, spoke in a similar vein. Even before then, Conrad Haußmann, Chairman of the Constitutional Committee, had said that 'no people in the world has a freer constitution'.[6]

By what yardstick can the superiority of the Basic Law be measured? If democracy is placed in the forefront, one measure will surely be the range of decision-making powers entrusted to the people themselves. But in that respect

[5] See Horst Dreier, 'Das Grundgesetz – eine "Anti-Verfassung"?' in Joachim Münch and Alexander Thiele (eds), *Verfassungsrecht im Widerstreit. Gedächtnisschrift für Werner Heun* (Mohr Siebeck, 2019) 13.

[6] The quotations appear in Jörg-Detlef Kühne, *Die Entstehung der Weimarer Reichsverfassung* (Droste, 2018) 57.

the Weimar Constitution was clearly superior to the Basic Law. All of the authors highlight the anti-plebiscitary nature of the Basic Law. If fundamental freedoms are used as a criterion, the Weimar Constitution had a considerably more extensive bill of rights than the Basic Law. A justification for the claim of superiority would therefore have been necessary, the more so since the Basic Law, following its adoption, was regarded in scholarly circles as a flawed constitution that was unlikely to last long,[7] a point that escaped the attention of all the authors.

This suggests that the historians' verdict is an ex post assessment, made in the knowledge of its subsequent realisation – further confirmation that the entry into force of a constitution is not the end of the story and that the process of realisation plays a crucial role. If realisation is the criterion, the selective focus on the Basic Law becomes conspicuously detrimental, because it complicates any identification of the Basic Law as a contributory factor in the subsequent course of events or as a cause of subsequent problems. Where knowledge of the Basic Law is incomplete, it will also be overlooked as a factor in situations, developments and events that seem important from a historian's perspective.

[7] Some voices are quoted in Christian Waldhoff, *Das andere Grundgesetz* (Carl Friedrich von Siemens Foundation, 2019) 23 ff.

3

The Beginnings of Constitutional Adjudication

I. Establishment of the Court

Once the Basic Law had entered into force and the Parliamentary Council had also adopted the statute governing elections to the first Bundestag, the constitutional organs could be established and take up their duties. On 14 August 1949, the Bundestag was elected, and it held its constituent sitting on 7 September. On the same day, the Bundesrat convened for the first time. On 12 September, the Federal Convention elected the President of the Federal Republic. On 15 September there followed the election of the Federal Chancellor by the Bundestag, and on 20 September he and the cabinet he had now formed took the oath of office. Thus the new state was able to function. The only thing missing was the Federal Constitutional Court (FCC). That was because the rules governing the Court in the Basic Law were fragmentary. It had been left to the Bundestag to fill in the details. As long as it did not fulfil that mandate, there could be no Constitutional Court.

In point of fact, quite a lot depended on those details. The Parliamentary Council, it is true, had defined the function of the FCC and conferred on it a number of powers which it needed in order to perform that function. It had also determined who would select the justices of the Court, namely the Bundestag and Bundesrat, each of which would elect half. The Bundestag could no longer alter those arrangements. There were still a great many things to regulate, however, and some of them were no mere technicalities but concerned the conditions for successful judicial oversight of the political institutions. In particular, these included the Court's independence of the political institutions which it was to oversee and the procedures for the election of justices. The two are linked, because institutional arrangements serve little purpose if the office bearers themselves are not independent. The rules governing their election are therefore of the utmost importance.

Politicians, whose conduct would henceforth be subject to judicial oversight, were well aware that the performance of the Court's function would depend on their decisions on that matter. However consensual the establishment of a Constitutional Court had been in the Parliamentary Council, its shape now became a bone of contention in the Bundestag. Deliberations on the FCC were no longer conducted behind the 'veil of ignorance' that had hitherto facilitated a fair balance between diverse visions and interests. In the Parliamentary Council, the Christian Democratic Union (CDU) and Social Democratic Party (SPD) contingents had been equal in size, but the CDU had won the first Bundestag election. Power considerations now came into play. The opposition SPD favoured a strong Court, which was also in the interests of the *Länder*. Within the CDU, which had become the main governing party, there were reservations.

A bill tabled by the SPD competed with a government bill, to which the Bundesrat had subsequently proposed amendments. It was, nevertheless, common ground that the FCC was to be a judicial organ, not a political one. The contested point was whether, unlike the judiciary in general, it was to be an organ of state ranking alongside the Federal President, the Bundestag, the Bundesrat and the Federal Government. That was not a mere question of protocol. It had a bearing on the independence of the Court, which, unlike the other law courts, had the task of assessing the constitutionality of political activity. The independence of its adjudication was unquestioned, being guaranteed by Article 97 of the Basic Law. But that independence did not extend to the basic conditions in which it would operate.

As a body administering justice which did not have the status of a supreme organ of state, the FCC would be part of the departmental structure of the Federal Ministry of Justice. Its staff would be under the ultimate authority of the Minister of Justice, not the President of the Court. Above all, however, the Court would depend for its funding on the competent government minister, who would thus possess a certain leverage. As a supreme organ of state, on the other hand, the Court would be in direct contact with the other organs of state without having to go through a government ministry; on budgetary matters, in other words, it could deal directly with the Bundestag, where the opposition also has some say. The Minister of Justice, Thomas Dehler (FDP), however, attached great importance to having the Constitutional Court within his portfolio. He regarded himself as minister for the constitution, from which he inferred certain powers of oversight.

There were also varying views regarding the composition of the court in terms of both the number, election and term of office of the justices and the formation of the adjudicating bodies. Since the constitution represents the formal and substantive common ground between political rivals, and since adjudication partly involves enforcing the prescripts of constitutional law against the current majority, it seemed logical to require a supermajority for the election of justices, just as the constitution cannot be amended unless the majority and minority are in agreement – provided at least that no party has won a supermajority at the polls. Accordingly, the bills provided for a three-quarters majority vote in both electing bodies – the Bundestag and the Bundesrat – which was even higher than the majority required for constitutional amendments.

Under the government bill, however, failure to obtain the required supermajority would result in a second round of voting, in which a simple majority would suffice. That would have been tantamount to an invitation to the majority to withhold their consent to opposition candidates in the first round so as to pack the

Court with their own candidates. The SPD could not accept that and lodged a successful objection, thanks primarily to CDU member Kurt-Georg Kiesinger, who later became Federal Chancellor. He managed to persuade his party that a statute with such profound implications for the democratic process should be adopted by consensus between the majority and the minority. Both sides, therefore, had to make concessions.

It was by no means easy, however, to reach a compromise, and it took time. The facts refute Conze's assertion that the statute was quickly drawn up and that the election of judges was the only source of delay (120). Nineteen months elapsed from the start of the legislative work to its completion. The Legal Affairs Committee of the Bundestag needed no fewer than 26 meetings to deliberate on the bill. After the Bundestag had reached its decision, against which only the Members of the Communist Party of Germany (KPD) had voted, a mediation procedure was only just avoided when the Bundesrat opted to refrain from trying to assert its numerous amendment wishes with the aid of a mediation committee. On 16 April 1951, the Federal Constitutional Court Act was finally promulgated, and it entered into force the next day.

The Act provided for 24 justices, divided beween two senates. For the first election, it had been agreed that the number of candidates which each party could nominate would be proportionate to its share of Bundestag seats. Since the parties of the governing coalition agreed on a joint list of candidates, there was a government and an opposition list, which was liable to create the impression that the party-political fronts were to be replicated in the Court. Four months after the promulgation of the Act, the justices were finally appointed to the Bench. Justices nominated by the SPD were in the majority in the First Senate, while most of the justices in the Second Senate had been nominated by the governing coalition. That led to talk of the Court having a black and a red chamber. On 8 September 1951, two years after the other organs, the Court was able to take up its duties. Its first order dates from the following day.[1]

If the FCC had already been neglected in the description of the Basic Law, the wrangling over the Federal Constitutional Court Act and the election of its justices receives scarcely any attention in the historical works, although that was the very point at which the political explosiveness of the new institution came to light after having played no part in the thinking of the Parliamentary Council. Only Conze mentions the Federal Constitutional Court Act (120), though without going into the contentious issues and their resolution. The election of the justices, he says, was preceded by 'horse-trading' (*Kuhhandel*) between the parties. He adds, however, that the justices' political leanings and sympathies should not be overestimated (120).

[1] Decisions of the Federal Constitutional Court (BVerfGE) 1, 1 (1951) – *Süd-West-Staat*. Winkler moves the date on which the Court was constituted to 28 September 1951 (152, English 84). That was the date of the formal opening ceremony. Because of the urgency of the south-western state issue, the Court had been constituted and had taken up its duties earlier.

Why 'horse-trading' occurred is not revealed. That there were trade-offs was inevitable, given the adopted arrangement. The three-quarters majority prescribed by the Act served to prevent the Court from becoming a government puppet. Since no party came anywhere close to achieving that supermajority, the arrangement compelled the government and opposition to reach an understanding. The rules did not prescribe how that was to be achieved. On the contrary, it only established conditions in which a practice then had to be developed. What emerged was an apportionment of the nomination of candidates between the two major parties. It was known which seat was a CDU seat and which was an SPD seat, but that did not mean that only party members entered the arena.

Simply nominating a candidate, of course, was not enough. He or she needed the approval of the other side. Candidates were thus sought from the outset on the basis of their acceptability to the political adversary. That was a barrier to staunch party loyalists and turned the spotlight on candidates' aptitude for such office. This, however, was not an automatic consequence of the arrangement or by any means inevitable. Things could have taken a different turn if it had been agreed to accept every candidate without question. What Conze calls horse-trading would thus have been rendered superfluous, but it would also have produced a different breed of justices and a Court which is likely to have found it more difficult to maintain the distance from politics and the professionalism in interpreting and applying the constitution which are expected of a court.

Who was to become a justice of the Constitutional Court was therefore settled between the major political parties before his or her election. In these circumstances, the only significance of the division of voting rights between two organs was that *Land* politicians were involved in the nomination process within their respective parties. That, too, was anything but inevitable. It is equally conceivable, and indeed maybe more plausible, that there could have been two separate search processes, one for the Bundestag seats and one for the Bundesrat seats, probably resulting in decidedly pro-centralising justices having the best prospects in one process and decidedly pro-decentralising justices in the other. In that case too, a different type of court would have emerged, a kind of arbitral tribunal, at least when seized of disputes relating to the federal system.

How was it nevertheless possible for a 'red' and a 'black' Senate to emerge, which Conze mentions and which, in his view, was conducive to the politicisation of the Court (120)? Since the Court and its Senates had an even number of members, it would have been logical to provide for parity in each Senate. Behind the decision, however, lay a party-political stratagem. The CDU expected that the politically relevant disputes would concern the organisational part of the constitution, for which the Second ('black') Senate was competent, and wanted to secure a majority there, while the SPD assumed that greater importance would attach to the Bill of Rights, which fell within the jurisdiction of the First ('red') Senate. Although no one sought to interfere with the independence of the justices, there was nevertheless an evident assumption that their party leanings would have implications for their adjudication.

The history books, in so far as they deal with the FCC, agree that a strong court was created. Almost all of them emphasise that it possessed a great deal of authority and enjoyed a high degree of public acceptance. Once again, however, that represents an *ex post* perspective. When the Court opened in 1951, such an outcome was far from certain. The legal provisions created the conditions for such a reception but offered no guarantee of it. How things progressed from there depended on whom the political parties would send to Karlsruhe, how the justices would understand their function, what cases would come before the Court, how the justices would interpret the Basic Law in the light of those cases and how politicians would respond to the Court's rulings. The historians, however, pay no heed to the membership of the Court. Only the name of its first President, Hermann Höpker-Aschoff (Free Democratic Party; FDP), is mentioned in some of the works.

Yet it surely had significant implications for the authority of the Court that the great majority of the justices were not recruited from the judiciary which had compromised itself under the National Socialist regime but which was still serving with virtually the same personnel. The intention was to avoid any such tainting of the Constitutional Court, precisely because it was supposed to be bound to the new order. Willi Geiger was the only justice known to have a National Socialist past, but he was a favourite of Thomas Dehler, who could not be accused of any link with National Socialism. The great majority of the justices, however, were members of the legal profession who had emigrated after 1933 or had been ousted from office or banned from practising. Those backgrounds were moral capital which contributed to recognition of the Court.

II. Early Struggles

Recognition, however, did not depend on that moral capital alone but also on how the other organs of state would respond to the new organ, especially if they suffered defeats at Karlsruhe. It must be constantly borne in mind that constitutional courts are particularly vulnerable institutions. Their oversight function is focused on the conduct of the supreme political organs of state, which have the coercive instruments of the state at their command. In contrast to the ordinary courts, in constitutional adjudication the addressee and the guarantor are thus one and the same. If Parliament and the Government do not comply with a judgment, the Court has no coercive means of enforcing it. Accordingly, the story does not end with the constitution of the Court. That is only the beginning, and, if the course of events is traced, it becomes apparent that things could have gone quite differently from the outset.

Talk of the red and the black Senate, which, given their composition, was not entirely fanciful, implied a risk of politicisation. Could the Court still have acquired the authority that the historians attribute to it if the impression had arisen that decisions in Karlsruhe were based on political rather than legal criteria? It took less than a year before the Court was first confronted with that question because politicians were trying to make tactical use of the different hues of the Senates. The case arose in connection with Konrad Adenauer's policy of integration into the West and rearmament of the Federal Republic, its *Wehrbeitrag*, or contribution to the defence of Western Europe, which was unquestionably a matter of the utmost political importance, for which reason it is not omitted from any of the histories.

Adenauer's policy led to the first major clash between the Government and the opposition. The SPD opposition was not absolutely opposed to an attachment to the West. It had no sympathy at all with the system that had been established in the German Democratic Republic. The forced fusion of the SPD and the Communist Party of Germany (KPD) into the Socialist Unity Party (SED) in the Soviet zone of occupation set it fundamentally at odds with the East. It feared, however, that the Government's policy would cement the division of Germany. But even within the CDU the policy led to strains. Gustav Heinemann resigned his post as Federal Minister of the Interior over the rearmament plans and founded a new party, together with some followers. The controversy greatly preoccupied West German society too. After all, only seven years had passed since the end of the war, and the universal cry of 'war no more' was equated by many with 'military forces no more'.

What the history books only mildly hint at, however, is that the Court also played a part in the dispute. Government and opposition not only locked horns politically over the General Treaty – the Convention on Relations between the Three Powers and the Federal Republic of Germany – and the defence contribution; they also wrangled over whether rearmament required an amendment of the constitution. If it did, the Government did not command a sufficient majority. The only reason why the judicial aspect of the controversy assumed political importance, however, was that there was now a Constitutional Court which, if seized of the matter, could decide the issue with binding effect on the political institutions. Without that option, it would have been inconsequential to insist on the constitutional obstacle, for it was clear how the odds were stacked: the Government commanded a majority in the Bundestag and took the view that a simple majority sufficed to ratify the two agreements.

Without the option of bringing an action in Karlsruhe, then, the parliamentary debate would have culminated in a decision in favour of the Government's policy, regardless of the constitutional reservations. The holder of power takes precedence, as Bismarck said in the Prussian constitutional conflict. Consequently ratification, and hence the fate of the two agreements and – indirectly – rearmament and integration into the West, at least in the form negotiated with the victorious powers, depended on the constitutional issue. For that reason, the political spotlight now focused for a period of several months on the constitution and the Constitutional Court. The FCC was not even a year old when its judicial decision became crucial to the resolution of a political issue regarded as essential.

The Federal Government had signed the General Treaty and the European Defence Community Treaty in May 1952. They now awaited ratification by the Bundestag and signature by the Federal President. In that situation, both sides sought confirmation by the FCC of their respective views regarding the legal position. In so doing, they relied on the different colours of the two Senates.[2] Back in January 1952, the members of the parliamentary group of the SPD in the Bundestag had already filed a request for judicial review with the FCC, seeking a ruling that rearmament without prior amendment of the Basic Law would be unconstitutional. After the signing of the agreements, they had extended the request to cover the pending ratification act.

Under the allocation of responsibilities at that time, the First ('red') Senate had jurisdiction for judicial reviews. That considerably unnerved the Federal Government, since the Federal President had let it be known that he would await the Court's decision. It therefore attempted to have the matter taken out of the First Senate's hands. To that end, the Federal Chancellor urged the Federal President to obtain an advisory opinion from the FCC, which he was legally entitled to do at that time. Advisory opinions were to be delivered by the Plenary of the Court, in which the justices nominated by the CDU were in the majority. The request for an opinion coincided with the Court's oral hearing of the SPD action. Even before the opinion was drawn up, the SPD action was dismissed as inadmissible on 30 July 1952 on the grounds that an action could not be brought against a law which had not yet been adopted.[3]

On the same day, the Court decided to begin its deliberations on the advisory opinion. Rumours were soon circulating in Bonn that the opinion of the Plenary was set to be unfavourable to the Government. So as to pre-empt any SPD move to bring a permissible action before the First Senate, the Government decided, contrary to all practice, to suspend the ratification process after the second reading, which had taken place from 3 to 5 December 1952, and to bring the matter before the Second Senate. On 6 December 1952, the parliamentary groups of the governing coalition brought an *Organstreit* action (an action brought by one supreme federal body against another over their respective rights and duties) against the SPD group, asserting that, by contesting the right of the Bundestag to assent by a simple majority to the ratification of the agreements, it was in breach of the Basic Law. The Second ('black') Senate had jurisdiction for that action.

On 8 December 1952, however, the Plenary of the Court, patently irritated by the transparent manoeuvre, ruled that the advisory opinion procedure would first be completed, declaring at the same time that the plenary decision bound both Senates.[4] The Court's order caused a sensation. The request for an advisory opinion had thus boomeranged on the Government. This triggered a flurry of activity in Bonn. Meeting followed meeting in quick succession. In the end, the Federal

[2] A comprehensive account can be found in Richard Häußler, *Der Konflikt zwischen Bundesverfassungsgericht und politischer Führung* (Duncker & Humblot, 1993); Uwe Wesel, *Der Gang nach Karlsruhe* (Blessing, 2004) 54 ff; Justin Collings, *Democracy's Guardians. A History of the German Federal Constitutional Court, 1951–2001* (Oxford University Press, 2015) 14 ff; Aurore Gaillet, *La Cour constitutionnelle fédérale allemande* (La Mémoire du droit, 2021) 223 ff; documentation in Friedrich August Freiherr von der Heydte (ed), *Der Kampf um den Wehrbeitrag*, 3 vols (de Gruyter, 1952–58).

[3] BVerfGE 1, 396 (1952).

[4] BVerfGE 2, 79 (1952).

Government once more pressed the Federal President, this time asking him to withdraw the request for an advisory opinion. President Theodor Heuss let himself be persuaded again. This meant that the *Organstreit* proceedings brought by the parliamentary groups of the governing coalition were now the only pending case.

Their line of argument was spurious. The fact that statutes, including ratification statutes, could be adopted by a simple majority was absolutely beyond dispute. The only question was whether the ratification process involved a statute with unconstitutional content. In that case, its validity depended on a prior amendment of the constitution. Whether a statute has unconstitutional content is a question of constitutional law, on which, in the event of a dispute, it is for the FCC to decide. Its judgment of 7 March 1953 was a lesson in parliamentary democracy for the governing groups. 'It is not only the opposition's right but, in a parliamentary democracy, its absolute duty to voice its constitutional reservations besides its political objections.'[5]

The whole of the proceedings were accompanied by the heaviest of criticism, some of it abusive, from Federal Minister of Justice Thomas Dehler. With the order handed down by the Plenary, he said, the Court had 'deviated appallingly from the path of justice'. He claimed that the justices were not qualified to administer the law and implied a leaning on their part towards 'socialism'. That assertion, needless to say, also targeted the justices nominated by the government groups, for they were in the majority in the Plenary. Dehler announced, 'We will never recognise the order. This order is a *nullum*.' Adenauer, who agreed with the substance of Dehler's remarks but regarded the form in which he had expressed them as inappropriate, clothed his cautious rebuff of Dehler in the witty remark that the proper word was *nihil*, not *nullum*. There were veiled threats to dissolve the Court.

The effect was a different one. The FCC had warded off the political institutions' attempts to instrumentalise it. The so-called red Senate had ruled against the SPD, the so-called black Senate against the CDU, and the Plenary had declared both of them bound by the advisory opinion, making it impossible henceforth to play off one Senate against the other. Dehler's incessant invective had put public opinion on the Court's side. Even pro-government newspapers rebuked Dehler and praised the Court for having furnished proof of its autonomy and its party-political independence. The legal dispute was ultimately resolved by the course of events and not by judicial means, when the EDC Treaty was rejected in the French National Assembly, which opened the door to West German membership of NATO, and when the governing parties won an electoral victory which gave them the majority required to amend the constitution.

This gain in prestige served the FCC well in the dispute over its legal status, which developed alongside the Western integration and defence contribution controversies but was not resolved until later.[6] No agreement had been reached on

[5] BVerfGE 2, 143, 170 f (1953).

[6] The status conflict is documented in the *Jahrbuch des Öffentlichen Rechts*, Vol 6 (Mohr, 1957) 110.

the status issue in the legislative procedure. The occasion to take up the issue again was provided by the attitude of the Federal Minister of Justice, coupled with inadequacies in the Court's working conditions. Requests from the Court were being dealt with sluggishly in Bonn. That had to do with the fact that the FCC was not recognised as a supreme organ of state but as part of the judiciary, which fell within the portfolio of the Federal Minister of Justice, who, following the conflict over the defence contribution, was less inclined than ever to do the FCC any favours.

Accordingly, in June 1952, the Plenary of the FCC adopted an advisory opinion drawn up by Justice Gerhard Leibholz, in which he explained how it followed from the function of the FCC as defined in the Basic Law that its status was that of a supreme organ of state. The opinion was adopted by 20 votes to two; one of the dissenting votes came from the President of the Court, Hermann Höpker-Aschoff, who belonged to the FDP, and the other from Justice Willi Geiger, a close associate of Federal Justice Minister Dehler who, as a senior civil servant at the Federal Ministry of Justice, had drafted the Federal Constitutional Court Bill. To reaffirm that the FCC was not part of the departmental portfolio of the Federal Minister of Justice, it sent the advisory opinion direct to the supreme organs of state. Dehler was beside himself and dismissed the proposition as 'hubris'.

The Court did not stand alone, however. The opposition, which had already pressed for clarification of the status issue when the Federal Constitutional Court Act was being formulated, supported it unreservedly. And even members of the governing parties lined up against the Federal Minister of Justice, as did the Bundesrat, which saw it as one of the Court's functions to defend the rights of the *Länder* against central government. The cabinet therefore acquiesced. In the Bundestag debate, only Dehler spoke against recognising the Court as a supreme organ of state. On 14 July 1953, the Bundestag voted by a large majority to allocate the Court a budget of its own, which meant that it no longer depended on the goodwill of the Minister of Justice. Dehler's abusive remarks also prompted the justices to threaten to resign if he remained in office. The Federal Chancellor had no wish for it to come to that. When the Government was formed after the Bundestag election of 1953, Dehler was no longer considered.

Politically, Adenauer had achieved his goal, but he never forgot the defeat inflicted by the FCC. For that reason, attempts were made to bring the Court to heel. Several possible ways of strengthening the government position in the Court were considered. Adenauer wanted justices to be appointed by the Government in future, as in the United States; at the very least, a simple parliamentary majority should suffice for their election. In 1956, the Bundestag, through a motion carried by the groups of the governing coalition, adopted an amendment to the Federal Constitutional Court Act whereby justices could be elected by a simple majority. It was vetoed by the Bundesrat. The only changes that materialised were a reduction of the required supermajority from three quarters to two thirds and a downsizing of the Court from 24 to 20 justices; these were later followed by a further reduction to the present number of eight justices in each Senate and a standardisation of their terms of office.

III. Authority and Acceptance

The status dispute and the governing parties' attempts to bring the Court under control are passed over in the historical works, even though they would have changed the constitutional state for ever if their outcome had been different. The judicial dispute over rearmament features in most of the history books. Yet neither the drama of the situation nor the breadth of its implications are discernible. Herbert writes, without any recognisable relation to events, in connection with Adenauer's style of government, that his approach was 'not particularly gentle' if his main objectives were at stake, 'as in the case of the newly established Federal Constitutional Court'. But here Adenauer soon came up against the limits of his power (648, English 524 f). Herbert alludes to the need for a constitutional amendment before the Bundeswehr could be established (649, English 525), but that was the very basis of the dispute before the Court.

Most of the other works make do with the observation that the Court was seized, but not all of them say by whom and to what ends (Görtemaker 320, Morsey 33, Recker 40, Winkler 152/English 284, Wolfrum 113). Almost no mention is made of the outcome of the proceedings. Birke only says that it came in for criticism (77, Birke/Wengst 89). Only Conze is more specific, referring to the case, as does Hans-Peter Schwarz, as the '*cause célèbre* of German constitutional adjudication' (120). Adenauer, Conze writes, had tried to exploit the division of the Court into a 'red' and a 'black' Senate. The attempted 'party-political usurpation' had threatened to do serious harm to the Court, to the political culture and to the stability of the institutional structure (82 f). It was foiled, however, by the justices 'who, in their decisions, had let themselves be guided not by political but by legal considerations' (120).

Would the conflict over the defence contribution have merited greater consideration in the historical accounts? There was no shortage of potential starting points. The importance of integration into the West and the associated rearmament of West Germany were unquestionable. Without exception, the works under examination here put the utmost emphasis on those issues. They are regarded as fundamental to the subsequent development of the Federal Republic. Through the title he gave his book, Winkler even makes Germany's Western integration the leitmotif of his entire presentation. Herbert explains that, 'During the 1950s, the conflict over rearmament and the "defence contribution" was the dominant domestic political issue in the Federal Republic, and it went beyond the limits of parliamentary discussion' (649, English 525).

If that is taken as read, the question arises whether these watershed decisions owed something to the existence of constitutional adjudication and to the attitude of the Court. Could it be that the development of the Federal Republic took a different course on account of the FCC? There are several levels to examine. On the global political stage, the possibility that Western integration and rearmament could have been thwarted by a Court judgment can surely be ruled out. More powerful forces were at play there than a constitutional court. As far as the domestic political controversy is concerned, it may be considered at least equally certain that the legal view of the majority would have won the day without further ado. The opposition would have had no means of asserting its contrary legal view effectively.

As for the realm of foreign policy, if the actions brought by the SPD had succeeded, a serious crisis would certainly have erupted, which would have compelled the Federal Government and its constituent parties to take a decision, which would in turn have been impossible without consideration of the Allies. In the absence of sovereignty, which had not yet been granted to the Federal Republic, the Allies would have been able to exercise command. The easiest option would have been to wait for the Bundestag election, since, at the time of the Court's order, election day was only half a year away. But neither was it certain that the Allies would agree to that, nor was it foreseeable that the election would deliver a majority for the governing parties that sufficed to amend the constitution and so eliminate the problem.

If waiting for the election had been regarded as unenforceable or too risky, the Federal Government and the victorious powers would have been forced to seek an alternative, or else the Federal Government would have had to ignore the ruling of the Constitutional Court and base the milestone decision that was crucial to the future of the Federal Republic on a breach of the constitution. That could not be ruled out. There was too much at stake for Adenauer not to consider that option. Satisfying a demand made by the United States was not his sole concern. On the contrary, the demand also presented him with a lever to achieve sovereignty, a prime political goal in his eyes. Even if any possibility that the FCC could ultimately have blocked rearmament may be ruled out, such was the situation in 1952 and 1953 that the history of the Federal Republic could have taken a different course, which would have been due to the FCC.

Even without undue speculation, it may be assumed that historians would have highlighted the judgment of July 1952 if the Court had endorsed the legal view of the SPD and barred the ratification of the agreements. That can be deduced from the fact that constitutional judgments thwarting a political aim to which politicians and the public attach importance do feature in the histories, an example being the abortion judgment, which is not missing from any of the works.[7] The observation, moreover, cannot be dismissed with the argument that, from a judicial perspective, the FCC had absolutely no option but to rule as it did. The SPD had put forward grounds for its action, which were considered in Karlsruhe. The uproar in Bonn was by no means incomprehensible.

In point of fact, involving the Court in the political dispute only caused a delay. The ultimate outcome was what the majority wanted. Does that make the role of the Court any less significant? What is striking, of course, is the fact that a court has the last word on such a highly political matter. Nothing could show more clearly

[7] See ch 9 below.

that a new actor had entered the political stage and had done so with a mandate to uphold the requirements of the Basic Law, even against democratically elected majorities, and no less remarkable was the fact that that actor was not willing to let the interpretation of the constitution be guided by the wishes of the Government. This was already a sign that political events could no longer be described by focusing only on Parliament, the Government, political parties, special-interest groups and the public. The FCC had to be included in the equation.

The historians do not fail to make the general observation that, in the Court, a powerful actor had emerged which enjoyed a great deal of authority and recognition. Neither of those, however, are natural attributes of a court of law. They must be earned. How did that happen in the Federal Republic? Conze refers in that context to the fact that the FCC was not part of the portfolio of the Federal Minister of Justice. 'From that alone derives its authority', he writes (121). He is not wrong there, but the Court's independence of the Ministry was not born of the Basic Law or of the Federal Constitutional Court Act but was the result of a struggle waged over the course of a year, in which the Court was finally able to assert itself. Independence is a prerequisite for authority but does not suffice to explain it.

Wolfrum likewise associates the Court's authority with its relationship to the political institutions. He writes that the Court had gained its authority in spite of many conflicts into which it had been drawn and in spite of constant attempts to continue lost political battles in the courtroom (113). There too, however, the basis of that success remains unexplained. In its handling of those conflicts it could, of course, have failed or incurred public disapproval. What is more, should Wolfrum's comment not read 'because of' rather than 'in spite of'? How could the Court have gained authority and proved its independence if it had not been drawn into political conflicts? The foundations of its authority and recognition must surely have come from other sources too.[8]

When its turbulent beginnings are examined, in fact, the question arises whether the Court could have acquired the authority and repute to which the authors attest if the 'red' Senate had fulfilled the expectations of the opposition and the 'black' Senate those of the Government, or if the Federal Government had come to treat the Court with open contempt. That would possibly have put an end to the innovation of constitutional adjudication, so warmly acclaimed by the historians, when it was barely out of the cradle. Is it not actually possible that it was precisely in that early phase with the dispute over Western integration and the defence contribution and with the successful struggle for status that one of the key foundations was laid for the authority of the Court?

[8] This point is addressed again in ch 15 below.

4

Constitutional Evolution Through Amendments to the Basic Law

I. The Rules Governing Constitutional Amendments

Constitutions structure the political process and lay down conditions for political behaviour. They lend solidity and direction to political business, with its short time frames. They form the consensual basis for the resolution of political conflicts. For that reason they are designed to last longer and are harder to amend than ordinary statutes. Since constitutional amendments affect the rules of competition between political parties, they normally require a supermajority. They are often raised above the level of ordinary legisation through the involvement of other actors. In accordance with the understanding of the constitution as expressing the will of the people, from which those in public authority derive their legitimacy, numerous constitutions make amendments dependent on a referendum. Others, while leaving amendments to the legislature, interpose parliamentary elections between the decision and its confirmation.

Such mechanisms are not a necessity. The constituent power is free to frame the rules governing constitutional amendments. Past experience, however, is available to guide it. If the bar for constitutional amendments is set very high, it becomes more difficult to adapt the constitution to changing conditions. Anachronistic-sounding provisions remain in force. The temptation to circumvent the constitution increases. The onus of keeping the constitution abreast of the times is placed on the constitutional judges. As a result, the line between making and applying the constitution is liable to become blurred, causing the legitimacy of the court to suffer. All of this is well illustrated by the constitutional history of the United States. If, on the other hand, the bar is set too low, the difference between amending the constitution and legislating is blurred. That diminishes awareness of the fact that the constitution is there to govern the conduct of politics, not to be at politicians' disposal.

The Basic Law regulates amendment of the constitution in Article 79, prescribing that it may be amended only by a law. The actors and procedures are therefore the same as in the case of ordinary legislation. The people, to whom constituent power is attributed, play no part in the process. The only difference between amendment and legislation is that a two-thirds majority of both Houses is required. That supermajority, however, is often required for ordinary decisions – de facto though not *de jure* – when a statute needs the consent of the Bundesrat and the opposition has a majority there. However, the practice adopted in the Weimar Republic of constitutional override (*Verfassungsdurchbrechung*), whereby a statute adopted by a two-thirds majority could override constitutional provisions, has been precluded. Constitutional amendments are permissible only if the amending law expressly amends or supplements the text of the Basic Law. Constitutional overrides are breaches of the constitution.

The most important innovation in relation to the Weimar Constitution, however, stems from the provision in Article 79(3) which renders inadmissible any amendments affecting the supreme principles of the Basic Law, that is to say democracy, the rule of law, the social state and federalism, or the guarantee of human dignity. The purpose of this provision is to prevent any perversion of the constitution by legal means, as occurred through the Enabling Act of 1933. Article 79(3) of the Basic Law thus brings into the constitution, which itself establishes a hierarchy of norms, an additional internal ranking. There are now supernorms, which even bind the legislature when it seeks to amend the constitution. As a consequence, constitutional amendments may be unconstitutional, which also implies that the Federal Constitutional Court (FCC) has the power to review constitutional amendments for constitutionality.

The Parliamentary Council was particularly keen to stress the provisional nature of the Basic Law. That intention was reflected, for example, in the concluding provision, which stated that the Basic Law would cease to apply on the day on which a constitution freely adopted by the German people took effect. The Basic Law is thus a rare example of a constitution that provides for its own invalidation. The people within the meaning of that provision were the people of the whole of Germany. For the eventuality that an enlargement of the Federal Republic might occur before then, the second sentence of Article 23 provided that, in the parts of Germany other than the founding *Länder*, the Basic Law would enter into force 'after their accession'. Until reunification, that provision had only ever been applied in the case of the Saarland. Article 146, the concluding provision, was retained in modified form after reunification, for which it had been designed but never applied.[1]

II. Major Amendments to the Basic Law

As far as constitutional provisions not covered by Article 79(3) of the Basic Law are concerned, their amendment is therefore a comparatively simple process in the Federal Republic. Accordingly, the Basic Law has undergone frequent amendment. The first constitutional amendment was enacted as early as 1951.[2] By the time of reunification,

[1] For more details, see ch 6 below.

[2] The amendments are comprehensively documented in Angela Bauer and Matthias Jestaedt, *Das Grundgesetz im Wortlaut. Änderungsgesetze, Synopse, Textstufen und Vokabular zum Grundgesetz*

the point at which most of the historical works end, that amendment had been followed by another 35, of which three, affecting a total of 36 articles, were adopted in 1968, and no fewer than eight, affecting 24 articles in total, were adopted in 1969. The most frequent subject of amendment was the federal system of government. Some amendments were minimal, and some were of great significance. The subject of the last amendment before reunification was reunification itself. It contained the modifications that arose from the Unification Treaty, including the amendment of the concluding article, the amendment of the preamble and the amendment of Article 23, the accession article, which had now served its purpose.

Besides those amendments that were required for reunification, three amendments merit special emphasis first and foremost, on account of their political significance. Two of them may be regarded as belated constitution-making, namely the constitutional regime for the armed forces (*Wehrverfassung*) of 1956 and the constitutional regime of emergency provisions (*Notstandsverfassung*) of 1968.

A. The *Wehrverfassung*

In 1949, the rearmament of the Federal Republic was not yet on the agenda. When it became a critical issue, it gave rise to the bitter clash between government and opposition that was addressed in the previous chapter. It was resolved when the governing coalition of Christian Democratic Union (CDU)/Christian Social Union (CSU), Free Democratic Party (FDP), the German Party (DP) and the All-German Bloc/League of Expellees and Disenfranchised Persons (GB/BHE) won a supermajority in the Bundestag election of 1953 and made instant use of it to pave the way for rearmament by means of an amendment to Article 79 of the Basic Law, the insertion of Article 142a and the addition of 'defence, including compulsory military service' to the catalogue of matters under exclusive legislative power of the Federation in Article 73.

Once the dispute over the defence contribution had been settled in favour of the CDU by these constitutional amendments, the SPD came to terms with the new reality. It gave up its resistance and played an active part in the efforts to shape the federal armed forces – the Bundeswehr. The subsequent amendments of the Basic Law, establishing the actual *Wehrverfassung*, were thus adopted by a large majority in 1956, although the SPD could have blocked them, since the governing coalition had lost its supermajority in the meantime through the secession of the FDP and the BHE. Seven provisions of the Basic Law were amended, and nine new provisions were inserted. The amended provisions took account of the fact that there were now military forces. The new ones integrated the Bundeswehr into the

(CF Müller, 1997). For the period up to 1980, see also Alexander Roßnagel, *Die Änderungen des Grundgesetzes. Eine Untersuchung der politischen Funktion von Verfassungsänderungen* (RG Fischer, 1981), and Stefan Schaub, *Der verfassungsändernde Gesetzgeber 1949–1980* (Duncker & Humblot, 1984).

constitutional framework, regulated such important matters as the state of defence and command of the armed forces, and provided for a standing parliamentary defence committee as well as a parliamentary commissioner for the armed forces.

B. The *Notstandsverfassung*

The Parliamentary Council had originally dropped plans for a constitutional regime of emergency provisions without discussion, presumably at the request of the Allies. It became an urgent necessity in 1955, however, when the Allied control rights were largely abolished. The formulation of the emergency provisions, however, was a bone of contention between the Government and the opposition and made no headway because of the need for a two-thirds majority. The *Notstandsverfassung* was finally adopted under the Grand Coalition which took office following the collapse of the government of Federal Chancellor Ludwig Erhard. The process was accompanied by extensive protests, in which trade unions, student organisations and intellectuals played a leading part, resulting in the emergence of the extraparliamentary opposition as a major factor in German politics at that time. Memories of the use of Article 48 of the Weimar Constitution in the latter phase of the Weimar Republic and fear of the emergence of an authoritarian regime in the Federal Republic played a key role in the campaign against the emergency rules.

The emergency powers that were initially envisaged had to be substantially watered down to obtain the consent of the SPD. It set particular store by the continuous involvement of parliament and the limitation of restrictions of fundamental rights in emergencies. The last reservations were overcome through the insertion of the right of resistance in Article 20 of the Basic Law. The wording of the inserted provision reveals, however, that its significance lies mainly in the symbolic effect associated with the concept of a right of resistance. The legal conditions for its exercise were tightly framed. All Germans have the right to resist any person seeking to abolish the constitutional order defined in Article 20, but only if 'no other remedy' is available, in other words if the defensive resources of the state have already been immobilised. Whether resistance can still achieve anything in those circumstances is questionable.

C. Reform of Federalism

The third significant constitutional amendment of that period did not serve to complete the Basic Law but altered it considerably.[3] Its origins lay in the first

[3] A comprehensive account can be found, for example, in Stefan Oeter, *Integration und Subsidiarität im deutschen Bundesstaatsrecht* (Mohr, 1998) 259 ff.

recession – a mild one, it may be said in retrospect – that the Federal Republic experienced in 1966 and 1967. It had already contributed to the fall of Federal Chancellor Ludwig Erhard, who could not bring himself to satisfy the perceived need to refocus the country's economic policy along Keynesian lines. The Grand Coalition, which took office on 1 December 1966, then quickly tackled the reform. It benefited from the availability of proposals made by the Troeger Commission, which had been appointed by the Federation and the *Länder* in 1964 and which owed its creation to discontent on all sides with the preceding limited financial reform of 1955.

The Commission's mandate was to provide for a restructuring of the financial settlement between the Federation and the *Länder*. The impetus came from a particularly striking example of an unfolding parallel constitutional reality alongside the Basic Law, a reality which, for some observers, had already transgessed the bounds of constitutionality. Soon after the founding of the Federal Republic, a unitarising tendency had already started to emerge there, driven by a growing need within society for uniform living standards rather than the cultivation of regional differences. Once Konrad Hesse had depicted that trend concisely in 1962 in a small volume with big impact,[4] a concept of federalism developed which diverged considerably from the model that had prevailed in the Parliamentary Council.

As mentioned above, West German federalism was less dualist from the outset than, for example, the US or Swiss versions. Nevertheless, sufficient dualism was retained to ensure that governmental tasks were assigned to either the Federation or the individual *Länder*. No provision had been made for the joint performance of governmental tasks or for *Land* laws that applied uniformly throughout the country. As the years went by, however, the balance between the Federation and the *Länder* shifted further and further away from that model. In the area of concurrent legislation, the Federation had made almost maximum use of its legislative powers. However, since most federal laws were executed by the *Länder*, there was also a growing need for uniformity of administrative practice among the *Länder*, which resulted in the Federation making increasingly frequent use of its power under Article 84 of the Basic Law to regulate the organisation and procedures of *Land* administrations.

Furthermore, the Federation was making increasing use of its superior financial power to provide the *Länder* with financial assistance for the performance of the tasks with which they were still entrusted but was combining that financial assistance, for which no provision had been made in the Basic Law, with the exertion of influence over the use of the funds and hence over the performance of *Land* tasks. Even the *Länder* themselves had ultimately yielded to the need for uniform living standards by taking coordination measures by means of state treaties or administrative agreements, of which the Standing Conference of Ministers of Education and Cultural Affairs of the *Länder* is but the best known of many examples. Some

[4] Konrad Hesse, *Der unitarische Bundesstaat* (CF Müller, 1962).

constitutional scholars have therefore described the Federal Republic as a tripartite federal state, in which a level of uniform *Länder* law arising from voluntary coordination has inserted itself between the federal and *Land* tiers of government.

The *Länder* found compensation for the reduction of their autonomy in an increase in the importance of the Bundesrat. What the *Länder* lost individually, they gained collectively in the form of their federal organ. The main source of that gain was Article 84 of the Basic Law, which required the consent of the Bundesrat for federal regulations that applied to *Land* administrations. The FCC increased that territorial gain still further by ruling that a single norm requiring the consent of the Bundesrat was enough to make an entire statute require such consent.[5] This made the federal political institutions increasingly dependent on the *placet* of the *Länder*. The term used to describe the creeping departure from dualism was 'cooperative federalism', which in the report of the Troeger Commission was enthroned as the contemporary model of a federal state.

In view of the economic crisis, the Commission's proposals quickly led to legislative measures, at the heart of which was the Economic Stability and Growth Promotion Act of 8 June 1967, although the Act was dependent on a constitutional amendment, which was passed that same day. The reform of the federal system followed on 12 May 1969 in the form of three bulky statutes amending the Basic Law which covered a total of 18 provisions and recast the financial settlement, watered down the principle of separate federal and *Land* budgeting in the interests of a concerted short-term economic policy, gave financial assistance a constitutional basis and provided for joint *Bund-Länder* tasks for the first time. The Federal Republic remained a federal state, and there was no impingement on Article 79(3) of the Basic Law, but the face of West German federalism had changed considerably.

The constitutional reforms had a profound effect on the constitutional framework of federal politics over the next few decades. At the same time, the tendency to create new areas of federal competence continued. Since, under Articles 30 and 70 of the Basic Law, every new sovereign task devolves automatically on the *Länder*, even if they are not best equipped to perform it, a constitutional amendment was required whenever a power was assigned to the Federation. The list of matters under exclusive legislative power of the Federation is set out in Article 73 of the Basic Law. By 1990 it had undergone three amendments, while the list of matters under concurrent legislative powers had been amended seven times, and a new Article 74a had been added. As constitutional amendments, these changes all required the consent of the Bundesrat, and the price of that consent was the extension of its right to grant or withhold consent to legislation. In addition, the Federation and the *Länder* made extensive use of the constitutionally created instrument of joint tasks.

[5] BVerfGE 8, 274 (1958), 24, 184 (1968) and 37, 363 (1974); these rulings made clear that the Bundesrat could refuse to consent to a statute even if the reason for refusal related to a provision of the statute which did not itself require consent.

In this constellation lay the reason for an immobilism that characterised politics in the Federal Republic for many years. Through the interaction of constitutional amendments, institutional practice and consitutional adjudication, the rule-exception balance between bills to which the Bundesrat could object and those which required its consent was reversed.[6] The rule was now that the Federation needed the consent of the *Länder* for its statutes. That had no implications as long as the same parties were in the majority in the Bundestag and Bundesrat, as it had become established that the party-political dichotomy overshadowed that of Federation and *Länder*. Party loyalty tended to override the interests of the *Länder*.[7] If, on the other hand, a majority of the *Land* governments were headed by the federal opposition, that majority possessed an instrument, in the Bundesrat, which could veto the federal political majority, an instrument that was used to the full, regardless of whether it was in CDU/CSU or SPD hands.

The price of that reversal, firstly, was a reduction in democracy. The party which emerged victorious from the Bundestag election could not deliver on the manifesto that had helped to win its mandate without the consent of the opposition. In those circumstances, the committee for which Article 77(2) of the Basic Law provided to mediate between the Bundestag and the Bundesrat became the most important legislative organ. Legislation increasingly became a matter for negotiation. To maximise the chances of compromise, the mediation committee does not meet in public, nor does it publish records of its proceedings. Who made what concessions, who defended what positions – such information does not reach the public domain. It therefore remains unclear where responsibility lies for the negotiated outcome. Each party could unverifiably claim the credit for successes and blame the other party for failures, leaving voters clueless as to whom they should reward or punish at the next election.

The second price was a loss of efficiency. Reforms that the Government and its component parliamentary groups intended to undertake were either delayed and diluted, or did not materialise at all. At times when there was little pressure for reform, the disadvantages were limited, because the great need for consensus ensured that neither side was favoured or disfavoured, which contributed to the absence of social strife. When pressure for reform grew, however, the disadvantages began to surface. The state was unable to respond to new challenges or to respond to them quickly or thoroughly enough. The decision-making process stalled, and public discontent grew. The consequences no longer had to be borne by one or other of the parties but by the democratic system as a whole. The catchword of the time was *Politikblockade*, signifying a logjam in the political process, and the reason for it lay in the constitutional arrangement.

[6] For details, see Friedrich Karl Fromme, *Gesetzgebung im Widerstreit*, 2nd edn (Bonn Aktuell, 1979).

[7] See Gerhard Lehmbruch, *Parteienwettbewerb im Bundesstaat* (Westdeutscher Verlag, 1976).

The same applied to the second element of the constitutional reform, namely the joint tasks which had been incorporated into the Basic Law through Articles 91a and 91b and the financial assistance which Article 104a of the Basic Law now expressly permitted. Both mechanisms interlaced the Federation and the *Länder* to an extent that constituted a reversal of the original arrangement in the Basic Law. There would have been no departure from that system if the distribution of tasks between the Federation and the *Länder* had been adapted to satisfy the new requirements and the allocation of funds had been made to reflect the distribution of tasks. Here too, however, the actors were compelled to take the negotiating route. Since unanimity was prescribed for the performance of joint tasks, they could only be tackled if the Federation and all 10 *Länder* reached agreement. The prospect of federal funds rather than the quality of the solution was often the key to unanimity.

The result was often a compromise based on the lowest common denominator, and it was not unusual for the achievement of the compromise to be regarded as a success in itself. The parliaments whose consent was ultimately required found themselves in ratification scenarios. Since any amendment proposal would have put the negotiated outcome in jeopardy, they had no choice in practice but to assent. If malfunctions occurred, it was difficult to remedy them, because amendments also needed consensus, and one participant or another would be benefiting from the malfunction. This was another area in which democratic responsibilities were difficult to pin down. Claimed successes and apportionments of blame were unverifiable. All of this was soon recognised, especially by political scientists, and criticised as a source of democracy and efficiency deficits, but that did not lead to change.[8]

The governing parties of the day bemoaned the logjam but were not prepared to give up their jamming instrument when they returned to the opposition benches. Matters finally became so intolerable that a *Bund-Länder* commission was appointed in 2003 to draw up proposals for reform of the federal system. It ended its work in 2004 having drawn up a full programme of reforms but without having formally adopted it.[9] The large, wealthy *Länder* led by the CDU or CSU withdrew their approval at the last minute. The reservations of the small, financially weaker *Länder* were disregarded. The Grand Coalition formed after the 2005 election then made the constitutional reforms possible in the 52nd amendment act, based on the programme of 2004. That turning point, however, is already outside the period covered by most of the historical works.[10]

[8] See esp Fritz W Scharpf, Bernd Reissert and Fritz Schnabel, *Politikverflechtung* (Scriptor, 1976) and *Politikverflechtung II* (Athenäum, 1977).

[9] Accounts are given by Rainer Holtschneider and Walter Schön (eds), *Die Reform des Bundesstaats* (Nomos, 2007), and Hans Meyer, *Die Föderalismusreform 2006* (Duncker & Humblot, 2008).

[10] But see Conze, 376.

D. Fundamental Rights

Compared with amendments to the organisational part of the Constitution, amendments to the Bill of Rights have been relatively rare. The reason for that is that the interests protected by the fundamental rights in their abstract wording are not disputed. In this case, it is not the norm that triggers disputes, but its interpretation. Some changes to the Bill of Rights were occasioned by rearmament. Article 12a of the Basic Law introduced compulsory military and alternative civilian service. Article 17a permitted additional restrictions of fundamental rights for military personnel. A number of amendments were adopted in 1968 in connection with the *Notstandsverfassung*. In some cases, they widened the scope for restriction to protect the free democratic basic order (Articles 10 and 11), while some limited the scope for restriction. The new third sentence added to Article 9(3) of the Basic Law stated that emergency measures must not be directed against industrial disputes.

Palpable changes in the realm of fundamental rights took effect following reunification. Some owed their existence to the new risk scenario following the changes of 1989/90 in the international political situation, and others had their roots in a keener awareness of disadvantage. The latter were not in any way controversial. They related chiefly to equality between men and women, which had been guaranteed from the outset in Article 3(2) of the Basic Law. Although it had ensured that disadvantages suffered by women on the basis of statutory law were invalidated, if only with the aid of Karlsruhe,[11] Article 3(2) in its original interpretation as a ban on discrimination did not help to remedy the numerous actual disadvantages to which women were exposed as a result of the traditional status and role allocation between the sexes and the conventional distribution of labour in marriage and family life and which adversely affected women's educational and career opportunities.

For that reason, a second sentence was added to that paragraph in 1994, which reads as follows: 'The state shall promote the actual implementation of equal rights for women and men and take steps to eliminate existing disadvantages.' Its innovative force was minimal, however, because the FCC had already interpreted the old version of Article 3(2) not only as a *prohibition* of discrimination, but also as a *prescription* of equal treatment, which 'also extends to social reality'. Article 3(2) of the Basic Law, the Court ruled, seeks 'not only to eliminate legal norms which attach advantages or disadvantages to gender characteristics but to enforce gender equality for the future. Its aim is the assimilation of living conditions'.[12] Rules designed to favour women, therefore, are not in breach of equal rights. Article 3(3), moreover, was expanded to include a ban on unfair treatment on grounds of disability.

[11] BVerfG, 3, 225 (1953); see ch 11 below.
[12] BVerfGE 85, 191, 207 (1992).

Great controversy, on the other hand, surrounded the new restrictions of fundamental rights. The first of these came with the constitutional emergency provisions – the *Notstandsverfassung* – and related to the privacy of correspondence, posts and telecommunications, which is protected by Article 10 of the Basic Law, and freedom of movement, guaranteed by Article 11. These may be more tightly restricted in an emergency. The *Notstandsverfassung* was adopted by a large majority of the Grand Coalition. That, however, did not instantly quench the resistance within society. On the contrary, actions were brought before the FCC. They essentially targeted the extension of the provisions regarding the privacy of correspondence, posts and telecommunications guaranteed by Article 10 of the Basic Law; in particular, they challenged the rule that the person affected by any of the restrictions introduced to protect the free democratic basic order was not to be informed of the restriction and the fact that recourse to the courts was to be replaced by a review conducted by bodies appointed by the legislature.

Since the challenged provisions were constitutional norms, the application for judicial review filed by the *Land* government of Hesse and the constitutional complaints lodged by several lawyers could only succeed if the constitutional amendment itself were unconstitutional. The complainants argued that the principle of the rule of law, which was one of the inviolable constitutional principles protected by Article 79(3) of the Basic Law, was compromised by the exclusion of recourse to the courts. In addition, the *Land* argued that it made the individual a mere object of state authority, which also violated the guarantee of human dignity. It was the first time that the Court had been confronted with the question of an unconstitutional amendment of the Basic Law. The justices could not reach agreement. Three held that the amendment to Article 10 of the Basic Law violated both human dignity and the principle of the rule of law. Five saw no infringement of Article 79(3). The action was thus dismissed.[13]

Further restrictions resulted from the growing threat of terrorism after the turn of the year in 1989/90 and from the rise in the number of asylum applications following the opening of previously sealed borders. These evoked a highly emotive public response and accordingly became the subject of heated political debates too, which culminated in 1993 in a root-and-branch reform of the right of asylum, hitherto guaranteed by Article 16 of the Basic Law, which also regulated loss of citizenship and extradition. The old provision made do with a single sentence: 'Persons persecuted on political grounds shall have the right of asylum.' The debatable point was what constituted persecution on political grounds. As long as a person was deemed to be subject to persecution on political grounds, however, asylum had to be granted. The granting of asylum was now made subject to a host of further conditions. In particular, the entitlement ceased to apply if an asylum-seeker had entered Germany from a 'safe third country'.

Five years later, the provisions on the right to inviolability of the home enshrined in Article 13 of the Basic Law were supplemented with a number of

[13] BVerfGE 30, 1 (1970).

intervention authorisations, some of which were focused on the dangers that had to be averted, while others broadened the range of technical means which could be employed for that purpose. The amendment was the umbrella under which numerous laws designed to facilitate intelligence gathering in the fight against terrorism were adopted in the period that followed, especially in the wake of the atrocities of 11 September 2001. The amendment of Article 13 gave rise to the second occasion on which the FCC was seized of a request to review the constitutionality of an amendment to the Basic Law. Once again, the Court did not find any infringement of Article 79(3). Two justices, however, explained in a dissenting opinion why they found the amendment to be unconstitutional, and thus null and void.[14]

In terms of their constitutional function, both amendments must be regarded as flawed. The new Article 16a on asylum is about 70 times wordier than its predecessor. Article 13, for its part, is four times longer than the original provision. Several lengthy passages read more like an administrative regulation than a constitution. Many commentators regard this as a cosmetic blemish. In truth, it is a democracy problem.[15] What a constitution regulates is removed, *ipso facto*, from the democratic process. A constitutional provision is a premise for political decisions, not their object. Elections are inconsequential in that respect. Changes of political course can only be made after the constitution has been amended. The balance shifts from the elected organs to constitutional adjudication.

III. The Constitutional Amendments in Historiography

Every amendment of the constitution changes the conditions in which politics is played out. But not every amendment changes them so sustainably that it is bound to be registered by historians. The more detailed a constitution is, the greater the need for amendments, but the fewer the number of amendments which cross the threshold of structural determinancy or value change. The Basic Law is one of the more detailed constitutions, particularly in its provisions governing the relationship between the Federation and the *Länder*. Accordingly, many of the amendments to that part of the constitution serve only to correct details and are of no historical significance. The same does not apply, however, to the three amendments of 1956, 1968 and 1969 that have been highlighted here. The amendments to the Bill of Rights are no secondary matter either, but judicial responses to effects of globalisation – hence the question how they impact on the historiography of the Federal Republic.

All three major amendments to the organisational part of the Basic Law were responses to particular developments and took place in particular constellations, the significance of which is recognised by the historians through the more or less

[14] BVerfGE 109, 279 (2004).

[15] See Dieter Grimm, 'Wie man eine Verfassung verderben kann' in idem, *Die Verfassung und die Politik* (CH Beck, 2001) 126.

comprehensive treatment they give them in their works. That is not equally true of the role that the constitutional amendments played in them, however, for the amendments receive widely varying degrees of attention. Readers sometimes receive absolutely no hint of the fact that a constitutional amendment was on the agenda; sometimes they are merely informed that it was enacted but are not told what it comprised; sometimes the substance is discussed, but not its impact on subsequent developments. Only rarely is there an explanation of what was at stake in the decision to amend the constitution. Failed attempts to amend the Basic Law usually receive no attention at all.

First of all, as regards the constitutional regime for the armed forces (*Wehrverfassung*) of 1956, all of the works explain the historical background to rearmament and describe the establishment and structure of the Bundeswehr. The essential amendment of the constitution receives no mention fom Herbert, Morsey or Wehler. Wolfrum refers to 'new armed forces legislation' (132), but not to the constitutional amendment that made it possible in the first place. Görtemaker also speaks of 'armed forces legislation' but does let it be known, at least indirectly, that the legislation in question was a constitutional amendment (the legislation, he writes, had to be 'fitted into the constitutional framework', 339). Winkler mentions the enshrinement of federal competence for defence in the Basic Law, placing particular emphasis on the creation of a commissioner for the armed forces (182, English 335). Only Conze (93–96) addresses the constitutional amendment in greater detail.

Now, it may be possible to explain this finding by arguing that the event of historic importance was the establishment of armed forces, not the amendment of the constitution. But there could have been no Bundeswehr without the constitution having been amended, just as there was no constitutional regime of emergency provisions for 10 years because of the absence of the supermajority that was required for an amendment of the Basic Law. The amendment was also more than a mere vehicle for rearmament, for authorising political action was not the end of the story. At issue, and sometimes bitterly contested, were the questions of what options were open to the politicians and how the armed forces should be shaped. Special importance attached to the principle, fiercely resisted by traditionalists, of shaping the Bundeswehr as a parliamentary army, which was intended to reconcile the re-establishment of military forces with democracy. The issue was resolved by the constitutional amendment. There would therefore have been good reason to write more about it than simply the fact of its enactment.

The same phenomenon is even more clearly recognisable in the case of the *Notstandsverfassung*. Like the *Wehrverfassung*, it was also dependent on a constitutional amendment. But the difference between the two lies in the fact that the amendment of 1956 had an objective beyond the bounds of the constitution which would have been unattainable without the amendment. The amendment was therefore a means to an end. The amendment of 1968 had no such objective outside the bounds of the Basic Law. It was not the prerequisite for the achievement of an external goal. The amendment itself was the goal. The amendment remained intrinsic to the constitution. The Basic Law was to be equipped to deal with exceptional situations, should they ever arise. But the questions whether and how were far more bitterly contentious than the *Wehrverfassung*. The constitutional amendment resolved the conflict and even calmed the public in the long run.

In Herbert, Wehler and Winkler, however, the emergency rules owe their mention to having coincided with another process, namely the protest movement of 1968, for they are not addressed in their own right. Wehler, indeed, makes no mention at all of the constitutional amendment. In his view, the only significance of the emergencies issue was that it added German fuel to the student revolts of those years, which were not confined to Germany (313, 316). For Winkler, too (250–52, English 451–54), the primary significance of the emergency rules was that the campaign against them marked the climax of the '1968 movement'. Unlike Wehler, however, Winkler stresses the need for a constitutional amendment and, as regards its substance, the reader is at least informed that, thanks to the SPD, rules were pushed through which were designed to guarantee 'maximum parliamentary and judicial control of the executive during emergency situations' (251, English 451).

Herbert (846–59, English 684–703), on the other hand, attributes this achievement to the protest movement. Their demands, he writes, were 'largely' taken into account. Citing Hans Günter Hockerts,[16] he sees the value of the protest movement in the fact that 'a great public constitutional debate' took place, which made up for the fact that there had been no debate when the Basic Law was promulgated. It was indeed a constitutional debate, because for the critics of the restrictions the country was faced with a choice between authoritarianism and democracy. The emergency rules were dubbed the 'NS (National Socialist) laws', and their adoption was equated with that of the Enabling Act in 1933. But it was not the same debate which had been missed in 1949, because it did not concern the Basic Law in its existing form but sought, on the contrary, to prevent a change in the Basic Law that would have unravelled the achievement of 1949.

The other authors consider the *Notstandsverfassung* not only in terms of its significance for the protest movement but as an entity in its own right, which they describe more or less comprehensively (Conze 343–45, Wolfrum 236 f and Morsey 110 f). But they likewise recognise that the protest movement influenced the content of the constitutional amendment. Görtemaker (453–57), who makes a point of stressing that precautions for an emergency are among the self-evident components of constitutions and that Germany was the only country where they met with resistance, considered the main practical purpose of those precautions to be the 'pooling of all aid resources in case of natural disasters and serious misfortunes'; the campaign, however, was certainly not being waged against such contingency planning but against the intended regime of provisions for an internal emergency arising from attacks on the constitutional order and for an external emergency arising from military aggression.

[16] Hans Günter Hockerts in *Geschichte der Sozialpolitik in Deutschland*, Vol 5 (Nomos, 2006) 24.

In the case of the reform of the federal system, the significance of the constitutional amendment in itself is patently obvious. Like the *Wehrverfassung*, it served a purpose beyond the bounds of the constitution, namely overcoming the crisis and creating the conditions for effective economic policies. Unlike the *Wehrverfassung* and the *Notstandsverfassung*, however, it did not close any gaps. The Basic Law regulated the subject matter, but the way in which it did so had proved to be an obstacle to crisis management. The reform of the federal system was the response to that problem. Two authors – Henrich-Franke and Wirsching – reveal nothing about it. The other 10 deal with it, albeit to widely differing extents and with widely differing emphasis. Eight of those 10 authors mention the Economic Stability and Growth Promotion Act of 8 June 1967, but only five of them give any indication that a constitutional amendment had to be enacted on that same day before the Act could be adopted.

Now it might be said that the amendment of Article 109 of the Basic Law, the article providing for separation of the federal and *Länder* budgets, was not sufficient to overcome the economic crisis. It took the Economic Stability and Growth Promotion Act to introduce the requisite measures. But without the amendment of Article 109 of the Basic Law, there could have been no such Act. The amendment, in turn, was only the vanguard of the following year's reforms of the financial settlement and the federal system, which effected the switch from dual to cooperative federalism. Readers are informed more or less comprehensively of the significance of the systemic change by eight of the authors, while Herbert deals with the Economic Stability and Growth Promotion Act (837 f, English 681 f) but leaves it at that. Yet two of the eight authors pass over the fact that this was a constitutional reform (Görtemaker 516 f and Recker 58), which leaves readers wondering how such a key component of the Basic Law as the federal system could have undergone such radical change.

It is Conze who deals most comprehensively with the innovations (370 ff). Citing Herbert Weichmann, he regards the amendments as 'the most thorough and far-reaching reform of the Basic Law in the 20 years of its existence' (375; the quotation is in fn 21 at 964). Conze also provides the most comprehensive analysis of the their consequences for the political system. The premises for the constitutional reform, he states, already ceased to apply only a few years after the switch to cooperative federalism. He emphasises the importance of differing majorities in the Bundestag and Bundesrat for the functioning of the federal system, but overlooks the interaction with institutional practice and with constitutional adjudication. Apart from Conze, only Birke (36) and Geppert (36) cite the constitutional reform as a cause of the '*Politikblockade*', the logjam in the political process, while Winkler assesses the constitutional reform favourably on the whole (256, English 460 f) and elsewhere emphasises the erosions of democracy resulting from government by a Grand Coalition rather than those stemming from cooperative federalism (268, English 480).

Wehler is in a category of his own. He provides a detailed portrayal of the unique nature of West German federalism, contrasting it on the one hand with the Prussian-dominated federal state of the German Empire and the decentralised unitary state of the Weimar Republic and on the other hand with US, Canadian, Swiss and Austrian federal systems (243). He also describes the high degree of joint political decision-making (*Politikverflechtung*) that ultimately spilled over into political logjams, but overlooks the *caesura* of 1968/69 and, unlike Conze, does not associate the prevailing constellation with the constitution. As for the Basic Law, Wehler makes do with the comment that 'Here and there the constitution was supplemented or repaired, though without altering its foundations' (244 f), which gives no inkling of the scale of the reform.

Some of the authors conclude their account of this historical phase with an assessment. Conze delivers a mixed verdict. The reforms, he writes, had built the constitutional basis for reformist policies but had also created the conditions for the subsequent political logjam (376). Wehler also paints a variegated picture but concludes with the statement that the Basic Law and the empirical conditions for the political process in the sense of Lassalle's 'real constitution' had proved their worth, thanks to their stability and flexibility (245). Winkler believed that the Grand Coalition had made the democratic system 'more resistant to crisis' (256, English 461) and finally judged unreservedly that the political system of the Basic Law had passed its first serious test (272, English 488). Yet how does this conclusion sit with the fact that the need for a total revision of the Basic Law was being widely proclaimed at that very time?[17]

As far as the amendments to the fundamental rights are concerned, Winkler is the only one who takes account of the addition to Article 3 (611, English 1055). Several of the authors, on the other hand, comment on the asylum issue, the most sharply focused remarks being those of Winkler (613 ff, English 1057 ff) and Herbert, who states that no other issue moved Germans as much as asylum policy during those years (1174, English 954). In connection with the 'asylum compromise' of 1993, some refer unspecifically to the fact that asylum law was amended, while Wehler writes that a 'restrictive asylum law' was enacted (43). But the problem was the unrestricted fundamental right. According to Wolfrum, the fundamental right of asylum was extended (475). But the 'extension' consisted, as it then emerges, in a drastic restriction. The framing of the constitutional amendment ultimately caught only Winkler's attention. 'Never before', he writes, 'had an article of the Basic Law been so freighted with procedural matters as the new Article 16a. Such an approach contradicted the basic nature of the constitution' (613, English 1058).

[17] See ch 5 below.

5

Moves Towards a Total Revision of the Basic Law

I. The 'Antiquated' Basic Law

The second half of the 1960s saw a rising tide of opinion that the Basic Law was 'antiquated' and had to be subjected to a 'complete revision'.[1] The formation of the Grand Coalition in 1966 fuelled such demands. It created the prospect, and indeed was partly motivated by the prospect, that a number of overdue reforms which required constitutional amendments and which had therefore fallen by the wayside could now be made. Yet there was more to the desire for a total revision than the specific interest in those reforms. Accordingly, the extensive constitutional amendments of 1968 and 1969 that were addressed in the previous chapter did not silence the objectors either. On the contrary, their voices grew louder, thanks in great part to the veritable missionary zeal of Christian Democratic Union (CDU) Bundestag member Hans Dichgans.[2]

As his engagement shows, the demands were not all addressed to the political institutions from the outside, but had internal advocates too. Paul Lücke, Minister of the Interior in the Grand Coalition, had a list of articles in need of amendment compiled which grew to more than 80 items. The Bundestag was clearly impressed by the massed demands and decided in October 1970, by which time the Social Democratic-Liberal coalition was in power, to appoint a study commission on constitutional reform, comprising seven federal and seven *Land* politicians as well as five experts, all of whom were recognised scholars of constitutional law. The commission was to examine 'whether and to what extent it is necessary to adapt the Basic Law – while preserving its fundamental principles – to meet present and foreseeable future requirements'.[3]

Such radical revision projects which do not relate to individual provisions or particular sections of a constitution, but to the entire document, are normally the

[1] See Helmut Lindemann, *Das antiquierte Grundgesetz. Plädoyer für eine zeitgemäße Verfassung* (Wegner, 1966).

[2] See Hans Dichgans, *Vom Grundgesetz zur Verfassung. Überlegungen zu einer Gesamtrevision* (Econ, 1970), based on numerous previous essays. The whole range of statements made on the subject can be gleaned from the almost two-page-long fn 8 in Friedrich Karl Fromme, '"Totalrevision" des Grundgesetzes' (1970) 17 *Zeitschrift für Politik* 90.

[3] Bundestag printed paper VI/1211.

result of deep-seated uneasiness. This can have various causes. It is possible that the constitution in its whole scheme is proving to be poorly framed. It may be that conditions have changed in the meantime, so that an originally satisfactory constitution is no longer fit for purpose. It is possible, finally, that a society's values have undergone change and that a discrepancy has developed between the values that underlie the constitution and those of a significant part of society. History books would be expected to give an account of any changes occurring on that kind of scale.

Which of those possible reasons fed the desire for a complete revision of the Basic Law? Helmut Lindemann favoured the first option. He saw the Basic Law as a constitution rooted in the past which did not satisfy contemporary needs (those of the 'atomic age'). But Lindemann found little support for his supposition. A shift in values, triggered or at least accelerated by the protest movement of 1968, is registered in every one of the historical works. That shift, however, relates more to society's perception of traditional moral standards and to the virtues it prized most at the time than to the values underlying the Basic Law, such as human dignity, democracy, the rule of law and the welfare state, which were not called into question but were, to some extent, redefined in a more progressive direction.[4]

The protest movement was more receptive to Adolf Arndt, the prominent legal expert, Social Democratic Party (SPD) politician and campaigner for constitutional adjudication who, back in 1960, had published a book entitled *Das unerfüllte Grundgesetz* ('*The unfulfilled Basic Law*'). The movement did not reject the Basic Law, but called for fulfilment of the promises which, it believed, were contained in its provisions, and in the current situation that meant, above all, democratisation of society and its main functional areas, especially the economy and education. A similar chord is struck in Willy Brandt's call, made in his first government policy statement, to 'risk more democracy'. Not all of the protesters' concepts of democracy may have matched those of the Basic Law, but groups that dreamed of radical systemic change were largely fringe players.

The great majority of the authors who called for a complete revision of the Basic Law considered, first, that it was no longer appropriate to speak of a provisional arrangement and, second, that socio-eonomic changes which had occurred since 1949 made it necessary to revise the Basic Law. In particular, it was the experience of the 1966/67 crisis that motivated the desire for revision, an experience which had already provided the impetus for the reform of the federal system and which now refocused attention on the more profound changes in the economy, which did not seem to have been mastered yet following the reform of 1969.[5] Above all, constitutional reform was supposed to create the conditions for a switch from reactive to proactive policymaking. Planning,

[4] A signigficant role was played in this respect by Wolfgang Abendroth, *Das Grundgesetz. Eine Einführung in seine politische Probleme* (Neske, 1966), a book that stands in sharp contrast to the traditional doctrine of public law.

[5] See ch 4 above.

hitherto regarded as part of the arsenal of communist regimes, was the great catchword of the time. The historical works also refer to a planning euphoria of the late 1960s and early 1970s.

The Study Commission began its work in March 1971. In accordance with its remit to preserve the fundamental principles of the constitution, it did not perceive its task as a 'total revision' but, leaving the state objectives and the fundamental rights untouched, focused primarily on the issues of parliamentary reform, the division of legislative powers between the Federation and the *Länder*, and the planning of state tasks. Before it could complete its deliberations, however, its mandate expired with the early dissolution of the sixth Bundestag in September 1972. All it could present, therefore, was an interim report.[6] However, the new Bundestag gave it the opportunity to continue its work. Continuity largely prevailed in terms of its composition, but the pool of experts was enlarged with the addition of two new members, one of whom was a political scientist.

The concluding report, a document of almost 300 pages, was presented to the Bundestag on 9 December 1976.[7] The recommendations were more restrained than the interim report had led anyone to expect. In the section on the Federation and the *Länder*, the Commission could not envisage any way to restore more autonomy to the *Länder*, such as returning legislative powers to them. It merely proposed a more stringent verification of the need for federal laws. It rejected the insertion of a third tier into the federal structure, because that would have been done at the expense of the distinct statehood of the *Länder*; of the benefits of federalism, it would have left only the separation of powers but not closeness to citizens or the competition that spurs innovation. The only option, then, was to continue on the path of cooperative federalism on which the country had set out back in 1969.

Although most of the proposals on the federal system were carried in spite of the dissenting votes of the *Länder* representatives, there was more consensus on matters of planning and legislation. The joint tasks, and hence joint framework planning by the Federation and the *Länder*, were to be extended. The idea of involving Parliament in the planning process, however, met with scepticism. The Federal Government had issued a stern warning against regulating planning in the constitution before enough practical experience of the planning process had been gathered. The Commission, on the other hand, sought to strengthen Parliament in its political role and therefore tried to increase its ability to provide for transparency and oversight. To avert the threat of a legitimacy crisis, the influence of voters was to be increased by means of the use of open lists in elections, but the idea of introducing plebiscitary elements did not find favour.

Some other thematic areas were not addressed for want of time, including constitutional adjudication, which had come in for fierce criticism at that time

[6] Bundestag printed paper VI/3829; *Zur Sache*, 1/73.
[7] Bundestag printed paper VII/5924; *Zur Sache*, 2/77 and 3/77.

on account of various rulings against reform projects of the Social Democratic–Liberal coalition.[8] The full list of proposals was lengthy: 22 articles were to be amended, three added and two repealed. In substance, however, the proposals turned out to be more moderate than originally expected. They did not look like the seeds of a completely new constitution.[9] The preface to the concluding report ended with the following appeal: 'In presenting its report, the Commission assumes that the Eighth German Bundestag will consider its recommendations. It combines this assumption with the expectation that the proposals will be examined and gradually implemented.'

At that point in time, the Eighth German Bundestag had already been elected and would hold its constituent sitting on 14 December 1976. Although the two governing parties – the SPD and the Free Democratic Party (FDP) – had lost votes, they still held a majority. The newly elected Parliament took note of the Study Commission's report, but fell short of the Commission's expectations. Apart from two rather technical suggestions that had already been accepted by the previous Bundestag, its proposals received no consideration. Six years had passed since the appointment of the Study Commission, and much had changed during that time. Reformist zeal had given way to a mood of crisis, which had prevailed since 1973.[10] In May 1974, Willy Brandt made way for Helmut Schmidt as Chancellor. Interest in a new Basic Law waned.

The need for reform of the Basic Law was no longer being discussed, but that was not all. There was also a slowly growing awareness of its virtues. Dolf Sternberger coined the term 'constitutional patriotism' – not on the occasion of the 30th anniversary of the Basic Law, as is mostly assumed, but much earlier, in 1970.[11] In the essay of 1979, it was intended as an exhortation to West Germans, since their nation was divided and was not available as a focus for patriotism, to identify with their constitutional order. By the time Jürgen Habermas, another seven years on, revisited constitutional patriotism in connection with the *Historikerstreit*, the dispute that arose in Germany over historiographic assessments of the National Socialist era and the Holocaust, and recommended it as a somewhat harmless variant of patriotism,[12] it had even become acceptable to the Left. Ubiquitous veneration of the Basic Law had begun.

[8] See ch 9 below.

[9] See Dieter Grimm, 'Die Revision des deutschen Grundgesetzes. Ursachen – Themen – Chancen' in *Österreichische Zeitschrift für Politikwissenschaft* 6 (1977) 397.

[10] For more details, see ch 12 below.

[11] Dolf Sternberger, 'Unvergleichlich lebensvoll, aber stets gefährdet: Ist unsere Verfassung nicht demokratisch genug?' *Frankfurter Allgemeine Zeitung* (27 January 1970); idem, 'Verfassungspatriotismus' *Frankfurter Allgemeine Zeitung* (23 May 1979) (also in idem, *Verfassungspatriotismus* (*Schriften* X, Insel, 1990). On the origins of the term, see Jan Werner Müller, *Verfassungspatriotismus* (Suhrkamp, 2010) 21 ff; English *Constitutional Patriotism* (Princeton University Press, 2007) 15 ff.

[12] Jürgen Habermas, 'Eine Art Schadensabwicklung' *Die Zeit* (11 July 1986); also in the volume of the same name (Suhrkamp, 1987) 115.

II. Attunement to New Requirements

Nevertheless, only five years after the term of the Study Commission had ended, another commission was appointed to examine the need for amendment of the Basic Law. There were considerable differences, however, between the two reform projects. The aim of the new commission's deliberations was not to transform the Basic Law but rather to supplement it in the light of problems which had not yet arisen in 1949, but for which political responses were now needed. The focus this time was on the substantive part of the Basic Law, which had been excluded from the total revision. The new Expert Commission, moreover, was not appointed by Parliament but by the Ministries of the Interior and of Justice and consisted entirely of professors of law, seven in number, compared with the 21 members of the Study Commission, where external experts had been in the minority.

Examination of the possible need to define new state objectives had already been announced in Federal Chancellor Helmut Schmidt's government policy statement in November 1980. The Chancellor had also referred to a number of subjects which, in the Government's view, required discussion. The commission, which held its constituent meeting in 1982, compiled a list of subject areas that could be considered and decided to examine the suitability of four of them for inclusion in the Basic Law, namely work, environmental protection, state protection and promotion of culture, and data protection. The last of these did not meet the commission's criteria, but it concluded that the other three should be incorporated into the constitution. The members, however, could not agree on the wording of the additional provisions, and the place where they should be inserted was also a contentious issue, and so the commission ultimately presented several options in its report.[13]

It was not a matter, then, of replacing provisions that had proved detrimental to the pursuit of urgent political goals. The political organs could have dealt with the subjects that were now to be given a place in the Basic Law without the need to amend the constitution. So what purpose would the constitutional amendment serve? In its statement on legal affairs policy of March 1981, the Federal Government referred to clarifying and supplementing the state objectives which were already enshrined in the Basic Law. These are not an imperative component of constitutions. The Basic Law in its original form was sparing with its state objectives. Not even the supreme purpose of the state – the internal and external security of its citizens – was mentioned. Of the principles listed in Article 20, the principle of the social state was the closest in nature to an objective. To it may be added the aims of reunification and European integration proclaimed in the preamble.

The need to enshrine more objectives in the Basic Law, in fact, arose from a combination of changes in the nature of the state and an increase in the importance

[13] Federal Ministry of the Interior and Federal Ministry of Justice (eds), *Staatszielbestimmungen, Gesetzgebungsaufträge. Bericht der Sachverständigen-Kommission* (1983).

of the constitution, chiefly as a result of constitutional adjudication. The change in the nature of the state can best be described as a transition from a state focused on the status quo to one focused on the future. A state whose function is confined to preserving from disturbances an existing order deemed to be fair is replaced by a state that continually strives towards particular standards of justice. The replacement, it is true, is not an event but a lengthy process, though it was accelerated by the manifestations of crisis in 1966/67, and to a greater extent by those in 1973, which altered people's perceptions at those times.

If such a process occurs under a constitution which is recognised by society as a binding formulation of its aspirations and values, a constitution which, moreover, through influential constitutional adjudication, can constantly be perceived as a significant determinant of political and social conditions, society will quickly seek affirmation of its political expectations in the constitution. Those who believe they have an important interest will want that interest to be recognised in the constitution, which they can then play as a trump card in the political debate. The character of the constitution itself is thereby altered. It is then understood not only as an instrument for the legal organisation and regulation of political activity but also as a programme and a mandate to act for politicians and as an appeal to the political actors.[14]

But why were those three subjects chosen as worthy of treatment in the Basic Law from a wider selection of thematic areas which had been seen as important and given due consideration? If it is assumed, as the commission did, that these were the most pressing issues to which political responses were needed at the start of the 1980s, the history books would surely provide some relevant information. For that reason, another look may be taken at the works under examination at this point. What do they say about the state of work, environmental protection and culture in the late 1970s and early 1980s? Do they recognise *desiderata* in those areas? Do they relate the subjects themselves to the constitution? Is the work of the commission assessed, unlike that of the previous study commission?

A. Work

The Federal Republic had soon recovered from the economic crisis of 1966/67 thanks to the new set of instruments and had quickly achieved full employment again. The serious crisis was yet to come. It erupted in 1973 as a result of the Yom Kippur War. The oil-producing countries drastically cut their extraction volumes, thereby sharply increasing the price of oil. The term 'oil shock' or 'oil price shock' is not absent from any of the history books. The consequence was a deep recession, described by some of the historians as the worst since 1929, which quickly

[14] See Uwe Volkmann, *Grundzüge einer Verfassungslehre der Bundesrepublik Deutschland* (2013) 23 ff.

sent unemployment soaring. Aggregate demand management (*Globalsteuerung*), introduced in 1969 by way of a constitutional reform, could not stem the tide. Fear of joblessness and of declining living standards is described as the overriding issue of that time.

Only when the economy began to recover without a reduction in unemployment figures did it become clear that this was not just a cyclical crisis. Several works mention the English term 'jobless growth'. The oil price crisis had coincided with a profound structural change. Not much later, the service sector ousted the manufacturing sector from top place in the employment statistics. The end of the industrial age was proclaimed. The development is given ample space in the historical works, Herbert's treatment (887 ff, English 721 ff) probably being the most comprehensive, whereas Wehler gives it little coverage, even though he, unlike the other authors, presents a social history, in which the economy forms a central axis together with political rule and culture.

The subject of fundamental economic and social rights had never entirely disappeared from the constitutional debate. Now it acquired fresh topicality, particularly as regards the right to work. It is therefore understandable that the commission put the subject of work at the top of its agenda. It was certainly well aware that, in a system in which the conduct of private business is a fundamental right, there can be no individual right to a job. The 'right to work' could therefore be at most an obligation of the state to pursue an active labour market policy. That was the form in which the commission proposed it as the subject of a constitutional amendment. Some of the members regarded Article 12 of the Basic Law, which guarantees occupational freedom, as the right place for a new provision, while others preferred the insertion of a new Article 37b.

B. Environment

Just as the oil price shock is not missing from any of the history books, none of them fails to mention the first Club of Rome report of 1972 on *The Limits to Growth*. It is regarded as a wake-up call for protection of the environment and of the natural foundations of life. Accordingly, environmental protection is not absent from any of the works, although in this case, too, it takes a painstaking search of Wehler's work to find a reference. His subject index does not have *Umweltschutz* (environmental protection) as an entry, and although one would hope to find something under *Grüne* (Greens), the reference there directs the reader to a section entitled 'New political culture', where, in a somewhat throwaway remark, one learns that the Greens are 'an ecologist and pacifist protest party' (293).

Wolfrum, by contrast, describes environmental protection as 'the most significant issue of that time' (401). Back in 1974, the state had responded to the issue by establishing the Umweltbundesamt, the German Environment Agency. Some *Land* constitutions had already led the way with environmental protection clauses. Calls were being made in academic literature for the inclusion of environmental protection in the Basic Law. It was therefore natural for the commission to list it. This was, of course, another case in which it was difficult to clothe the desired protection in the garb of an individual right. An intact environment is a collective interest. For that reason, the commission opted once again for definition of a state objective, the majority preferring an addition to Article 20(1) of the Basic Law, while a minority favoured a new Article 37a.

C. Culture

It is harder to associate the proposal for a clause on state protection and promotion of culture with a current event or process. Nevertheless, the year 1973 is treated in all of the histories as a watershed year, the importance of which went far beyond the economic upheavals.[15] It was also culturally significant, not only in the cultural spheres such as education, research, art and religion, but also in terms of mentalities, lifestyles and value systems, either as a consequence or as a concomitant of the economic crisis. 'Post-modern' and 'post-materialist values' are the catchwords most often used to characterise this change, along with the term 'post-industrial era'.

The commission did not spread its net as far as that. It pointed out that, since the emergence of a tendency to unitarise the federal state and the constitutional amendments of 1969, the *Länder* had no longer had sole responsibility for cultural affairs, which had become an area of shared competence, particularly in the realm of higher education. It also mentioned that a 'change in favour of greater candour in conceptions of art'[16] had taken place, which had legal implications in areas such as the protection of families, youth welfare and the moral criminal code (*Sittenstrafrecht*). Ultimately, however, it was the growing degree of public authorities' activities in the fields of education, research and cultural policy which prompted the commission to propose that the cultural mission of the entire state be enshrined in the Basic Law.

The proposals met with the same fate as the far more comprehensive proposals made by the Study Commission. They were not incorporated into the Basic Law. Between the appointment of the commission and the presentation of its proposals came the change of government of 1982, which put an end to many reform efforts. Protection of the environment would not be included in the constitution until after reunification. A clause on state protection and promotion of culture was proposed as a new Article 20b by the Study Commission on Culture in Germany in 2005, but the proposal was similarly unsuccessful. The right to work returned to the agenda in the course of the reunification process, likewise to no avail. The commission itself had opted not to make proposals on data protection and the

[15] See also ch 12 below.
[16] Expert Commission (n 13) 115.

protection of personal privacy, because it could only have reproduced existing rulings of the Federal Constitutional Court (FCC).

III. The Revisions of the Basic Law in Historiography

The historians predated the praise that later came the way of the Basic Law. The fact that it was to be abolished and replaced by a new constitution entirely escaped their attention. Perhaps the failure of the project explains its lack of historiographic impact. But is the failure sufficient reason for silence? After all, the factors that gave rise to the reform efforts are mostly mentioned in the books. The assumption that they rendered a constitution unfit for purpose when it was barely 20 years old is no small matter. At that time the need to renew the Basic Law was a subject of general interest. The commission, moreover, was not by any means working in secret. Its deliberations were accompanied by a flood of published material, not only in scholarly journals but in daily newspapers too.

The Commission on State Objectives and Legislative Mandates, however, has met with the same fate in the history books as the Study Commission on Constitutional Reform, in that it does not feature there. Yet there were conspicuous differences between the two commissions. The remit of the Study Commission was to examine whether the legal basis that the Federal Republic had created for itself 20 years before should be replaced. The very fact that such endeavours were able to develop and received official blessing through the commission's mandate was historically significant. Had the proposals been implemented, that would not merely have created a differently worded constitution with internal consequences for the body of law but would have meant a different structure for political activity in the Federal Republic. The fact that this did not happen in the end does not make the process irrelevant; on the contrary, it demands a historiographic explanation.

For the Commission on State Objectives and Legislative Mandates, by contrast, it was not about a change in that dimension. It would not have brought about substantive changes but would have legitimised – like a constitutional notary, as it were – a situation which already existed but did not feature in the text of the constitution. The fact that the state pursued a labour market policy to the best of its ability went without saying, given the threat to its legitimacy from unemployment. Stronger forces were behind that effort than a constitutional norm could generate. Nor was there any remaining doubt about environment policy, which had long ago been set in motion, given the electoral successes of the Greens. As for the clause charging the state to protect and promote culture, the commission itself described the situation, saying that it would have been no more than an 'enshrinement of the stage of development that has already been reached' and an affirmation of the cultural responsibility of the state.[17]

[17] ibid 120.

That is not to say that it was a purely symbolic gesture which would have had no legal implications. Putting a constitution into practice today demands, to a great extent, balancing exercises between constitutionally recognised or guaranteed interests that come into conflict. What is defined as a state objective in the constitution weighs more heavily in the balance. In individual cases, then, something may certainly depend on recognition as a state objective. But in view of the fact that, in some of the areas under discussion, the achievement of the objective has more traction than the constitution, the effect would probably seldom exceed the threshold at which it started to demand the attention of historians.

One might choose to state that a process of importance to the constitutional history of the Federal Republic, namely the project for a total overhaul of its constitution, which was barely 20 years old, did not register with historians or was regarded as dispensable information and leave it there. Yet that meant squandering an opportunity to combine the juridical and the historical analyses, because, if the perspective is widened from either of those disciplines to the other, it emerges that both move along parallel paths. At the same time as belief in the need to revise the Basic Law was surfacing, the need emerged to adapt the self-image of the Federal Republic in the light of new realities. At least the more comprehensive historical works register that point.

The new reality that had dawned in 1961 took the form of the Berlin Wall. The erection of the Wall dashed the hopes of early reunification that the founding generation of the Federal Republic had cherished. Attitudes to the Federal Republic began to change. For Winkler, who addresses the situation in the greatest detail (243 ff, English 437 ff), an interview given to *Die Zeit* by Franz Josef Strauss on 8 April 1966, to which Görtemaker also refers (424), marks the turning point. In that interview, Strauss, who did not hold any governmental office at the time, called for a break with the German nation state, the restoration of which in the boundaries of the four zones of occupation he regarded as unrealistic. Instead, he argued, there was a need to refocus the policy of the Federal Republic on Europe and on a Europeanisation of the German Question, which, however, could only be achieved at the expense of national sovereignty.

Other voices followed suit. The thrust of their message was that national sentiment must not cling to pre-war Germany, which had ceased to exist and which could not be restored within the foreseeable future either. That, writes Winkler (245, English 442), quoting M Rainer Lepsius, was the only way to heighten the Federal Republic's 'internal legitimacy', which is precisely what was being challenged at that time by the student movement. What was needed, according to those voices, was the development of a West German patriotism. Similarly, Conze observes the emergence of a West German political identity and a release from the provisional arrangement of a partial state (329). Herbert observes 'the Federal Republic's recognition of itself as not just a transitory phenomenon but a state and a society which would last for a long time' (760; English 615). Wolfrum sees a paling of the idea of the whole nation. For its contemporaries, he writes, the Federal Republic had become a 'lasting provisional arrangement' (185).

The meeting point of the two phenomena – the need for a new self-esteem and the desire for a new constitution – lay in the conviction that the provisional arrangement was over. The two even intersected at certain points. Walter Scheel, as chairman of the realigned FDP, expressed the wish that the provisional nature of the Federal Republic should be overcome not by looking backward to the nation state but by looking ahead towards a united Europe. As he said, however – plainly targeting the calls for a total revision – that did not require fundamental amendment of the Basic Law. Conversely, Hans Dichgans, the promoter of total revision, gave a juridical twist to the Federal Republic's self-analysis when he expressed the view that the time had come for the people of the Federal Republic alone to be the German people within the meaning of Article 146 of the Basic Law who were entrusted by that article with the right to adopt a new constitution.[18]

If both strands are drawn together, the total revision no longer seems like an isolated phenomenon. On the contrary, it fits into a prevailing trend, which escapes legal historians, however, if they focus only on the constitution. A general historian, on the other hand, might find in the total revision the point at which the change in thinking crystallises and becomes politically relevant, provided that he or she attaches importance to the law. There are also explanations for the ultimate failure of the attempts to put a final end to the provisional arrangement, partly through a new national sentiment and partly through a new constitution. One reason was that the patriotism of the West German people was successfully redirected towards the constitution, and the other was that Willy Brandt's *Ostpolitik* reconciled recognition of the new reality with the goal of reunification enshrined in the Basic Law.

The fact that the goal of reunification did not become an empty phrase was ultimately down to the FCC, which, in its judgment on the Treaty on the Basis of Relations between the Federal Republic and the German Democratic Republic (GDR), rejected the Dichgans view and reaffirmed the original meaning of 'the German people' in Article 146 of the Basic Law.[19] The judgment confirmed the constitutionality of the treaty, albeit with the following proviso:

> It follows from the reunification clause that no constitutional organ of the Federal Republic of Germany may abandon the restoration of German unity as a political aim; all constitutional organs are obliged to work towards the achievement of this aim in their policies – including the obligation to keep the claim to reunification alive domestically and to persistently defend it externally – and to refrain from doing anything that would prevent reunification.[20]

The judgment is one of the few that is referred to in almost all of the works, with only Wirsching omitting any mention of it. The accentuation differs, however.

[18] Hans Dichgans, 'Eine verfassungsgebende Nationalversammlung' in *Zeitschrift für Rechtspolitik* I (1968) 62.

[19] BVerfGE 36, 1 (1973).

[20] Loc cit, Headnote 4.

Some authors confine themselves to indicating the outcome. Others emphasise the compatibility of the treaty with the goal of reunification (Görtemaker 361, Wolfrum 394). Several attach particular importance to the binding nature of that goal for West German political action. Winkler expresses the view that the judgment went further in that respect than the Parliamentary Council had done (313 f, English 557 f). As for the consequeces, Herbert emphasises that the judgment excluded any recognition of the GDR under international law (875, English 712). Others dwell primarily on the fact that the 'German Question' (Conze 452) or its 'nation state solution' (Winkler 313 f, English 557 f) had been left open. Rödder, by contrast, emphasises that the judgment narrowed the room for political manoeuvre (42).

The judgment became relevant later, when increasing support was being expressed, particularly in the SPD, for recognition of the GDR and its citizenship.[21] CDU governments were always able to invoke the unconstitutionality of that demand (Wehler 301, 303). In the reunification scenario, moreover, it assumed pivotal practical importance. Had the goal of reunification been sacrificed and the GDR been recognised as a separate state, the latter would no longer have been one of the 'other parts of Germany' within the meaning of Article 23 of the Basic Law in the version which applied at that time. Article 23 would have become redundant. Had that happened, the simple route to reunification would no longer have been available to the Federal Republic. Reunification would not have been an intra-German process but a merger of states under international law. That was prevented by the judgment.

[21] See also ch 1 above, 13f.

6

The Constitutional Question in the Reunification Process

I. A New Constitution for the German Democratic Republic?

New definitions of state objectives and fundamental social rights had not vanished for ever from the agenda after the rejection of the expert commission's proposals. They were back on the table when the Berlin Wall came down. That reappearance initially happened in the German Democratic Republic (GDR). After the Politburo of the Socialist Unity Party (SED) resigned and the Wall was opened, the talk did not turn immediately to reunification. Whoever was already thinking in those terms envisaged reunification as the possible culmination of a lengthy convergence process. A 'contractual arrangement' or a 'confederation' were mooted as transitional frameworks. In the minds of the groups which had brought about the revolution, the primary aim was for the GDR to be reformed under its own steam, after which it would still be a socialist state, but with a democratic and liberal system of government. In short, they envisaged a 'Third Way'.

On 1 December 1989, the Volkskammer – the People's Chamber – deleted the words 'under the leadership of the working class and its Marxist-Leninist party' from Article 1 of the GDR Constitution. On 7 December, the Central Round Table convened for the first time. It comprised 19 representatives of the old establishment forces, namely the SED, the bloc parties of the GDR National Front and the Free German Trade Union Federation (FDGB), and 19 representatives of the new forces. Its meetings were moderated by representatives of the churches. Its first act was to appoint a commission to draft a new constitution for the GDR.[1] Definitions of state objectives and fundamental social rights played an important part in the commission's deliberations, as did elements of direct democracy. That reflected the ideals of the East German reformist forces, though they also received encouragement from some of their West German advisers, who sensed an opportunity to realise in the GDR their unfulfilled hopes of reforming the Basic Law.

[1] See Uwe Thaysen (ed), *Der Zentrale Runde Tisch der DDR, Wortprotokoll und Dokumente*, 5 vols (Westdeutscher Verlag, 2000); idem, *Der Runde Tisch* (Springer Fachmedien, 1990) 52 and 143; Peter Quint, The Imperfect Union (Princeton University Press, 1997) 22 ff, further constitutional deliberations 35 ff.

The aims of the demonstrating masses, however, quickly diverged from those of the civil rights groups that had initiated the uprising. The slogan '*We* are the people!' gave way to 'We are *one* people!'. A large part of the population pressed for the fastest possible reunification in the sense of incorporation of the GDR into the Federal Republic. The elections to the Volkskammer – which had originally been scheduled for May 1990 but, following the demise of the political leadership, had been brought forward to 18 March 1990 – established clarity regarding the party-political balance. With a turnout of 93.4 per cent, the elections delivered a comfortable victory for the Alliance for Germany, an electoral partnership linked with the West German Christian Democratic Union (CDU)/ Christian Social Union (CSU), as well as a crushing defeat for the Social Democratic Party (SPD) and marginalisation for the citizens' movements. That rendered the deliberations on reform of the GDR pointless.

The earlier election date made it impossible for the Constitutional Commission to complete its draft before the election. Only some parts of it were ready in time for the last meeting of the Round Table on 13 March 1990. The Chamber instructed the commission to complete its work but had no opportunity to adopt the final text formally.[2] It declared, however, that the constitution was to be put to a referendum with a view to its entry into force on 17 June 1990 – the anniversary of the popular uprising of 1953 in the GDR, which was also a national holiday in the Federal Republic. The adoption decision, however, was for the newly elected Volkskammer to make. The group of Alliance 90/The Greens there took ownership of the adoption process and tabled a motion for its provisional entry into force, to be followed on 17 June by the referendum on the text drafted by the Constitutional Commission of the Round Table.

The Volkskammer rejected the motion. Given the outcome of the elections, it was clear that the draft had no part to play in the ongoing unification process. At the same time, the GDR Ministry of Justice set to work on drafting an alternative constitution, on the basis of which unification with the Federal Republic was to proceed. The Volkskammer put an end to that attempt too; instead – still adhering to the symbolic date – it chose 17 June as the date of entry into force of a Constitutional Principles Act, in which the GDR was defined as a 'liberal, democratic, federal, social and environmentally oriented state based on the rule of law'. The provisions of the old GDR Constitution were to be interpreted in accordance with those principles. The Constitutional Principles Act remained in force until the moment of reunification.

II. Accession or New Constitution?

The more the population of the GDR united behind reunification, the more sharply the population of the Federal Republic became divided over its desirability. The

[2] The draft constitution is reproduced in the *Jahrbuch des öffentlichen Rechts* 39 (Mohr, 1990) 319, with a commentary by Peter Häberle.

right–left dichotomy was only one of the dividing lines; the other ran between the generations. Very clear positions were adopted by the conservative forces and the Greens, with the former in favour of reunification and the latter opposed to it. The SPD was split. Many younger people, who had only ever known Germany with two states – the eastern one of which was more alien to them than foreign countries in the West – saw no reason to change that situation. Of course the GDR should become 'free', but not as part of the Federal Republic. In the SPD, Oskar Lafontaine, the party's candidate for the chancellorship, was its fiercest opponent of reunification, while Willy Brandt was its staunchest advocate.

After the Volkskammer election it was clear that everything pointed to a reunification, and within the shortest possible time, at least as far as the Germans themselves were concerned. It would have been impossible, on constitutional grounds alone, for the Federal Republic to reject the unification decision of the GDR. The preamble to the Basic Law was legally binding, as the Federal Constitutional Court had ruled in 1973 when reviewing the Treaty on the Basis of Relations with the GDR.[3] The next steps depended on the Allies. From that point, what was at stake in the unification conflict was not *whether*, but *how*. Under the constitution of the Federal Republic, the options were accession of the GDR under Article 23 of the Basic Law or the adoption of a new constitution for the united country under Article 146. These alternatives now took centre stage in the West German discussion.

Bernd Guggenberger and Tine Stein, who collected the main contributions to that debate, write in the introduction to their volume:

> Surely in none of the other salient constitutionally significant stages in the development of the Federal Republic – from rearmament to the debate on the emergency rules, from the extraparliamentary opposition to *Ostpolitik*, from the debates on parliamentary reform, cooperative federalism and party funding to the suppression and prevention of terrorism, and finally from the campaign against nuclear power stations and the host of citizens' objections motivated by environmentalism and the desire for peace to the enduring conflicts over the rules governing pregnancy terminations – has the difference of opinions ever escalated into such a vehement, rigorous and fundamental debate on the scope and limits of the constitution and on the basis and duration of its validity as in 1990.[4]

If the difference between the two pathways to unification were seen only in terms of their likelihood of achieving the desired purpose, the significance of that discussion would certanly have been underestimated. In reality, there was much more at stake. Accession under Article 23 of the Basic Law meant that the GDR would enter into the West German state structure which had been established in the Basic Law. That did not rule out the possibility of expressing wishes with regard to the

[3] See ch 5, section III above.

[4] Bernd Guggenberger and Tine Stein (eds), *Die Verfassungsdiskussion im Jahr der deutschen Einheit* (Hanser, 1991) 9.

Basic Law at the negotiations on the conditions of accession. Such wishes, however, would have to be treated in accordance with the rules of that Basic Law governing constitutional amendments. Article 146, on the other hand, would have meant convening a constituent assembly, in which delegates from both states would have agreed on a constitution for united Germany and would not have been bound by the Basic Law when formulating its provisions.

The extent of the difference between Articles 23 and 146 of the Basic Law cannot be measured without ascertaining the function of the constitution. If it were merely a judicial regulatory framework for the establishment and exercise of public authority, there would be no reason to put the Basic Law up for discussion because, according to the general consensus, it had proved its worth as a judicial regulatory framework. But the importance of the constitution does not lie in its judicial function alone. It also has significance as the self-description of a society and a definition of that society's goals. A successful constitution therefore serves as an integration medium too. Particularly in the Federal Republic, where the customary integration factors were missing,[5] it had performed that metajuridical function to a high degree, as encapsulated in the collocation 'constitutional patriotism'.

This identity-building and integrating effect, however, did not attach to the Basic Law from the outset. On the contrary, it evolved as the result of a development which was due to the conjunction of several favourable factors and which reached its zenith in precisely that watershed year of 1989, when the Federal Republic celebrated the 40th anniversary of the Basic Law, though with no notion yet of what was about to unfold. The people of the GDR were excluded from that development. They could not experience it, let alone influence it. The Basic Law undoubtedly enjoyed a good reputation among the East German population, and the majority wanted to live in future in a system which was largely in line with the one established by the Basic Law. But they had no way of knowing exactly what that meant, and the Basic Law was not attuned to their specific experiences and expectations.

There were, therefore, reasons, arising at least from the metajuridical function of the constitution, to reopen the discussion on the constitution of the united country with the participation, on an equal footing, of the GDR citizenry. But the Federal Republic also had reason to take stock of the new situation and decide, now that the state objective of reunification had been achieved, how it wanted to see itself as a nation state. The old preamble, which was, of course, based on the premise that the Basic Law would only cover the period up to reunification, could not remain in place. There was no doubt about that. Replacing a preamble, however, is no mere exercise in rhetoric. It also implies a change in meaning. The routine pathway to amendment of the constitution through decisions of the Bundestag and Bundesrat is not appropriate for such a step.

[5] For more details, see ch 15 below.

It was logical that the opponents of reunification now found themselves on the side of Article 146 of the Basic Law. That gave them an opportunity to align the future German constitution more closely with the unfulfilled hopes of reform in the old Federal Republic. But it would be too simplistic to equate opposition to reunification with advocacy of a new constitution. There were also advocates of reunification who spoke out in favour of the Article 146 route. This had to do with the conviction that, if reunification was to succeed, it was important to avoid the impression of an annexation in which the East Germans would be unable to influence their future political and social order. A joint new beginning, by contrast, would have signalled respect for the East German population and counteracted any sense of winners and losers that might subsequently have arisen.

No one could foresee at that time whether such an effect would have occurred, and even in retrospect it is impossible to ascertain whether the fusion process would have taken a different course if the reconstitution route had been followed rather than that of accession. For many West German supporters of accession, the symbolic effect of a new constitution was not worth pursuing at all, because they assumed that the people of the GDR themselves, through their mass demonstrations and their vote in the election, had opted for the Basic Law. Others preferred to see reunification as a voluntary merger and, for that reason alone, saw no need to ask the constitutional question. Others again boasted that the Basic Law had stood the test over 40 years of West German history and that reunification should not be burdened with the risk of a constitution that might be inferior.

In the end, the time factor proved to be the most persuasive argument in favour of Article 23. Reunification, of course, was not a purely German affair. It could not have been realised against the will of the wartime Allies. That will, however, could not by any means be taken for granted. Only the United States unreservedly advocated reunification. Britain and France would have preferred continued division. The Soviet Union pursued a vacillating course but was finally won over to the German vision of reunification. Yet the political leadership did not in any way enjoy the undivided approval of the party and the military command. For many, relinquishing the GDR seemed like a belated defeat in the Second World War. Some Western states would have happily hidden their aversion to a united Germany behind a Soviet refusal.

There was sufficient reason, then, to assume that the chance of reunification could quickly trickle away. Consequently, swift action was needed, and Article 23 was the only option that allowed for swift implementation. The advocates of accession, however, managed to present the two variants as mutually exclusive. It boiled down to a stark choice, they argued, and in that scenario it was obvious that the accession route had to be taken; only in point of fact the variants were not mutually exclusive. It would have been possible for accession to take place under Article 23 and be combined with the subsequent convocation of a constituent assembly. In these circumstances, those who favoured the content of the Basic Law would not automatically oppose the Article 146 route, and those who favoured the Article 146 route were not thereby bound to come out against the Basic Law.

All that remained of that hybrid option was the recommendation made to the Bundestag and Bundesrat in Article 5 of the Unification Treaty that they should deal with the questions regarding amendments or additions to the Basic Law as raised after German unification. That promise made it easier for the SPD to consent to the Unification Treaty. And so, for the time being, changes were confined to the amendments to the Basic Law which had been adopted in the treaty itself. Those related to the preamble, which now stated that the unity and freedom of Germany had been achieved; Article 23, the accession article which had now served its purpose, was repealed, for leaving it in place would have created the impression of further territorial ambitions. In addition, besides two transitional arrangements, the composition of the Bundesrat was adapted to take account of the new situation.

Heinrich August Winkler describes the discussion as to whether Bonn or Berlin should be the future capital – another issue that was deferred to the period after reunification – as an *ersatz* debate (609, English 1051) on the significance of unification. That is true, for behind the question of the capital city stood the question whether unification was only to be an enlargement of the old Federal Republic or whether it entailed a joint new beginning. An open debate on the subject was avoided by the politicians. The debate on the future capital, however, was not the only *ersatz* debate. The more important *ersatz* debate was about the choice between extending the Basic Law to the territory of the former GDR and drawing up a new constitution for the united country. The question as to what concessions the Federal Republic was prepared to make to East German sensitivities and expectations could not then have been avoided.

The hopes of those who were unable to win the argument with their views on the constitution of united Germany now rested on the revision of the Basic Law which was recommended in Article 5 of the Unification Treaty and which was to take place within two years following the date of accession. The Unification Treaty specified the subjects which, in the opinion of the contracting parties, merited discussion, namely the Federation-*Länder* relationship, restructuring of the political divisions in the Berlin/Brandenburg area, new state objectives, and even the question of applying Article 146 of the Basic Law 'and of holding a referendum in this context'. The hopes of those who had lost out in the reunification debate were pinned especially on the discussion of the last-named subject, because simple majorities suffice in referendums, whereas a two-thirds majority is required for constitutional amendments under Article 79 of the Basic Law. Work was carried out on drafts for the eventuality of a referendum.[6]

The revision of the constitution did not begin until November 1991, a year after unification.[7] The reason for the delay was that the constitutional debate from the

[6] See, for example, Kuratorium für einen demokratisch verfassten Bund deutscher Länder in cooperation with the Heinrich Böll Foundation (eds), *Vom Grundgesetz zur deutschen Verfassung. Denkschrift und Verfassungsentwurf* (Nomos, 1991).

[7] See Helge Lothar Batt, *Verfassungsrecht und Verfassungswirklichkeit im vereinigten Deutschland* (Leske + Budrich, 2003) 127 ff.

unification phase was now repeated as a dispute over the aims of the commission, its composition and its procedures. While the SPD envisaged a 'Constitutional Council' of 120 members, including non-politicians, the CDU and FDP favoured a small commission comprising 16 members of the Bundestag and 16 Bundesrat members. The latter variant won the day, albeit with an amendment whereby each House was to send 32 members. Among the Bundestag members appointed by the CDU and FDP, there were no East Germans; in the case of the SPD, there were two. The 13 Minister-Presidents who belonged to the commission were almost all absent from its meetings.

The appointment of this Joint Constitutional Commission pre-empted any retrospective application of Article 146, including any subsequent referendum. The commission further restricted the scope of its deliberations by deciding only to make proposals which stood a chance of adoption by the Bundestag and Bundesrat, thereby committing itself to two-thirds majority voting. Its organisation and procedures thus ensured that matters arising from the views of the East German citizens' movement had no prospect of inclusion on the agenda and that not even a scaled-down version of a jointly drafted legal basis for the reunited country could ever materialise. At the time, I described that as 'constitutional reform in the wrong hands'.[8]

Nevertheless, the proposals made by the commission were not insignificant and included the extension of Article 3(2) to cover the actual implementation of equal rights and of Article 3(3) to cover the prohibition of discrimination on grounds of disability, a new Article 20a on protection of the natural foundations of life, an Article 20b on respect for the identity of ethnic, cultural and linguistic minorities, a new Article 23 on the European Union to take the place of the repealed accession article, an addition to Article 24 which permitted the transfer of sovereign powers of the *Länder* to European regions, the right for non-German nationals to vote in local elections and an addition to the rules on new delimitation of the federal territory. Not all of these were adopted by the Bundestag and Bundesrat. Those that were adopted had nothing to do with reunification.[9]

III. The Constitutional Question in Historiography

What significance do historians attach to the constitutional debate? None of the authors fails to mention that reunification was effected by the accession of the GDR to the Federal Republic. Almost all of them refer to Article 23 of the Basic Law, the norm that made accession possible. Only Recker fails to mention it. By

[8] See Dieter Grimm, 'Verfassungsreform in falscher Hand' in *Merkur* (Klett-Cotta, 1992) 1059; also in idem, *Die Verfassung und die Politik* (CH Beck, 2001) 58.

[9] German Bundestag (ed), Report of the Joint Constitutional Commission (in German) in *Zur Sache* 5/93.

contrast, the fact that another option was available in the form of Article 146 of the Basic Law, which was actually conceived expressly for the event of unification, is not widely reported. Only half of the works mention Article 146 at all. Wehler only states that there would, 'in theory', have been another way (337) but does not specify which way. But even where Article 146 is mentioned, the mention is not always accompanied by an explanation of what the difference meant. Rödder, for example, limits himself to the remark that unification took place on the basis of Article 23 of the Basic Law instead of Article 146, in other words without a new constitution. For the lay reader, these remain no more than two numbers.

Görtemaker adds to his mention of both articles that the question of the future constitution was one of the 'main topics' of discussion in the spring of 1990 (751). If that was the case, it would have been worth examining why the discussion was ignited by that issue and what views were held by each side. Without such an explanation, the statement has little information value. Wolfrum, on the other hand, without expressly referring to Article 146, finds that the debate on the future of the constitution had been quickly settled (448). But then how did the issue arise at all? Herbert's readers do not even learn that there was such a debate. He asserts that there was no interest in a new constitution on the part of the CDU and CSU (1128, English 917). That, however, applies only to those whose views prevailed and so is not an accurate portrayal of the situation.

In curious contrast to the economy shown by most of the authors in their examination of the constitutional question is the space they devote to the presentation of the capital city issue. Even details of the removal from Bonn to Berlin, the fact that some older journalists remained in Bonn, how the Federal Chancellery was housed until its new building was ready or Christo's wrapping of the Reichstag building sometimes receive more attention than the constitutional question (Geppert 85 ff). Others who quickly dispatched the constitutional question and stated that there were no lengthy discussions on the future of the Basic Law, which had stood the test of time, find it worth mentioning that, as a consequence of reunification, the national holiday was no longer 17 June but 3 October (Wolfrum 448).

One could, of course, overlook the imbalance if the constitutional debate had only been an internal discussion within legal circles about the juridical details of the unification process. But on that point it is necessary to refer again to Guggenberger and Stein. After the sentence quoted above, they continue as follows:

> Perhaps even more remarkable is the fact that it did not remain just a debate among experts. Granted, the tracks of viewpoints, opinions, criticisms and proposals cut a broad thematic swathe through all of the relevant journals and periodicals devoted to public law and constitutional theory – but also through the entire range of German publications … And not only scholars and writers set out their stall but also 'the citizen', also groups, associations and organisations within society.[10]

[10] Guggenberger and Stein (n 4) 9.

Few of the authors convey an impression of that debate and also focus on its consequences. One reads in Wirsching, for example, that the fact that, through the decision in favour of Article 23 of the Basic Law, 'the entire political, economic and legal system of the Federal Republic was extended to the territory of the former GDR within a short time' was sharply criticised by more than a few in East and West (121). He dismisses the term '*Anschluss*', however, as 'polemical' and goes on to justify the decision, calling it 'a necessary condition for the stabilisation that East Germany urgently required'. 'A long and agonising debate on a new constitution would have been prejudicial to such stabilisation', he writes (122). That is by no means certain. The fact that the two routes were not mutually exclusive is not discussed.

Conze reports in greater detail (732 ff) that there were voices in East and West in favour of a new constitution. But both governments, he states, were against it. The decisive factor in the selection of Article 23, he writes, was that it made rapid accession possible. It was also agreed that the Basic Law had stood the test and should not be put at risk. The alternative route via Article 146 had thus been ruled out. Ultimately, Conze concludes, it was a matter of extending the West German system to the GDR. A similar assessment is made by Wehler. In his view, the outcome of the Volkskammer elections, the 'proven' Basic Law and the pressure of time were sound arguments against any other solution. He records the result in the laconic sentence, 'The Federal Republic enlarged itself to include the GDR' (321).

It is basically Winkler alone who highlights, in his detailed presentation of the problem, the fact that the alternatives of Article 23 and Article 146 were not simply two paths to reunification but two blueprints for reunification (553 ff, English 959 ff). He not only mentions that the '23 or 146' question was the subject of a heated controversy, but also outlines the positions and names their proponents. Winkler is also the only one who emphasises that there was no contradiction between the two paths (553, English 960). Rapidity, he concludes, was the reason why Article 23 prevailed. That path, however, left a 'normative deficit', which could have been remedied after accession by the aforementioned means of a constitutional assembly of the united country. That this was where the real *ersatz* debate took place, however, is not stated by Winkler either. As indicated above, he uses the term in connection with the question of the capital city (609, English 1051).

Few of the authors address the fact that there was another constitutional debate after the decision in favour of accession under Article 23. That, of course, was the concession made to the SPD, many of whose members would have preferred the Article 146 route. The Joint Constitutional Commission, which began its work in November 1991, is mentioned by Birke/Wengst (59), Conze (734), Görtemaker (773), Recker (202) and Winkler (611, English 1055), and also indirectly by Herbert (1131, English 920). References to it are absent from most of the works. Almost no one has recognised how its procedural arrangements prejudiced its results. In Winkler's book, at any rate, the individual results are set out. It is also the only work to mention that the wishes of the East German parliamentarians were not given a platform. Only Conze (733) tells the reader anything about the constitution drafted by the Board of Trustees for a Democratically Constituted Federation of German *Länder* (Kuratorium für einen demokratisch verfassten Bund deutscher Länder).

The fact that there was also a debate about a new constitution for the GDR, which culminated in a final draft and primarily reflected the ideas of the reformist groups, is indicated only by Conze (733) and Winkler (557 f, English 964). The main differences between that draft and the Basic Law were the additional definitions of state objectives and the proposed inclusion of fundamental social rights and plebiscitary elements. Görtemaker states that the Volkskammer rejected a new constitution in April 1990 (752). He does not indicate, however, whether the rejected draft was that of the Round Table or that of the Ministry of Justice. The Constitutional Principles Act which was adopted instead does not feature anywhere. The constituent processes in the five new *Länder* have attracted no attention either, even though a comparison with West German *Land* constitutions would have been a promising source of enlightenment about East German conceptions.[11]

Notwithstanding the considerable differences in depth of detail and problem awareness between the various accounts, they still leave the impression that the import of the constitutional question has not been grasped. When a problem is juridified, the focus narrows onto the problem, but not the problem as such. That narrower focus is necessary for a retrospective judicial review of political decisions, the sole purpose of which is to determine lawfulness or unlawfulness, but not for a historical appraisal. The constitutional question was a legal question, but only at face value. In answering it, the Federal Republic also made a choice between two basic understandings of reunification. From the historical perspective, one would expect the answer not to remain on a superficial level but to reveal precisely what purpose the narrower juridical focus served and what its effects were.

Many of the accounts, moreover, appear success-focused. They consider the reunification process from the standpoint of its completion. The views of those who won the argument over the pathway to reunification largely dominate the portrayals. Whatever failed to gain acceptance is disregarded in most of the histories. That eliminates any need to look for reasons. History's losers suffer another defeat at the hands of historians. The reunification process raises numerous counterfactual questions. Most of them are unanswerable. The constitutional question marks a fork in the road. Thirty years after reunification, the fusion of the two halves seems further away than in 1990. Whether the outcome of the constitutional debate is partly responsible for that is uncertain. The possibility cannot be dismissed out of hand.

[11] An overview is provided in Peter Häberle, 'Die Verfassungsbewegung in den fünf neuen Bundesländern' (1993) 41 *Jahrbuch des öffentlichen Rechts* 69 and (1994) 42 *Jahrbuch des öffentlichen Rechts* 149.

7

The Liberalisation of Society as a Question of Fundamental Rights

I. Peculiarities of the Interpretation of Fundamental Rights

Whether the Basic Law of 1949 has been altered more by the formal constitutional amendments made under Article 79 or by the quiet change resulting from constitutional adjudication is a moot question. In some areas, however, the answer is unequivocal. In the organisational part of the Basic Law, the federal system of government has been the subject of numerous far-reaching constitutional amendments, whereas the structure of the constitutional organs at the federal level has been spared any major amendments. The Bill of Rights, by contrast, has been altered by Constitutional Court rulings in a way that would have been inconceivable back in 1949. Although amendments to the text have not been entirely absent,[1] they are far inferior in number and significance to the changes wrought by interpretations of its wording.

Compared with most of the norms in the organisational part of the constitution, the fundamental rights, on account of their terse wording, are particularly open to, and in need of, interpretation. As indicated above, the interest protected by a fundamental right is usually defined in a single word, such as faith, expression, family, occupation, home or property. No more is said, as a rule, about the object of protection except that it is 'free' or 'guaranteed'. There then follows an authorisation to limit the free exercise of the right. Sometimes it comprises only a requirement to adopt a statutory basis for restrictions. Sometimes the statute restricting the fundamental right or the implementation of that statute is subjected to additional conditions. In exceptional cases, a requirement for a statutory basis is lacking. Fundamental rights, then, constitute a promise, the real value of which depends on the extent of the limitations.

In this respect, the constitutional text leaves many questions unanswered. What is covered by the term used to describe the protected interest, and what it excludes, are a matter of interpretation, as is the meaning of 'free', for example with regard to the press or property. The same applies to the limits of fundamental rights. Can it

[1] See ch 4 above.

be concluded from the limitation clause of such an elementary fundamental right as the right to life, which may only be interfered with pursuant to a law, that any random law may permit killing, whereas in the case of a far less important right such as inviolability of the home in Article 13 of the Basic Law, extensive safeguards are prescribed to qualify the restrictions? Or does the absence of a requirement to enact a specific statute limiting freedom of the arts mean that the arts enjoy absolute protection and therefore must not be subjected to any restriction?

These are questions that arise from the wording of specific fundamental rights. Even more open-ended, however, are the questions concerning the meaning and function of the fundamental rights as such. The beneficiaries of fundamental rights are usually defined in the text as 'every person' or 'all Germans'. Who is bound by them is not conclusively discernible from the text. Are they only enforceable against the state, or do they also apply in relations between private individuals? What do they require of the state – only to refrain from violations of freedom, or also to act to protect freedom? Is their protection afforded only to individuals, or do certain sectors of society with their specific rationality, such as the academic system or the media, enjoy the protection of fundamental rights? Entire theories develop around such questions and, in their turn, guide the understanding of fundamental rights in specific disputes.[2]

It is clear that these questions can be answered in one way or another without desecrating the text of the norm, and indeed they have been answered in various ways over time or are answered in different ways from one country to another. This does not imply an infinite choice of answers. The whole of legal scholarship, in so far as it is focused on doctrine, revolves around how such questions are to be answered 'correctly'. But what is 'correct', in terms of both the method of interpretation and its result, is itself a bone of contention too and can change over time and from place to place. As a rule, however, the scholarly discussion of these questions and the ways in which they are answered in real cases deliver preferred and proven practices and solutions which mostly endure in the longer term.

One must always reckon with the possibility, however, that a promising catalogue of fundamental rights will prove irrelevant in practice, whereas a meagre catalogue may hold the key to a wealth of scope for interpretation. What this means for historians is that they cannot simply consider the text of the constitution and leave it at that. They must also enquire into its practical relevance; in systems with constitutional adjudication like that of the Federal Republic, this means examining rulings of the Constitutional Court. Since constitutional courts can only determine the meaning of constitutional provisions when seized of a specific case, that makes dealing with cases unavoidable – not, of course, in the same way as legal scholars, for whom the judicial correctness of the decision is what matters, but by looking

[2] See, eg, Ernst-Wolfgang Böckenforde, 'Grundrechtstheorie und Grundrechtsinterpretation' in idem, *Staat, Gesellschaft, Freiheit* (Suhrkamp, 1976) 221; Uwe Volkmann, 'Rechts-Produktion: Wie die Theorie der Verfassung ihren Inhalt bestimmt' (2015) 54 *Der Staat* 35; Ino Augsberg, *Theorie der Grund- und Menschenrechte* (Mohr Siebeck, 2021) 1 ff.

at the impact of the Constitutional Court's interpretation of fundamental rights on the conditions, developments or events which appear relevant to historians.

The works under examination in this volume, as already indicated, give short shrift to the fundamental rights when describing the Basic Law, even though the Parliamentary Council was anxious to elevate their importance decisively in view of their relatively low relevance in earlier eras and the utter contempt with which they were treated under National Socialist rule.[3] This neglect continues in the accounts of the period following the entry into force of the Basic Law. The rulings of the Federal Constitutional Court (FCC) on the fundamental rights arouse little interest, even though they significantly influenced various events and processes which are reported by the historians, and which could well have turned out differently without the Court's interpretation of fundamental rights.

II. *Lüth* and its Consequences

The key ruling for the understanding of fundamental rights in general, as opposed to the interpretation of individual fundamental rights, is the *Lüth* judgment of the FCC.[4] The case concerned the fundamental right of freedom of expression. The complainant, Erich Lüth, head of the Press Office in the Hamburg Senate and chairman of the Hamburg Press Club, was outraged to learn that Veit Harlan, the notorious director of anti-Semitic films in the Third Reich, had returned to the German film scene shortly after his denazification with a new film, entitled *Unsterbliche Geliebte* ('Immortal Lover'), and he called publicly, though not in his official capacity as head of the Senate Press Office, for all cinema owners and all 'decent Germans' to boycott that film. Cinema owners were not to include it in their programmes, and cinemagoers were to steer clear of it.

The producers and distributors of the film – though not Veit Harlan, as is frequently assumed – brought a civil action against Lüth's boycott call. The civil courts found Lüth's conduct to be inflicting damage on the plaintiffs in a manner offending common decency, within the meaning of section 826 of the German Civil Code, and ordered him to refrain from his campaign on pain of a fine or imprisonment. Lüth's objection that he had exercised the fundamental right to freedom of expression which, under Article 1(3) of the Basic Law, bound all three branches of government was rejected by the courts on the grounds that the fundamental rights produced their effects only in relations between citizens and the state, not between private individuals. In relationships governed by private law, they ruled, only civil law was applicable, not constitutional law.

The Hamburg courts cannot be faulted. They had decided the case as it had to be decided, in accordance with the generally accepted interpretation of the German

[3] See ch 2 above.
[4] BVerfGE 7, 198 (1958), which is the source of the quotations cited below.

Civil Code. Lüth lodged a constitutional complaint and hired as his legal counsel Adolf Arndt, the parliamentary torch-bearer for constitutional adjudication. Veit Harlan's film went on release in cinemas in 1950. The Regional Court delivered its final decision on the merits in November 1951. Before the year was over, the FCC received Lüth's constitutional complaint. The case lay there for six years. The First Senate, which had jurisdiction in matters relating to fundamental rights, was fully occupied by the proceedings for the prohibition of the Communist Party of Germany (KPD), which were completed in August 1956. The *Lüth* judgment was delivered on 15 January 1958.

To understand the significance of the judgment, it is necessary to recall how fundamental rights were understood at the time when the First Senate was seized of the case. There had been fundamental rights in Germany since the time of the earliest constitutions, dating from the start of the nineteenth century. Their juridical importance remained minimal, however. In the German Empire, whose constitution did without fundamental rights, whereas most of the *Land* constitutions contained a bill of rights, the view had become established that fundamental rights did not bind the legislature. In those circumstances, their effect was confined to the rule that the executive could not interfere with fundamental rights without a statutory basis. The legislature, however, was free to frame that statutory basis. Consequently, for the courts only the statute was relevant. That remained the prevailing view in the Weimar Republic, although it was no longer as unchallenged as it had been in the Empire.

The limitation of the effect of fundamental rights to the executive was ended by the Basic Law. Under Article 1(3) of the Basic Law, the fundamental rights bind the legislature too, and do so 'as directly applicable law', in other words not only as an exhortation. In addition, the fundamental rights, according to the prevalent view, were characterised by three properties. They were *subjective* rights, meaning that they entitled individuals, they applied *vertically*, meaning that they were enforceable against the state, and they were *negatory* in effect, meaning that they were defensive rights against state interference. The FCC was vested with the power to review the constitutionality of laws. If they were found to be constitutional, the Court's business was completed. The interpretation and application of laws was a matter for the competent ordinary courts alone.

Had that view been upheld, Lüth would have lost in Karlsruhe too. The FCC, however, used the case as an opportunity to ask afresh the question about the significance and special nature of the fundamental rights in the context of the Basic Law. There was no doubt that a norm which prohibited inflicting damage on third parties in a manner offending common decency, as section 826 of the German Civil Code did, was not unconstitutional. Accordingly, only its interpretation and application by civil courts in specific cases could be problematic in terms of fundamental rights. That, it is true, depended on the fundamental rights having not only vertical effects but horizontal effects too, meaning that they also had to be taken into account in disputes in the realm of private law. Only if that were the case did the question arise whether the civil judgments had violated fundamental rights.

The FCC preceded that question with another one, through which it hoped to shed light on the extent of the effects of fundamental rights. It was the basic question as to the legal nature of fundamental rights. 'Without doubt' they were first and foremost defensive rights of the individual against the state. That, however, was not the full extent of their legal effects. Since the Basic Law was not intended to be a value-neutral order, as the Weimar Constitution had supposedly been, it had established an 'objective order of values' in its Bill of Rights. That 'value system' had to be regarded as a fundamental constitutional decision for all areas of the law, 'self-evidently' including civil law. 'No provision of civil law may be inconsistent with it; each one must be interpreted in its spirit'.

The question of the *Drittwirkung* (the horizontal effect, literally the 'third-party effect') was thus decided by the roundabout route of the objective order of values. Fundamental rights applied not only vertically but horizontally too. That finding, however, did not yet establish how such an effect was to be understood. The FCC answered that question by ruling that the effect was not direct, because positing a direct effect would amount to reinterpreting the fundamental rights as obligations. On the contrary, regulating relations between private individuals remains a matter for private law. But private law has to be interpreted 'in the light' of the fundamental rights whenever its application affects fundamental rights. They have a 'radiating effect' on private law. This means that the effect of fundamental rights no longer ends with the law but extends to its interpretation and application.

The only point left to clarify was whether that also applied to the first sentence of Article 5(1) of the Basic Law, the provision at issue in the *Lüth* case. The question arose on account of the unusual limitation clause attaching to that fundamental right. Under Article 5(2) of the Basic Law, freedom of expression finds its limits in the provisions of general laws, to which section 826 of the German Civil Code undoubtedly belonged. That could be read as stating that freedom of expression could only come into play in so far as ordinary laws permitted. Such a situation would, of course, have overturned the precedence of fundamental rights over the provisions of statutory law. The FCC held, on the contrary, that freedom of expression, 'as the most direct expression of the human personality in society', was 'one of the most precious rights of man' and was 'absolutely constitutive' for a free democratic system of government. Accordingly, it could not be subjected to relativisation at will by the legislature.

On the basis of this redefinition of the meaning of fundamental rights, Lüth won his case in Karlsruhe. The contested decisions were set aside. The civil courts, the justices said, should have taken the fundamental right of freedom of expression into account when interpreting section 826 of the German Civil Code. Had they done so, Lüth's freedom of expression would have outweighed the economic interests of the film companies which were protected by section 826 of the Code. Lüth's call for a boycott would still have constituted damage to those interests, but not damage that could be regarded as offending common decency within the meaning of section 826 of the German Civil Code. At a time when the National Socialist past was still widely hushed up in the Federal Republic, the FCC had prevented a suppression of free speech regarding that era. The case was thus settled. In factual terms, it had been settled long before, for by 1958 no cinema was screening *Unsterbliche Geliebte* any more.

But the significance of the *Lüth* judgment is not limited to the Court's decision. It was now settled case law for all future litigation that the fundamental rights were to be regarded as supreme values of the legal order and, as such, demanded observance in all branches of the law and that the FCC could review such observance. No decision of the FCC has so radically changed the understanding of the constitution as that judgment. Asked to name the most important judgment of the FCC, surely there is scarcely a legal scholar who would hesitate to reply, 'the *Lüth* judgment'. But even foreign scholars of comparative constitutional law are all familiar with the German *Lüth* judgment. It profoundly influenced the understanding of fundamental rights both at home and abroad. Many of its innovations have been incorporated into other legal systems.

Further consequences of the *Lüth* judgment followed. At that time, the last of the three characteristics of the traditional understanding of fundamental rights, the purely negative effect of limiting state power, was still open to interpretation. It played no part in the *Lüth* judgment, which was about defence against interference with fundamental rights by the civil courts; in other words, the classical defensive function of fundamental rights. A few years later, however, a dispute over the reform of section 218 of the German Criminal Code[5] gave the Court an opportunity to clarify that third characteristic too. Once again, the basis of the decision was the understanding of the fundamental rights as values: if the fundamental rights were not only subjective defensive rights against the state but also objective values, it would not suffice to protect them from menaces posed by state authority; they also had to be defended against threats emanating from third parties. Only the state, however, could provide that protection. Accordingly, besides obligations to refrain from certain actions, fundamental rights also impose on the state protective obligations, which are for the legislature to fulfil.[6]

Just as *Lüth* would have culminated in a different decision without the horizontal effect of fundamental rights, the outcome of the abortion dispute would also have been different without the protective obligation imposed by fundamental rights. The fundamental rights would have amounted only to defensive rights of the individual – in that case the foetus – against the state. The state itself, however, neither performed nor ordered abortions. The right to life of the foetus, in fact, was threatened by the pregnant woman who decided to have an abortion as well as by the doctors or other persons who performed it. But they are not the addressees of the fundamental right to life. Fundamental rights are directed towards the state. No court rulings had altered that. So there would have been no interference with fundamental rights. That, in actual fact, is how the Austrian Constitutional Court

[5] For the context, see ch 9 below.
[6] BVerfGE 99, 1 (1975).

ruled at the same time on the basis of the traditional purely defensive understanding of fundamental rights.

The protective obligation imposed by fundamental rights was developed in response to the abolition of an existing safeguard, namely the prohibition of abortion in the German Criminal Code. As it quickly transpired, however, its real significance lay in another area. Today the protective obligation applies above all against the risks to freedom that arise from scientific and technological advances and their commercial exploitation. Such progress typically entails both benefits and risks. Without the protective obligation, interests in the immediate benefits would prevail over the indefinite future risks. The protective obligation compels the state to strike a reasonable balance between the two. The state violates the constitution not only by going too far in restricting fundamental rights but also by doing too little to protect them.

The interpretation of the fundamental rights as value-based objective principles rather than mere subjective entitlements is also the source of the assumption that particular fundamental rights apply not only to individuals or associations of persons but also to those functional systems within society in which individuals exercise their respective freedoms. In those circumstances, the freedom of such systems is also guaranteed. This quite simply means that the functional systems within society are protected in their inherent logic or rationality, in other words safeguarded against hijacking for alien purposes, particularly by the powerful political and economic systems. Rulings to this effect were made at an early date for the press, then, with particular force, for radio and television, and lastly for academic and research activity.[7]

Finally, it was also a consequence of the understanding, established by the *Lüth* judgment, of fundamental rights as the highest order of values of the community that the FCC abandoned the assumption that fundamental rights did not apply to persons in special relationships of subordination (*besondere Gewaltverhältnisse*) – now generally defined as relationships based on special status (*Sonderstatusverhältnisse*).[8] Special relationships of subordination, in contrast to the general relationship between individuals and the state, are relationships in which individuals, mostly of necessity, are enrolled or detained in state institutions, such as prisons, reformatories, psychiatric institutions, schools or the armed forces. If fundamental rights were the supreme values of society, they could not be withheld from the members or inmates of those institutions.

An extension and an enhancement of the protection of fundamental rights, which did not date from the *Lüth* judgment but which, in combination with *Lüth*, contributed to the unprecedented increase in the importance of fundamental rights, should also be mentioned to complete the picture. A year before *Lüth*, the FCC, in the *Elfes* case, had already extended the protection of fundamental rights

[7] BVerfGE 10, 118 (1959), 12, 205 (1961) and 35, 79 (1973).
[8] BVerfGE 33, 1 (1972).

far beyond the rights set out in the Basic Law.[9] Wilhelm Elfes was a politician who had been expelled from the Christian Democratic Union (CDU) and who was a fierce opponent of Konrad Adenauer's policy of Western integration and rearmament; for that reason, he was in great demand as a speaker in the German Democratic Republic (GDR) and other socialist countries. In 1953, Elfes' application to extend his passport was rejected on the ground that he was endangering 'significant interests of the Federal Republic'. That was specified as a ground for rejection in the Passports Act (*Passgesetz*).

The administrative courts confirmed the decision of the passport authority in all three instances. Elfes regarded this as a violation of his freedom of movement, guaranteed by Article 11 of the Basic Law, and lodged a constitutional complaint. The FCC saw no way of overriding the unequivocal wording of Article 11, whereby the right to move freely 'throughout the federal territory' was guaranteed. The Basic Law did not contain an equivalent guaranteed right to leave the federal territory. If the fundamental right were interpreted narrowly on the basis of the wording, the case would thus have been settled. Fundamental rights could not be invoked against a refusal to issue a passport. Recourse to the administrative courts was therefore the end of the road, and Elfes had already exhausted that remedy in vain.

The FCC, however, did not leave it at that, but considered whether free development of the personality, guaranteed by Article 2(1) of the Basic Law, might be applicable to the case at hand. Unlike Article 11, however, Article 2(1) was extremely vague about what it protected and to what extent. Its wording begged the question whether the opportunity to travel abroad was of such considerable significance in terms of development of the personality that it merited the protection of that fundamental right. The FCC did not pursue that sharply case-focused approach, however, but undertook to clarify once and for all, as it were, regardless of the case, what was to be understood by 'free development of one's personality' and then, on the basis of that abstract clarification, to rule on the concrete case.

The Senate was confronted with two possible understandings – one was narrow and concerned the autonomy of the individual in an extremely moral sense, and one was broad, encompassing all the actions of the individual which did not enjoy the protection of an explicitly listed fundamental right. The latter view prevailed, with the consequence that freedom to travel out of the country, because it had not been granted protection in a specific fundamental right, fell within the general protection of freedom under Article 2(1) of the Basic Law. Elfes was thus able to rely on a fundamental right, yet the FCC did not find that right to have been violated by the refusal to renew his passport. If each and every form of human conduct enjoyed the protection of a fundamental right, it followed logically that the scope for limiting that right also had to be broadly defined.

[9] BVerfGE 6, 32 (1957). On the sometimes dramatic genesis of that judgment, with its many twists and turns, see Dieter Grimm, 'Das Elfes-Urteil' in Florian Meinel (ed), *Verfassungsgerichtsbarkeit in der Bonner Republik* (Mohr Siebeck, 2019) 155; also in Dieter Grimm, *Verfassungsgerichtsbarkeit* (Suhrkamp, 2021) 204; English *Constitutional Courts and Judicial Review* (Hart, 2024) 140.

Little though the broad interpretation of Article 2(1) served the complainant in that case, its general implications were immense. The protection of fundamental rights which the Basic Law had granted selectively was thereby made comprehensive. Free development of the personality meant freedom of action, with the result that every conceivable restriction, encumbrance or hindrance by the state of individual actions could now be challenged by means of a constitutional complaint. Access to the FCC, which was already easy, was thus extended still further. That was the procedural consequence of the substantive interpretation of the fundamental rights. At the same time, by broadening the interpretation of fundamental rights protection, the Court obtained a right of review over all state activity that impacted in any way adversely on individuals' conduct of their lives.

Even more consequential than the derestriction of Article 2(1) of the Basic Law was the adoption of the proportionality principle into constitutional adjudication. The principle was familiar to every legal scholar, but as a principle of administrative law which was relevant to the executive, not as a principle of constitutional law. The Prussian Higher Administrative Court had developed it in the late nineteenth century in an effort to reinforce the principle of the rule of law. Its purpose was to limit the broad discretionary powers that the laws granted the police. The Higher Administrative Court restricted those powers by permitting police actions that affected people's liberty and property only if the actions were appropriate and necessary means of achieving their purpose. The criterion of necessity in particular acquired considerable significance, because it prevented overreactions by police forces.

The FCC now elevated that principle to constitutional status. As a result, it was no longer only the police who had to pay heed to the proportionality of their actions but also the legislature when operating in the area protected by fundamental rights – but when did it not operate there after the *Elfes* judgment? At the same time, the Court extended the proportionality principle by adding another criterion, which had only occasionally been discernible in rulings of the administrative courts, namely appropriateness. This meant that laws must no longer only satisfy the conditions for the restriction of fundamental rights which were defined in the text of the Basic Law but were now also required to serve a legitimate purpose, to be a suitable and necessary means of achieving that purpose and to ensure a reasonable balance between the cost of restricting the fundamental right and the benefit of achieving the regulatory purpose.

The FCC never explained how that additional hurdle for the legislature was derived from the Basic Law. The proportionality principle slipped quietly into the Court's rulings, amid general unawareness of its immense importance, and only gradually assumed the form in which it has been routinely applied down to the present day. Accordingly, unlike the innovations associated with *Elfes* and *Lüth*, the proportionality principle cannot be traced to a single landmark decision but to a chain of decisions. Today it bears the main onus of protecting freedom. When laws are rejected in Karlsruhe, the most common reason is that they breach the proportionality principle. Without the proportionality principle, considerably more laws would pass the constitutionality test.

Legal scholars may argue about whether all of these effects could be derived from the Basic Law or amounted in substance to constitution-making. For historians they are a given fact. If one wishes to explain the significant role played by fundamental rights today in determining the actions of political and administrative bodies on the one hand and the scope of individual freedom on the other, that cannot be done without considering *Lüth*, *Elfes*, the protective obligation and proportionality. Nor can the weight of the FCC in the political system of the Federal Republic be understood without knowledge of those judgments. Although it is quite often written that the introduction of constitutional adjudication has proved in retrospect to be the most momentous innovation in the Basic Law, that was not already preordained when the Basic Law entered into force but is the result of its subsequent judicial interpretation and application.

III. The Fundamental Rights in Historiography

How do the historical works deal with these trailblazing decisions? The *Lüth* judgment is not encountered in any of the histories under examination in this volume. The same applies to *Elfes* and to the order on the restriction of prisoners' fundamental rights, the decision which abolished restriction based on the special relationship of subordination. The proportionality principle does not feature either. The abortion judgment of 1975 is mentioned in almost every work, because it concerned a question that deeply divided society and because it thwarted a major reform project of the Social Democratic–Liberal coalition, but not on account of the revolutionary innovation of the protective obligation. Of the television judgments,[10] the first features in connection with the end of the Adenauer era as a painful defeat for the Federal Chancellor. Once again, however, none of these judgments is mentioned on account of effects that transcended the adjudicated case.

Would they have merited a mention? Probably not, if the decisions had only proclaimed in the specific cases what was already prescribed in general terms in the Basic Law. But that was manifestly not the case. Nor would they have merited a mention if their impact, though seismic, had only been felt within the legal system. The reach of the *Lüth* judgment and of the other decisions grouped around it, however, extends far beyond the realm of legal doctrine. In the fundamental rights, basic conditions for social interaction within a political entity are formulated. To what extent may individuals and their associations make autonomous decisions about their lives and lifestyles, and to what extent can the state impose restrictions on them for the sake of the common good? In the fundamental rights, these conditions are defined in abstract and general terms. What they mean in practice is a subject of social debate, political wrangling and and often – since fundamental rights are, after all, rights – judicial proceedings.

[10] For more details, see ch 8.

In the rulings of the FCC, these basic conditions have been decisively reformulated by comparison with earlier eras. Through them, the protection of liberty which the fundamental rights guarantee for individuals has become more extensive, more finely grained and more effective. It is more extensive, because the interests protected by the existing fundamental rights are broadly interpreted and because the gaps between the various fundamental rights have been closed by the upgrading of Article 2(1) of the Basic Law into a general freedom. In particular, however, the protection of freedom is more extensive because, following the disappointment of liberal hopes in the ability of a society liberated from the chains of feudalism and authoritarianism to govern itself, that society has been freed from a situation in which it was protected only from threats to its liberty emanating from the state, and that protection is now extended to cover threats emanating from within society.

The protection of fundamental rights has become 'more finely grained' because the proportionality principle compels the legislature to ask what means are necessary to achieve a particular aim in the public interest and what means will overshoot the target (known as the *Übermaßverbot*, or prohibition of excessive measures), but above all because it requires the legislature to balance the gains for the legally protected right for the sake of which the fundamental right is being restricted against the losses for the restricted fundamental right. The protection is made more effective by the fact that these considerations, which must be made by politicians and sometimes by administrators, can be reviewed by the FCC on the initiative of affected persons or associations or political forces that consider alternative solutions to be more consistent with the constitution.

For that reason alone, the extralegal relevance of those developments is surely beyond doubt. The matter does not end there, for institutional issues are also associated with the extension and enhancement of fundamental rights protection. Every increase in the significance of fundamental rights that results from an interpretation of the constitution widens the Court's sphere of influence at the same time. That is not the intention behind judicial acts but certainly their effect. To some extent the increase in influence affects the rest of the judiciary. Within the ambit of the constitution, all adjudication is subject to review by the FCC, but how far the ambit of the constitution extends is determined by that same court when it interprets and applies the constitution. The process has not always been conflict-free, because many a constant ruling has not stood up to judicial review. In the meantime, however, it has become normality.

The widening of influence, however, is not confined to the judicial system but also spreads to the political system. One institution's gain in significance necessarily entails a corresponding loss in the significance of other institutions. When expansive interpretation of fundamental rights by the FCC has the effect of increasing its scope for decision-making, that of the political institutions – parliament and the government – is reduced by the same degree. That is more than just a shift in competence. Since a democracy gap exists between parliament and government on the one hand and the Constitutional Court on the other – the Court's justices possess less democratic legitimacy than members of parliament and government ministers and are not democratically accountable for the performance of their function – the shift in relative weight also poses a democracy problem, the 'countermajoritarian difficulty', discussion of which has become veritably obsessive in the United States.[11]

Would there have been starting points in the historiographic works for consideration of the constitutional rulings based on *Lüth*? Changes of that magnitude do not go unnoticed. They trigger discussions. The FCC's rulings on fundamental rights were by no means undisputed in legal circles. The understanding of fundamental rights as values was attacked, partly by the Right as a threat to the rule of law and partly by the Left as a threat to democracy. Similar objections were raised to the protective obligation and the proportionality principle. The FCC was accused of transgressing the boundary between interpretation and amendment of the constitution. There were calls for a return to what was termed the classical understanding of fundamental rights of the pre-*Lüth* era.[12]

Such internal discussions among legal scholars may escape the attention of historians, although critics took part in it whose names are not only known in legal circles, such as Carl Schmitt, Ernst Forsthoff and Ernst-Wolfgang Böckenförde.[13] The discussion did not remain confined to legal scholarship, moreover. Jürgen Habermas, for instance, presented a general critique of the jurisprudence of the FCC.[14] The discussion reached the public through catchwords such as *Richterstaat* ('judge state') and *Hypertrophie der Grundrechte* ('hypertrophy of fundamental rights'). When some of the reforming laws of the Social Democratic–Liberal coalition were quashed or watered down in Karlsruhe, the FCC came under severe public pressure for a time.[15] That might have been an indicator of problems that were not merely inherent to the law but affected society in general.

The Court's doctrinal constructs were not in any way exempted from that criticism. In the judgment of 1975 on the time-limit rule for abortions, the Court had not only established an obligation of the state, inherent in fundamental rights, to protect the developing life but had also prescribed the means which it regarded as

[11] The expression first appeared in Alexander Bickel, *The Least Dangerous Branch* (Bobbs-Merrill, 1962); see also ch 3 above.

[12] Made, for instance, in Bernhard Schlink, 'Freiheit durch Eingriffsabwehr – Rekonstruktion der klassischen Grundrechtsfunktion' in *Europäische Grundrechte Zeitschrift* (NP Engel, 1984) 457; but see Dieter Grimm, 'Rückkehr zum liberalen Grundrechtsverständnis?' in idem, *Die Zukunft der Verfassung* (Suhrkamp, 1991), 221; English 'Return to the Traditional Understanding of Fundamental Rights?' in *Constitutionalism: Past, Present, and Future* (Oxford University Press, 2016) 183.

[13] See Ernst Forsthoff, 'Die Umbildung des Verfassungsgesetzes' in *Festschrift für Carl Schmitt zum 70. Geburtstag* (Duncker & Humblot, 1959) 35; Carl Schmitt, *Die Tyrannei der Werte, Ebracher Studien* (1967) 53; English *The Tyranny of Values and Other Texts* (Telos, 2018); Ernst-Wolfgang Böckenförde, 'Zur Kritik der Wertbegründung des Rechts' in idem, [*Recht, Staat, Freiheit*] (Suhrkamp, 1991) 67.

[14] Jürgen Habermas, *Faktizität und Geltung* (Suhrkamp, 1992) ch VI, 292 ff; English *Between Facts and Norms* (MIT Press, 1996) ch 6, 238 ff; but see Dieter Grimm, 'Justiz und Gesetzgebung. Zur Rolle und Legitimität der Verfassungsrechtsprechung' in Peter Koller and Christian Hiebaum (eds), *Jürgen Habermas: Faktizität und Geltung* (Walter de Gruyter, 2016) 99.

[15] See ch 9 below.

constitutionally necessary for its fulfilment. Since the issue concerned the supreme value of human life, the Court ruled, the strongest means had to be employed to protect it, namely criminal law. The dissenting opinion did not challenge the protective obligation of the state but rather its obligation to use the threat of criminal punishment.[16] That issue became the subject of public debate. It arose again 15 years later, when it threatened to derail the unification process between the Federal Republic and the GDR. The Federal Republic felt bound by the 1975 judgment, but the GDR did not want to join the Federal Republc under that condition.[17]

There is no shortage of starting points in historiography for consideration of constitutional jurisprudence. Almost without exception, the histories identify a liberalisation surge in the Federal Republic in the late 1950s or early 1960s, even referring to it in some cases as a 'fundamental liberalisation' (Conze 183, Recker 44, Wehler 277 and Wolfrum 13) or a 'historical turning point' (*Zeitenwende*, Conze 219) and 'of epochal significance' (Wehler 277). That liberalisation, often linked with pluralisation, individualisation, democratisation and even westernisation, related to value compasses, lifestyles and mentalities. The trend ranged from so-called secondary virtues to post-materialist values. Some speak of a 'denormalisation process' (Rödder 29). Self-fulfilment, they say, was the new ultimate value. It is but a small step from there to fundamental rights.

Rödder provides a kind of definition, accepted by other sources:

> Essentially, changing values means a general shift in the system of standards that governs society as a whole away from values based on duty and acceptance (acceptance in the sense of unquestioning acquiescence to the status quo) such as willingness to work, devotion to duty, discipline, punctuality and thrift, obedience, subordination and authority as well as middle-class moral standards, to self-fulfilment values such as independence and co-determination, criticism, free will and indiviual autonomy, to self-determination in place of binding external obligations (29).

Almost all of the historians identify gender roles and sexual mores as areas in which the shift was most conspicuous.

As reasons for the change, almost all of the authors cite the elimination of the post-war shortages and the replacement of the founding generation by a generation no longer marked by wartime experiences, processes which were occurring at that stage. Of the new generation, it is said that they were free of the baggage burdening their parents, that they were prompted by high-profile criminal trials and television series to quiz their parents and rebel against parental authority. The replacement of the industrial society by a service society and the associated dissolution of traditional milieus are also cited. Almost all of the authors see the protest movement of 1968 as a consequence of liberalisation and changing values, not as their source.

[16] BVerfGE 39, 1, 68 ff (1975).
[17] See ch 13 below.

Now it would undoubtedly be wrong to present the FCC as the originator of that liberalisation. But the idea that there might be a link between the liberalisation and the interpretation of the freedoms enshrined in the Basic Law is as plausible as it is intangible. The main reason why it is so difficult to pin down lies in the wide discrepancy between the degree of abstraction of the observed liberalisation and the concrete cases on the basis of which the FCC has to articulate its understanding of freedom. But in view of the fact that jurisprudence is not confined to the adjudication of individual cases but defines a general framework of freedom, it is certainly possible to ask how liberalisation would have proceeded without the Karlsruhe rulings on fundamental rights.

The change in values, of course, did not run smoothly. The new values had to gain ground gradually in the face of fierce opposition, which not all of the historical works reveal. Some of the ensuing disputes led to judicial proceedings. One area in which clashes were frequent was that of free speech and freedom of the press. It was observable when civil courts heard prohibitory actions, as well as when criminal courts heard slander, libel and other defamation cases, that the courts were tending to subordinate freedom of expression. The FCC set aside many such civil and criminal judgments in response to constitutional complaints from convicted persons and gave precedence to the communicative freedoms, drawing heavy criticism from legal scholars as well as from politicians.[18]

The contribution of the FCC to the liberalisation of the Federal Republic is almost even more conspicuous in the case of freedom of assembly. That freedom is part of the classical catalogue of fundamental rights, at least in democratic constitutions. In the Basic Law it is guaranteed in Article 8. In spite of that constitutional guarantee, however, demonstrations were predominantly seen as a threat to public order. The Assemblies and Processions Act of 1953 was not free of that attitude either. With the anti-nuclear movement and the peace movement, mass demonstrations made their entrance as a form of protest. Politicians and the forces of law and order were unprepared for that development. The more heavy-handed the police engagement, the more militant the forms of demonstration became.

It is a surprising fact that 36 years had elapsed since the entry into force of the Basic Law before the FCC had to deal with its Article 8. Until then, public gatherings had evidently not been the subject of any major legal controversies. The reason for the Court's adjudication was a mass demonstration on 28 February 1981 against the construction of Brokdorf nuclear power plant. The protest action had been banned by the county authority responsible for public assemblies. The administrative courts confirmed the assembly ban. Nevertheless, some 50,000 people turned out to demonstrate in Brokdorf. Numerous clashes occurred with the police, some of them heavy. A number of constitutional complaints were lodged against the ban

[18] An overview is provided in Dieter Grimm, 'Die Meinungsfreiheit in der Rechtsprechung des Bundesverfassungsgerichts' in *Neue Juristische Wochenschrift* (1995) 1698.

and the decisions of the administrative courts, and those were received by the FCC in the course of the same year. The Court gave its ruling in May 1985.[19]

The Court adopted an innovative, democratically founded position on Article 8 of the Basic Law. It placed that fundamental right alongside the fundamental right to freedom of expression, the paramount importance of which it had demonstrated in the *Lüth* case. That right had been described in *Lüth* as 'absolutely constitutive' for a free democratic system of government. The description was now applied to freedom of assembly, which had to be understood as 'freedom to proclaim opinions collectively'. Its meaning was then further unfolded by the 'unique nature of the decision-making process in democratic society'. Large associations, wealthy donors and mass media, the Court stated, could exercise considerable influence on political institutions, whereas individuals were more likely to feel powerless.

As the Court said:

> In a society in which direct access to the mass media and the opportunity to communicate through them is limited to a few, the only outlet for individuals other than organised participation in associations and political parties is generally the exertion of collective influence through the exercise of freedom of assembly in demonstrations.

In view of the limited plebiscitary rights of participation in representative democracy, the Court held, freedom of assembly possessed 'the significance of a fundamental and indispensable functional element'. It stabilised the representative system, allowed the expression of discontent and operated as a political early-warning system which indicated disruption potential, revealed integration deficits and so enabled the political institutions to effect course corrections.

Once again, the decision that a demonstration which had taken place four years ago should not have been banned was not the end of the matter. On the contrary, the judgment marked a turning point in the perception of the fundamental right of freedom of assembly. Protest rallies were no longer seen primarily as disruptions, but as a legitimate expression of opinions and interests. They made a contribution to democracy. For that reason, an obligation was imposed on the state to guarantee the exercise of freedom, which it had to permit, not suppress. From this the Court deduced that the competent public authorities and the police were duty-bound to cooperate with the organisers of the demonstration so as to help avoid disruptions of the assembly on the one hand, and disruptions of the general public on the other. De-escalation was the aim.

Oliver Lepsius calls the order a 'landmark decision on the new forms of civil protest and on the integration of the anti-nuclear and peace movement into society'. He characterises it as a 'decision of symptomatic importance to the political system of the Federal Republic through constitutional jurisprudence'.[20]

[19] BVerfGE 69, 315 (1985).

[20] Oliver Lepsius, 'Versammlungsfreiheit und gesellschaftliche Integration' in Anselm Doering-Manteuffel, Bernd Greiner and Oliver Lepsius (eds), *Der Brokdorf-Beschluss* (Mohr Siebeck, 2015) 113.

Although the Assemblies and Processions Act of 1953 essentially remained in force, it had to be interpreted henceforth in accordance with the Brokdorf order. That radically changed not only the doctrinal basis of Article 8 of the Basic Law and the attitude to freedom of assembly but also police training and practice. It is a milestone in the liberalisation of the Federal Republic. Although demonstrations feature prominently in the historiographic works, none of them mentions the Brokdorf order.

In the realm of fundamental freedoms, historians thus had an adequate basis for a comparison between the situation with constitutional jurisprudence and the situation without it. Without the intervention of the Constitutional Court in favour of freedom of expression and freedom of assembly, and in favour of a democracy brought alive by free opinion-forming, free expression of opinion and free collective declaration of opinion, it would have been far harder for liberalisation to advance, at least for a certain period of time. It is true that every conviction for making statements or demonstrating concerns only one individual case, but the judicial line adopted in that category of cases can generate a deterrent effect on the exercise of fundamental rights, an effect which the FCC nullified.

Why, then, is the contribution of the FCC to liberalisation afforded so little attention in historiography? Part of the answer probably lies in the fact that most of the groundbreaking changes stemmed from unspectacular cases far from the world of high-level politics and so remained below the radar. A statement made by Conze might confirm this. The importance of the FCC, he writes, must not be reduced to its role in the major political disputes between government and opposition. 'In those years, the Karlsruhe justices made a decisive contribution to establishing the liberal state based on the rule of law and its fundamental principles' (121).[21]

The cases on which the historians have focused – the abortion time limit, the first television judgment – came under their microscope for reasons other than juridical innovations. What was decisive for them was the outcome, and hence the immediate effect on the political debate, not the long-term effect on social and political conditions, let alone the structural impact on entire areas of activity, such as the media.[22] Long-term effects, however, are precisely where judgments derive their relevance to historical developments. To track these down, it is necessary to consult the grounds of judgments. The operative part of decisions do not reveal them.

An expectation of historiographic awareness of that point is raised by the title of Konrad Repgen's essay, *Bundesverfassungsgerichtsprozesse als Problem der*

[21] The examples that he gives, however, do not relate to judgments but to subject areas, namely gender equality, labour law and the prison system, which differ from those that are emphasised here in connection with liberalisation.

[22] See ch 8 below.

Zeitgeschichtsforschung ('Federal Constitutional Court proceedings as a problem in modern-history research').[23] In that essay, Repgen writes:

> The Karlsruhe court was conceived by the Parliamentary Council as a new element of the constitution and was to guarantee 'comprehensive oversight of the law'. It very soon outgrew that task and also became, de facto, an organ for political decision-making. For four decades, its major cases have been the framework and road map for subsequent political occurrences with regard to many important issues and to that extent are truly 'political proceedings'.

From the fact that they had 'considerable consequences for subsequent political occurrences', Repgen concludes that 'according them due consideration is therefore a genuine task of modern historiography'. What comes next, however, is only a lament that there is no access to files. As a result, says Repgen, historians 'cannot answer the historically indispensable question of the internal opinion-forming and decision-making processes from the files'. The justices' deliberations are undoubtedly of great historical interest, but the historian's focus is on the 'considerable consequences for subsequent political occurrences', and those have slipped quietly out of sight because the court files cannot shed any light on them.[24]

The works analysed here do not give the impression that the judgments have been consulted. It must not be forgotten, of course, that court judgments are unwieldy sources. Their grounds are legal grounds. They explain why and how the decision follows from the constitution, and they do so in the language of legal doctrine. That does not make them unreadable for non-jurists, but the grounds do not reveal all the effects of the judgment. Without interdisciplinary cooperation, the identification of those effects is surely an impossible task. That cooperation has occasionally occurred. There is, for example, a substantial work devoted precisely to the *Lüth* judgment to which not only legal scholars but also historians and political scientists contributed.[25] It has left no mark, however, on the works examined in the present volume.

[23] In Karl-Dietrich Bracher et al (eds), *Staat und Parteien. Festschrift für Rudolf Morsey* (Duncker & Humblot, 1992) 863.

[24] Section 35b(5) of the Federal Constitutional Court Act, which was added in 2013, now provides for perusal of the Court files. See Florian Meinel, 'Das Bundesverfassungsgericht als Gegenstand historischer Forschung. Leitfragen, Quellenzugang und Perspektiven nach der Reform des § 35b BVerfGG' in *Juristenzeitung* 69 (Mohr Siebeck, 2014) 913. On the question of what historians can expect to find in the files, see Dieter Grimm, 'Das Elfes-Urteil' (n 9) 176. A good insight into the working methods of the Court is provided in Gertrude Lübbe-Wolff, *Wie funktioniert das Bundesverfassungsgericht?* (Universitätsverlag Osnabrück, 2015).

[25] Thomas Henne and Arne Riedlinger (eds), *Das Lüth-Urteil aus (rechts-)historischer Sicht* (Berliner Wissenschafts-Verlag, 2005).

8

Influence of the Constitution on the Media System

I. The Significance of the *Spiegel* Affair

In connection with the liberalisation of the Federal Republic, there is one episode that virtually none of the historical works omits, namely the *Spiegel* affair of 1962. Together with the presidential election of 1959, in which Konrad Adenauer initially wanted to stand before opting to remain Chancellor, and with the attempt in 1960 to create a pro-government television channel, which was thwarted in Karlsruhe, the affair stands for the decline in the Federal Chancellor's political instinct and his loss of authority. To an even greater extent, however, it represents an important driving force for that very liberalisation process, because – as the authors generally agree – in the wake of the affair, the Federal Republic saw the emergence of journalism that was emancipated from Adenauer's control of the media and the formation of critical public opinion. This contributed in turn to the change of government in 1969, when the Social Democratic–Liberal coalition took office.

The trigger was a *Der Spiegel* article in which doubt was cast on the operational readiness of the federal armed forces – the Bundeswehr – in the event of hostilities. At the instigation of Defence Minister Franz Josef Strauss, who sensed an act of treason, the publisher of *Der Spiegel*, Rudolf Augstein, his publishing director and several editors were arrested, and the *Spiegel* offices were searched and closed for a time. None of the investigative and criminal proceedings against the publisher and staff of the magazine resulted in a conviction, because the details on which *Der Spiegel* had based its assessment were already public knowledge before the article appeared. The magazine had merely collated information from a variety of sources. Strauss had to resign his post as Minister of Defence and left the Federal Government.

Der Spiegel lodged a constitutional complaint against the search and closure of its premises. The Court did not, as Wehler states, refuse to admit the complaint for decision in the first place. The Court did adjudicate, but because of a tied vote in the First Senate the complaint was rejected.[1] For such an eventuality, which rarely occurs in practice in Karlsruhe, the Federal Constitutional Court Act prescribes

[1] BVerfGE 20, 162 (1966).

that the action is deemed unsuccessful. There is no provision for a President's casting vote. A decision against a contested act of state requires a majority vote. In the event of a tied vote, the legal views of both sides are given equal exposure in the judgment. The losing side is not restricted to producing a dissenting opinion. Wehler calls the judgment 'one of the few deplorable decisions in the history of the highest German court and guardian of the constitution' (273).

Whatever one's position on the matter, it is certainly revealing that the separate assessments of the two groups of four justices were preceded by a jointly formulated four-page passage which developed the semantic content of the freedom of the press enshrined in the second sentence of Article 5(1) of the Basic Law. It reads like a paean to the importance of freedom of the press in a democracy. 'A free press, not controlled by public authority and not subject to censorship, is an essential element of the liberal state; in particular, a free political press, appearing regularly, is indispensable for a modern democracy.' Drawing on the dual nature, expounded in *Lüth*, of fundamental rights as subjective rights and objective principles, the Court found that the fundamental right of freedom of the press not only guaranteed the freedom of publishers and editors but also 'the institution of the free press'.

The fact that *Der Spiegel* lost its case at that time because of a tied vote in the Senate is history. The passage on freedom of the press remains settled jurisprudence today and is cited time and again whenever cases involving the press are adjudicated. That escapes attention if judgments are examined for their outcome alone. The outcome is not an act of pure decision-making but the result of juridical reflections on the meaning of the relevant norm, which are set out in the grounds. They reverberate beyond the case at hand, not only as a precedent in isolated future cases with similar substantive features but also as a general synopsis of the legal position. Particularly in the realm of fundamental rights, with their laconic formulations that are open to interpretation, statements about the state of the law can no longer even be made without reference to constitutional jurisprudence.

II. Constitutional Jurisprudence on Freedom of the Media

The contracted appreciation of judgments is also observable in connection with the first television judgment, delivered by the Federal Constitutional Court (FCC) in 1961, which almost all of the historians mention and which thwarted Adenauer's plan for the creation of what he intended to be a pro-government second television channel, against which three Social Democratic Party (SPD)-governed *Länder* brought a successful action.[2] The FCC ruled that competence for broadcasting lay with the *Länder*. With that, the case was decided. No further explanation was

[2] BVerfGE 12, 205 (1961). The proceedings are documented in Günter Zehner, *Der Fernsehstreit vor dem Bundesverfassungsgericht*, 2 vols (CF Müller, 1964).

needed. Nevertheless, the Court deemed it appropriate to add that the creation of the proposed television company, Deutschland-Fernsehen-GmbH, was in breach of Article 5(1) of the Basic Law, the second sentence of which guaranteed the freedom of broadcasting from state control, meaning in particular freedom of programming, which a shareholders' agreement governed by private law could not adequately guarantee. It is this second ground which is of interest here.

In the history books, however, the opportunity to assess the importance of that ground is missed, because the authors focus on the judgment solely in terms of the painful defeat for Adenauer and not of its impact on the media in the Federal Republic, which is where its significance transcends the specific case. That judgment is likewise based on the concept of the twofold nature of fundamental rights which was developed in *Lüth*. The meaning of freedom of broadcasting is deduced from its impact on the formation of public opinion. The Court held that broadcasting – and television in particular – belonged to the 'indispensable modern mass communication media through which influence is exerted on public opinion and which helps to form that public opinion'. It was not only a medium, but also a factor in the formation of public opinion. For that reason, it was not enough to regard the second sentence of Article 5(1) of the Basic Law as an individual fundamental right of those who worked in broadcasting. As freedom of the press was already understood, namely as freedom of the whole institution, so must freedom of broadcasting be regarded.

Nevertheless, the FCC perceived differences between the press and broadcasting, which made it advisable to safeguard their freedom in different ways. One of those differences lay in the considerable higher financial outlay involved in the creation and operation of a broadcasting station compared with that required for a newspaper publishing house; the other lay in the limited availability of frequency bands, which meant that broadcasters were necessarily few in number. Accordingly, the Court stated, a market with numerous competing providers such as that which existed for the press could not emerge in the broadcasting sector. The legislature therefore had to take steps to ensure that broadcasting 'is not put at the mercy of either the state or one single group within society'. On the contrary, broadcasters had to be organised in such a way that 'all relevant forces can have influence in their decision-making bodies and can make their voices heard within the overall broadcasting schedule and that the schedule is subject to binding principles which guarantee a minimum degree of balanced content, objectivity and mutual respect'.

Under the prevailing conditions, the Court found, it was compatible with the second sentence of Article 5(1) of the Basic Law for broadcasting to be carried out by entities organised as institutions governed by public law, whose collegial bodies comprised 'representatives of all significant political, ideological and social groups'. The FCC thus sanctioned the founding ideal of the Western allies for broadcasting in democratic Germany, which was essentially modelled on the British Broadcasting Corporation (BBC) and followed a middle course between a state broadcasting corporation and a private broadcasting company – neither state-owned nor private, but simply an institution governed by public law. Because of the special situation of broadcasting, the Court considered that the second sentence of Article 5(1) of the Basic Law permitted, though did not require, a broadcasting monopoly to be held by an institution governed by public law. What was decisive, the Court ruled, was not the legal form but adherence to the principles. Adenauer's Deutschland-Fernsehen-GmbH, by contrast, was a state broadcaster in the guise of a private company and as such was incompatible with Article 5 of the Basic Law.

The historical works leave no doubt about the importance of television either. Around 1960, television had replaced radio as the dominant broadcasting medium. The authors focus on that development primarily on account of its social effects. They note that Germans' leisure time was largely spent watching television. In that way, they narrate, it came to exercise considerable influence on individuals' views of the world, as Niklas Luhmann sums it up in the first sentence of his book on the mass media: 'Whatever we know about our society, or indeed about the world in which we live, we know through the mass media'.[3] At the same time, the information received from television, through the combination of word and image and the possibility of transmitting both from the scene of the action in real time, created an aura of particular authenticity. That increased the credibility of the medium and thus its influence.

That influence reaches further, however, as almost all of the works emphasise. Not only views of the world but also values, standards of conduct, social conventions, tastes and role models are significantly influenced by television. That does not leave the world of politics untouched. On the one hand, television shapes attitudes that impact on political preferences and political commitment. Its effect is even more direct when it imparts information on political players and their programmes and achievements and the attitudes that develop in response to these. Accordingly, the way in which politicians present themselves must be tailored to television and the particular characteristics of that medium. In that dependence, however, lies the source of the temptation for political entities to guide the media system in the direction of their own objectives and projects. The broadcasting system governed by public law, in which the state is constitutionally bound to play no part but where 'socially relevant forces', which include the political parties, may become involved, is therefore a focus of party-political interests.

Many of the works also emphasise the homogeneity of West German society, which was fostered by television, or the integrating force that emanates from it. That integrating force, however, is not inherent in the medium as such but is due to the particular situation in the 1960s and 1970s in which the shortage of frequency bands that led to the broadcasting monopoly of the institution governed by public law permitted only a narrow programme schedule. In these

[3] Niklas Luhmann, *Die Realität der Massenmedien*, 2nd edn (Springer VS, 1996) 9; English *The Reality of the Mass Media* (Polity Press, 2000) 1. The changes that have been wrought by the internet and social media were not yet a factor in the period discussed here.

circumstances, integration resulted from the fact that everyone, whether high or low in the social hierarchy, whether rich or poor, rural or urban, old or young, had watched the same channel in the evening and had conversation material for the following morning which overcame other barriers to communication. It could also be assumed that there was a basic store of information which everyone shared.

Those days were over, however, when the means of transmitting programmes by cable and satellite put an end to the scarcity. That development was matched by growing interest in a wider range of channels as well as in alternative organisational forms of delivery. Business saw this as a new area of activity, while the Christian Democratic Union (CDU), which had a chronic sense of being disadvantaged by the public broadcaster, saw it as an opportunity to improve its image on entrepreneurially focused private television. The 'jeremiads of the cultural pessimists' (Herbert 980; English 796) had to give way to the goal of preserving power. The supporters of the public broadcasting monopoly, at least some of whom had a clearer vision of the consequences of commercialising the medium, had been forced onto the defensive, because the transmission of television programmes does not stop at national borders, and if private television were to be prohibited in Germany, programmes would be beamed in from Luxembourg.

The time came in 1981, says Wehler, when the FCC permitted private television (396). He is alluding to the Court's third television judgment, surely the most important in the ever-lengthening chain of television judgments from Karlsruhe.[4] In spite of its importance, the judgment is not mentioned in any other work, just as the media rulings in general receive scant attention. Wehler is the only historian to deem the judgment worthy of mention, but he misstates the reason for its importance. The fact that private television was compatible with the Basic Law had already been established in the first television judgment of 1961. The proceedings that culminated in the 1981 judgment, however, were the first in which the Court was asked to judge a *Land* law that allowed private TV in the light of the second sentence of Article 5(1) of the Basic Law. The importance of the judgment lies in the fact that it set out the conditions in which private television was constitutional. That is the reason why it is still relevant to the media system of the Federal Republic today.

To that end, the Court set about elaborating more precisely what the objective dimension of the protection of fundamental rights meant for the second sentence of Article 5(1) of the Basic Law. The formulation that was familiar from the press judgments, stating that protection applied not only – as a subjective right – to those working in the press but also – as an objective right – to the press as an institution, no longer featured. Whether this had to do with the fact that the concept of institutional protection had been borrowed from the constitutional doctrine of the Weimar era, when Carl Schmitt had introduced it into the discussion, attributing to it the effect of preserving the status quo, is uncertain. The FCC did not comment

[4] BVerfGE 57, 295 (1981).

on the omission of that formulation. Yet such an explanation is certainly not far-fetched, because in its grounds the Court went on to accord the legislature a broad margin of appreciation for shaping the broadcasting system, whereas the concept of institutional protection had restrained the legislature.

Instead of focusing on the institution, the Court focused on the 'task and nature' of the fundamental right. That, said the Court, consisted in guaranteeing the free formation of opinion. In the Court's view, that is the implicit reason behind the guarantees which are set out explicitly in the second sentence of Article 5(1) of the Basic Law. By contrast with the individual freedom of expression enshrined in the first sentence of Article 5(1), which, 'as the most direct expression of the human personality in society' (*Lüth*), is an end in itself, the freedom of the media enshrined in the second sentence of Article 5(1) thus derives its meaning from an extraneous purpose, namely permitting the free formation of opinion. The fact that broadcasting is a factor in the formation of public opinion and that freedom of broadcasting, therefore, must not be understood solely as a subjective right had already been apparent in the first television judgment. Now, however, the purpose was widened. Free media are a prerequisite for the formation not only of public but also of individual opinion.

On the basis of these two pillars – individual self-development and collective self-determination – the FCC now undertook a more precise definition of the protection of that freedom. Free opinion-forming, the Court held, takes place in a communication process. It presupposes both the freedom to express and disseminate opinions and the freedom to obtain information about the expressed opinions. The expressed opinion or message is conveyed and received as information, enters the opinion-forming process and generates statements in response. The media keep this process going. Only if it is itself free, however, can the process contribute to the free formation of opinion. The 'task' of the second sentence of Article 5(1) of the Basic Law therefore emerges as guaranteeing freedom of the communication process. The specific characteristic of freedom of broadcasting lies in the fact that it is a 'serving freedom' (*dienende Freiheit*).

With 'serving freedom' a new type of fundamental right enters the scene, a right which is anything other than self-evident and even sounds puzzling. 'Serving freedom' seems like a contradiction in terms. The contradiction is resolved, however, when the purpose for which the service is rendered is itself that of promoting freedom. That is the case with the implicit purpose of free opinion-forming behind the second sentence of Article 5(1), which is itself a prerequisite for free development of the personality and democracy, in other words for two key guarantees given by the Basic Law. As a 'serving freedom', the second sentence of Article 5(1) protects first and foremost the function performed by broadcasting in pursuit of the desired purpose. It protects those who work in broadcasting only to the extent that they exercise that function. That is why this freedom has also been described as a functional fundamental right.

The particular characteristic of a functional fundamental right lies in the fact that the function of the right-holders – in this case those who work in broadcasting – is prescribed. Unlike an individual fundamental right, a function cannot be exercised at will or be left unperformed. As an individual, one can express oneself on whatever subject one wishes or keep one's silence. Both modes of behaviour are covered by fundamental rights. One's function, however, must be performed. Those who work in broadcasting have no freedom to perform or not to perform their function. Their freedom relates only to how they perform it. How the function of broadcasters' employees is performed can only be determined by the employees themselves, exercising journalistic freedom. The free formation of individual and public opinion would not be served if the objects of media reporting were permitted to guide that reporting in support of their own interests.

In contrast to the first television judgment, the focus was now on privately operated broadcasting, and so an aspect came to the fore which had only been hinted at in 1961 in the statement that broadcasting must not be put at the mercy of either the state or one single group within society. Dangers to freedom of broadcasting, in that interpretation, not only emanate from the state. That is why the third television judgment states that the aim of freedom of broadcasting cannot be achieved by freedom from state control alone, 'for mere independence from the state does not yet mean that free and comprehensive formation of opinion through broadcasting becomes possible'. Freedom of broadcasting therefore affords protection from any instrumentalising of television for extraneous purposes, be they political, economic, religious or whatever in nature. From this, the FCC concluded that freedom of broadcasting needed legal framing to ensure that it achieved its goal. Only on that basis could private broadcasting then take place.

The relaxation of the special situation (high costs, scarcity of frequencies), the Court held, did not eliminate the need for such framing of freedom of broadcasting to guarantee the free formation of opinion. Even if that situation no longer existed, there was still a constitutional requirement for statutory measures to safeguard freedom. The FCC found these necessary because it did not trust 'the forces of competition' to deliver a range of content which met the requirements of Article 5 of the Basic Law. It came to that conclusion in the light of two considerations: first, the tendency of commercial television to prioritise entertainment with mass appeal, and, second, the scope for concentration, resulting in the creation of private opinion makers, which can lead to a loss of diversity and may develop into political power, which will then restrict democratic competition. The aim of Article 5 of the Basic Law remained the same, the Court ruled; at most, the means of safeguarding freedom might change for the private sector.

How that system was to be shaped in detail was for the legislature to determine, said the Court. The Basic Law did not prescribe any particular model for the regulation of broadcasting. The sole criterion was that 'free, comprehensive and truthful opinion-forming' must be ensured and undesirable developments avoided. In that context, the Court drew on the formula that it used in the first television judgment that broadcasting must not be put at the mercy of one single group within society. The Court went on, however, to list a number of issues that had to be resolved in the broadcasting laws of the *Länder*. Foremost among these, besides guidelines for the provision of appropriate, comprehensive and truthful information, were rules relating to access for and selection of private broadcasters. On that basis, the Court then reviewed the Saarland Broadcasting Act for constitutionality, which was the purpose of the case, and reached the conclusion, in its third television judgment, that the Act failed to resolve a number of the issues which required regulation and must therefore be declared unconstitutional.

On the basis of that third television judgment, broadcasting policy now began to take shape. Those *Länder* which sought to permit privately operated television channels enacted laws to that end. A dual model emerged there, in which the television service provided by institutions governed by public law and funded by users' fees co-existed with commercial television funded from advertising revenue. The laws imposed less stringent requirements on all private broadcasters regarding diversity of content and opinion. In place of the supervisory and control bodies, formed from the relevant groups within society, that oversee public broadcasting, *Land* media authorities (*Landesmedienanstalten*) are responsible for licensing private broadcasters and overseeing their compliance with programming requirements. In addition, safeguards were put in place against concentrations in the media industry.

Some of these laws were now the subject of judicial review in their turn, presenting the FCC with the task of specifying what the second sentence of Article 5(1) of the Basic Law required of the dual model chosen by the *Land* legislatures. That was done for the first time in the fourth television judgment of 1986, which concerned the *Land* Broadcasting Act of Lower Saxony.[5] In that case, the Court was confronted by two key elements of its own jurisprudence that were not easy to reconcile with each other. On the one hand, the special situation which had justified the public broadcasting monopoly had now at least partly ceased to exist with the advent of the new technological means of programme transmission. It was therefore politically possible to license private broadcasting companies. And if a company could be licensed, its licence must not be subject to conditions that would have made it impossible to exercise its freedom in practice. The profit motive of the new industry was legitimate. On the other hand, the funding method of commercial television, namely advertising, made it unlikely that it would offer programme schedules which fully satisfied the requirements of the Basic Law.

For that reason, the Court was prepared to accept a relaxation by the legislator of the diversity and even-handedness requirements for commercial television schedules, but only if public broadcasting was fully compliant with the constitutional requirements. It had to continue ensuring the undiminished 'basic provision' (*Grundversorgung*) of the population with content through the medium of television if the concessionary arrangement for private broadcasters was to be compatible with the Basic Law. *Grundversorgung* was the key concept. But it was an unfortunate choice of term, because it could be understood to mean

[5] BVerfGE 73, 118 (1986).

a minimal provision. The private broadcasters capitalised on this by interpreting 'basic provision' as legitimising a division of labour in which commercial television could concentrate on everything that was lucrative – in other words, popular entertainment and sport – while the sector governed by public law was expected to compensate for this imbalance by offering only news and cultural programmes.

For the FCC, by contrast, 'basic provision' meant 'full provision', because the Court did not succumb to the illusion that public broadcasting without entertainment and sport would not quickly vanish into a niche, so that even its funding by means of user fees would no longer be justifiable. Public broadcasters, the Court concluded, must continue to provide programmes in all categories, which made the private competitors' schedules appear like a 'supplementary provision'. That translated into a guarantee for the existence and development of public broadcasting in technological, organisational, staffing and financial terms, which ensured not only its survival but also its competitiveness.[6] Licensing of private competitors was thus conditional upon the viability of public broadcasting.

III. The Relevance of the Media Rulings

The foregoing is the dogmatic derivation of the judicial outcome and is not something into which historians need to delve. But what about the outcome itself and its implications for the media system as well as for the impact of that system on the knowledgeability of society and the public debate? A good authority on the media landscape says, 'With its interpretation of the fundamental right, the Court set its stamp on the development of the media system and on the media industry for decades to come'.[7] Would the critical public, whose emergence in the 1960s appears to be so important to the historians as a characterising factor for the Federal Republic, have materialised if the FCC had adopted a different position on Article 5 of the Basic Law? Would it even have been able to adopt a different position, or were the television judgments merely enforcements of the constitution, which would mean that the contribution of constitutional jurisprudence was confined to updating what had been determined in 1949?

Wehler asks such a question towards the end of his chapter on the media after concluding that 'an entirely favourable verdict must be delivered on the Fourth Power of the West German public domain between 1949 and 1990' (404). 'Why', he asks, 'did the political culture of the Federal Republic succeed – that is the crucial question which needs clarification – in developing an essentially consensually orientated public domain within a broad and by no means restrictive framework?' (404). Wehler

[6] This is most strongly emphasised in the sixth television judgment – BVverfGE 83, 238 (1991) – and in the radio and television user fee judgment – BVerfGE 90, 60 (1994).

[7] Christoph Degenhart, 'Realitätsprägung durch Verfassungsrecht' in Rupert Scholz et al (eds), *Realitätsprägung durch Verfassungsrecht* (Duncker & Humblot, 2008) 97.

answers that the main reason is obvious to historians, namely 'because the historical situation was so completely different in nature from the one that obtained after the defeat in the First World War'.

If that is what he means by the 'framework' within which the public domain developed, the answer has become far removed from the media system. Yet the framework in question may also be regarded as the legal framework for the media system. Could the judgment on the media have turned out equally favourable if a different legal framework had been in place, that is to say if freedom of the media had meant no more than the prohibition of state interference with the media? Or if there had been no Constitutional Court to oversee the preservation of the legal framework? Here, too, it is worth recalling that there is a limit to what can be said about any hypothetical course of events. On the other hand, it is not the case that such statements can only be based on pure speculation and therefore possess minimal academic value. The more concrete the starting point, the greater the probability of an accurate finding.

This much at least may be regarded as certain: if the FCC had not issued an injunction in December 1960 preventing Konrad Adenauer's Deutschland-Fernsehen-GmbH from going on air,[8] the company would have begun transmitting on 1 January 1961, in good time for the Bundestag election of September 1961. In the view of the FCC, that would have been seriously detrimental to the common good: 'If transmissions through a second channel, operated by Deutschland-Fernsehen GmbH, were to begin on 1 January 1961, a de facto situation of not inconsiderable political significance would be created.' In the decision on the main proceedings, delivered on 28 February 1961, the Court then confirmed that the creation of the company had breached fundamental constitutional principles. Had the decision been different, there would have been a permanent pro-government broadcaster with a pro-government programming schedule.

But the significance of the judgment went beyond the prevention of the television programmes which the Federal Chancellor wanted the company to transmit. Ever since then, it has been established that the transmission of television programmes directly by the state or under its influence is incompatible with the Basic Law. One of the essential functions of television is critical reporting of political activities, particularly those of the government. That function could not be performed if the object of observation and reporting were in control of both activities. Oversight of television programmes is a matter for society, undertaken by its relevant groups. That has served to prevent public television institutions from effectively becoming state broadcasters, a development which has been observable even in some democratic states. What proved to be a weak spot in the construct, however, was the allocation of seats on the supervisory bodies to the political parties. It was not until much later that the FCC had the opportunity to address that flaw.[9]

[8] BVerfGE 12, 36 (1960).
[9] BVerfGE 136, 9 (2014).

Similarly, the significance of the third television judgment of 1981 was not limited to the fact that the Saarland law on the organisation of private broadcasting was declared null and void and that the company Freie Rundfunk AG, which had applied for a licence under that law, was unable to commence operations. On the contrary, it was now established that private broadcasting in general could not be left to market forces in accordance with the press model but had to be tied into a system, even after the relaxation of the special situation, which ensured that private broadcasters served to foster free development of the personality and democratic rule and that a concentration of opinion-forming power was prevented. With such provisions, Silvio Berlusconi's amassing of opinion-forming power in Italy would have been impossible, as would the emergence of a broadcaster such as Fox News in the United States, where broadcasting was fully liberalised when the special situation ceased to apply.

Lastly, the fourth television judgment was not limited to enabling the establishment of the dual system by means of a few small adjustments to *Land* legislation. On the contrary, it was now established jurisprudence that the concessionary arrangement whereby the *Land* legislatures required less diversity of opinion and of subject matter from private operators on account of their funding method was dependent on undiminished performance of the classical broadcasting mission, at least by the public broadcasters. In that way, precautions were taken to ensure that public broadcasters did not vanish into a niche, as they did in the United States, but remained a significant factor in the formation of public opinion. It is easy to imagine what would have happened to the availability of informative and cultural programme options for viewers if that guarantee had not existed.

The Court was less successful with regard to the constitutional requirements for private broadcasters. It had, of course, only conceded that the obligation to ensure diversity of opinion and programming content could be relaxed but not waived. It was incumbent on both sectors of the dual system to perform the constitutionally guaranteed function of broadcasting. Only the public broadcasters, funded by user fees, had to meet that requirement in full, whereas certain concessions could be made for private broadcasters, which relied on advertising revenue. Exactly what that meant in practice was to be determined by *Land* legislation or by media services agreements concluded by the *Länder* and enforced by the *Land* media authorities. These did not always set ambitious standards. According to Herbert, 'The programmes produced by the private broadcasters competed with each other in triviality and shallowness' (980, English 796); Wehler speaks of an *Unterklassen-Programm*, a schedule for the lower classes (397).

It is not as though there was no alternative to the decisions reached by the FCC. All the Basic Law says is that the press and broadcasting are to be 'free'. As can be seen by looking at democratic countries which have that kind of freedom in their constitutions, 'freedom' may be interpreted in very different ways. The FCC opted for an ambitious definition of freedom. The conception of freedom of broadcasting as a 'serving freedom' and the extension of its protection to the social function performed by broadcasting were important innovations in the theory of fundamental rights which have no equivalent in the United States, for example, where the idea that fundamental rights are any more than subjective defensive rights of individuals against the state has never gained a foothold.

Even in Germany, however, the constitutional conception of freedom of broadcasting was by no means undisputed. The private providers fought it tirelessly. Some constitutional theorists criticised it vehemently and regarded the second sentence of Article 5(1) of the Basic Law as an individual liberty like any other, from which they inferred that, at least after the special situation had ended, there was no longer any justification for a constitutional differentiation between the press and broadcasting. Freedom of broadcasting would not then be serving the purpose of free opinion-forming but would amount to freedom of entrepreneurship for broadcasters. It may be supposed that a different public domain would have developed in those circumstances. Exactly what it would have looked like and what consequences it would have had, for democracy for instance, is a moot question. Examples from other countries provide at least some clues.

Now, however good the decisions of a Constitutional Court may be, they will naturally be worthless if they are not respected. But there can be absolutely no suggestion of non-compliance. The first television judgment of 1961 was regarded publicly as a sensation. It unleashed a torrent of extremely fierce criticism on the FCC from the parties of the governing coalition. In the Bundestag, Adenauer declared that the cabinet had examined the judgment and had come to a unanimous conclusion: 'The judgment is wrong, ladies and gentlemen.' But he submitted to it. And that remained so. Protests were made against decisions that harmed party interests or offended the sensitivities of large sections of the population. Justices were maligned. Occasionally, politicians would call for judgments to be disregarded. But never have the organs of state flouted any judgment. There are few constitutional states with similarly high compliance rates.[10]

[10] See Helmuth Schulze-Fielitz, 'Wirkung und Befolgung verfassungsgerichtlicher Entscheidungen' in Peter Badura and Horst Dreier (eds), *Festschrift 50 Jahre Bundesverfasungsgericht*, Vol I (Mohr Siebeck, 2001) 385.

9

The Social Democratic–Liberal Reforms under Scrutiny

I. A New Phase in Relations between the Court and the Political Institutions

What befell Adenauer in the television dispute had to be endured more than once by the coalition of Social Democrats and Free Democrats which came to power in 1969, after three years of a Grand Coalition of Christian Democratic Union (CDU)/Christian Social Union (CSU) and Social Democratic Party (SPD). The SPD–Free Democratic Party (FDP) coalition took office with far-reaching reform projects. In the field of foreign policy, its aim was a policy towards Eastern Europe – an *Ostpolitik* – based on rapprochement in place of demarcation. Domestically, the new Government intended to set about reshaping the education system, liberalising criminal law, particularly with regard to the abortion ban, making changes to family and marriage law, especially by basing divorce law on the principle of irretrievable breakdown instead of the fault principle and reforming the rules on the division of acquired assets and pension rights adjustment. It also intended to tackle pension and tax reform, to make amendments to the works constitution and to introduce worker codetermination. Willy Brandt listed the projects in his programme of government. *Mehr Demokratie wagen* ('Risking more democracy') was the slogan he used as a heading.

As the historians show, the foundations for some of these changes had been laid by the Grand Coalition. Nevertheless, Brandt managed to convey the impression of a deep caesura and, above all, to fuel the expectation that democracy was only now beginning in earnest in the Federal Republic. The existing democracy was presented as a merely state-centred, formal structure which was now to be transformed into a substantive form of democracy that would also imbue social institutions, particularly enterprises and educational establishments. There was indeed much that was new. For the first time, the SPD led the Government, the FDP coalesced with the SPD for the first time, and the CDU, despite winning the election, found itself in opposition for the first time. The changeover had been effected smoothly, following the pathway marked out in the constitution. The historians see that as another test passed by the Basic Law (Birke 39, Herbert 865/English 703), Görtemaker 475, Rödder 34, Winkler 272/English 488).

It is not only the smooth transition that made the period remarkable from a constitutional perspective, but also the judicial actions against those reform proposals which had come to fruition. These actions took the form of applications for judicial review made by the opposition or by the CDU/CSU-led *Land* governments or of constitutional complaints lodged by individuals. The political argument, then, was not settled by the majority decision but was continued before the Federal Constitutional Court (FCC). Which of the ambitious reform plans succeeded depended not only on what could gain acceptance in the democratic process but also on what could stand up in court proceedings. Since expectations were high and had even been overinflated by the promise of a 'democratisation of society', it was easily possible for the Court to slide into the role of the antagonist of democracy.

As for the question of the Court's attitude to the reforms, it is not insignificant that, in 1971, when the proceedings challenging the reform of higher education were already pending and, given the sharp conflicts over some other reform proposals, more judicial actions were to be expected, six justices of the FCC reached the end of their term of office: Gebhard Müller, who was President of the Court, Gerhard Leibholz and Erwin Stein, justices of the first generation, also justices Gregor Geller and Rudi Wand as well as the only woman on the Bench, Wiltraut Rupp-von Brünneck. Accordingly, the election of new justices aroused controversy and attracted an unusually high level of public interest. An additional complication lay in the fact that five of the six retiring justices had been CDU nominees. In view of the new party-political balance in Parliament, that had to change. The FDP, moreover, was pressing its coalition partner to let it nominate one candidate.

It was agreed that Wand should be re-elected, since he had only joined the Bench one year before to complete the term of Hans Kutscher, who had moved to the European Court of Justice. As for the other vacancies, the CDU and the SPD were each permitted to nominate two candidates, while the FDP was to propose the final candidate. The SPD proposed that Rupp-von Brünneck be re-elected and nominated Bundestag member Martin Hisch as a newcomer. The CDU selected the former Minister of the Interior, Ernst Benda, as President of the Court along with Hans Faller, a judge by profession. Joachim Rottmann, a departmental civil servant, joined the Court as the nominee of the FDP after the woman whom it had initially proposed had not gained the approval of the other parties. This meant that there was no longer a professor of public law on the Bench, the only academic lecturer being Hans Brox, a scholar of civil law.

II. The Reforms under Scrutiny

Of the reform proposals that were implemented, the magnanimous pension reform, understandably, was spared any constitutional challenge. The reform of marriage law, though fiercely contested, also remained unchallenged.[1] Actions were brought, however, against the Treaty on the Basis of Relations with the GDR, against the treaties with the Soviet Union, Poland and Czechoslovakia and against the abortion time-limit rule, the amendment of the Conscription Act and worker codetermination. Since education is primarily a matter for the *Länder*, the FCC also had to adjudicate on *Land* laws introducing the *Gruppenuniversität* – a university jointly managed by its teaching staff, students, academic assistants and other staff. The federal Framework Act for Higher Education had already been formulated in the light of the Karlsruhe judgment on the Higher Education Act of Lower Saxony and so was no longer the subject of judicial actions.[2]

A perusal of the Basic Law, it must be said, was not enough in these cases. Whoever seeks a ready-made answer there will seek in vain. If the judgment on pregnancy termination is taken as an example of the situation in which the Court found itself, the Basic Law simply does not state 'Abortion shall be punishable'. If it did, every political party which sought to decriminalise abortion would have known that it could only be achieved by amending the Basic Law. However, there is nothing at all about abortion in the constitution. What it does state is that every person has the right to life (first sentence of Article 2(2)). Does 'every person' include the foetus? Or does it mean only persons who have already been born? If the right also extends to the foetus, another question arises, namely at what moment the right begins. Is there possibly a time-based scale of entitlement to protection?

Once it has been established who enjoys the right, the next question is against whom the right is enforceable. It is established that fundamental rights are addressed to the state in all its manifestations. That is clear from Article 1(3) of the Basic Law. But only to the state, or to private individuals and entities too? That was the nub of the *Lüth* case.[3] Moreover, Article 2(2) of the Basic Law, in its third sentence, makes it possible to interfere with the right to life pursuant to a law. All the Basic Law requires for such interference is a legal basis, subject to the proviso set out in Article 19(2) of the Basic Law that no law may affect the essence of a fundamental right. Interfering with the right to life means killing. So there are evidently circumstances in which a holder of the right to life may be killed. What are those circumstances, under what conditions may someone be lawfully killed, and who is entitled to carry out or order such an act?

The matter is further complicated by the fact that the expectant mother is necessarily part of the picture. She also enjoys protection of her fundamental rights. The Basic Law, and indeed the selfsame Article 2, states that every person

[1] A number of proceedings did arise later, however, as a consequence of civil actions; see ch 11 below.

[2] Informative insights into the adjudication on the reforms, where it lay within the jurisdiction of the First Senate, are now provided by Fabian Michl's biography *Wiltraut Rupp-von Brünneck (1912–1977), Juristin, Spitzenbeamtin, Verfassungsrichterin* (Campus, 2002) 342 ff.

[3] See ch 7 above.

has the right to free development of his or her personality (Article 2(1)). Does that include the right to terminate a pregnancy? The FCC had already answered that question implicitly in the affirmative in its *Elfes* judgment by ruling that free development of the personality encompassed every action of the individual which was not covered by a specific fundamental right.[4] Since there is no sign of such a specific fundamental right relating to abortion, the individual's general freedom of action comes into play. Under Article 2(1) of the Basic Law, however, that right applies only in so far as its beneficiary does not violate the rights of others or offend against the constitutional order or the moral law. So how much remains of that right?

If the right to life of the foetus is affirmed, the FCC sees itself confronted with a conflict between fundamental rights. On the basis of one fundamental right, the foetus has a right to life, though not unconditionally; on the basis of the other right, the mother has a right to termination of her pregnancy, though not unconditionally either. The FCC tries to resolve conflicts between fundamental rights by means of a balancing exercise, the purpose of which is not to supplant one right with the other but to preserve as much as possible of both rights. At every stage in the resolution of a case, decisions therefore have to be made which are not preordained by the text of the Basic Law. The justices are faced with a choice – albeit a legal choice – and depending on which option they deem to be legally appropriate, the political decision stands or falls. The interpretation of the constitution determines the outcome.

The decisions taken by the Court affected the reform goals of the Social Democratic–Liberal coalition to differing extents. The coalition suffered a total defeat in its reform attempts regarding the abortion ban[5] and the amendment of the Conscription Act.[6] The Conscription (Amendment) Act, which abolished the need for conscientious objectors to appear before an examination panel, replacing it with a mere communication by the conscript of his refusal to perform military service on grounds of conscience, was declared incompatible with what the Court called *Wehrgerechtigkeit*, or equity of conscription, which it derived from the principle of equality enshrined in Article 3(1) of the Basic Law. In the abortion judgment, not only was the time-limit rule adopted by the Bundestag declared unconstitutional; the FCC also bound the legislature to protect developing life by means of criminal law. The permissible exceptions were narrowly defined.

The legislators' duty to act was based on the precept established in the *Lüth* judgment that fundamental rights are not only subjective defensive rights against state interference with guaranteed fundamental freedoms. If they were no more than that, the new legislation would not have raised any problems with regard to fundamental rights, because the state neither ordered abortions nor performed them itself. It only declared that abortions were no longer punishable. Now,

[4] BVerfGE 6, 32 (1957); see ch 7 above.
[5] BVerfGE 39, 1 (1975).
[6] BverfGE 48, 127 (1978).

however, fundamental rights were objective principles too and, as such, gave rise to state obligations to protect fundamental freedoms. That was new, although it was a direct consequence of *Lüth*. Accordingly, the duty to protect was not in dispute in the First Senate either. The two dissenting justices, Wiltraut Rupp-von Brünneck and Helmut Simon, expressly excluded that duty from their criticism, which was only levelled against the finding that the means of discharging the duty to protect, namely the criminalisation of abortion, could be deduced from the constitution.

The duty of the state to protect the guaranteed fundamental freedoms if they are threatened by private individuals or entities is now a part of Germany's constitutional heritage. It is understood as a second pillar of the protection of fundamental rights alongside defence against state interference and has been adopted by courts in many other countries and by the European courts. The choice of means to discharge the duty of protection, however, is left to the legislators' discretion. There will normally be more than one constitutionally permissible means to that end. Therein lies the difference between fundamental rights in their capacity as protective obligations and fundamental rights as defensive rights. The legislature must merely choose a suitable means and tailor the protection to the gravity of the danger. Just as a prohibition of excessive measures applies to interference with fundamental rights, a prohibition of insufficient action applies to the duty to protect. In that respect, the Court corrected itself in the second abortion judgment, given in 1993.[7]

In the case of the Higher Education Act of Lower Saxony, only part of the reform was struck down, but it was largely found to be constitutional.[8] That is only observable, however, if consideration of the relevant judgment is not confined to its outcome. Its significance, in fact, does not emerge until the general understanding of the fundamental right of academic freedom prior to that judgment is taken into account. On the basis of a constitutional doctrine carried over from the Weimar era, Article 5(3) of the Basic Law was regarded as the 'fundamental right of the German university'. In that context, 'German' referred to the university model which was traced back to Wilhelm von Humboldt, at the core of which was academic self-governance. According to the prevailing view, the fundamental right protected that model from legislative change. Had that view persisted, the *Gruppenuniversität* introduced by the legislature would have had to be declared unconstitutional, as it represented a departure from that model.

The FCC, however, did not embrace that understanding but stated that the legislature was free to determine the organisational form of universities, provided that academic freedom was not impaired. It saw the purpose of academic freedom as enabling the academic system and those working in it to adhere to the specific rationality criterion or the inherent logic of the system and preserving them from subjection to the rationality criteria of alien systems. It was, in other

[7] BVerfGE 88, 203 (1993).
[8] BVerfGE 35, 79 (1973).

words, the function of academic institutions, namely to generate scientifically sound knowledge – or, to put it in more old-fashioned terms, to seek the truth – which formed the core of what the fundamental right guaranteed. The jointly managed *Gruppenuniversität* was compatible with the performance of that function, provided that, in matters of teaching and research, the influence of the professors in university bodies was adequately safeguarded. That was the only respect in which the Act had to be remedied.

The Court upheld the Treaty on the Basis of Relations with the GDR in its entirety.[9] There were caveats, but they arose only from the grounds and concerned future policy; they did not affect the validity of the Treaty. The Court insisted that the goal of the reunification of Germany, which was primarily proclaimed in the preamble to the Basic Law, must not be abandoned.[10] The Court did not let the matter rest there, however, but extended the binding effect of the judgment, which would normally reside only in the operative part of the judgment and the grounds on which it is based, far into political territory by summarily declaring all grounds set out in the judgment, including the obiter dicta, to be part of the *ratio decidendi*. That was of no relevance to the Treaty itself, but it did have a bearing on future policy in view of the flagging will for reunification, which the historians register.

As for the constitutional complaints against the treaties with the Soviet Union and with Poland[11] and Czechoslovakia,[12] complaints that were chiefly directed against recognition of the existing borders, which would result, it was feared, in property losses, their merits were not even examined, for the complaints were rejected as inadmissible on the ground that they did not affect the fundamental rights of individuals. The Court held that the treaties neither created behavioural obligations for individuals nor deprived private individuals or entities of assets. The property losses, it stated, had occurred through acts of foreign states which could not be imputed to the Federal Republic. The complainants' higher expectation that the Federal Government would take account of particular private interests when negotiating an international agreement, the Court ruled, was not protected by any fundamental right. Otherwise the Federal Government's margin of appreciation in the field of foreign policy would be severely restricted.

Before the series of judgments on the reform acts was completed, another extensive shake-up occurred in the Court in July 1975. Once again, six justices reached the end of their term of office. The previous major changeover had taken place only four years ago, and the political parties still had scathing criticism of the selection process ringing in their ears, the selection of the judges having been significantly dictated by party interests. Efforts were made to do it better this time. Helmut Simon, a professional judge, was confirmed in office and was joined by

[9] BVerfGE 36, 1 (1973). Documentation from the proceedings is provided by Eve Ceislar et al (eds), *Der Streit um den Grundlagenvertrag* (Olzog, 1973).

[10] See chs 1 and 6 above.

[11] BVerfGE 40, 141 (1975).

[12] BVerfGE 43, 293 (1977).

three other judges from the highest federal courts. Two professors entered the Court – Helmut Steinberger, a scholar of international law, and Konrad Hesse, one of the most eminent experts in constitutional law; the latter succeeded Theodor Ritterspach, who had served on the Bench for 24 years and had been the rapporteur for the *Lüth* judgment. Of the founding generation, only Willi Geiger now remained in the Court. None of the new justices had ever held political office or a parliamentary mandate.

Contrary to a promise made by his party, the SPD, to Justice Martin Hirsch, a former Bundestag member who had been elected to the Court in 1971, he was not appointed Vice-President of the Court. That position went to Wolfgang Zeidler, who had previously been a justice in the First Senate before being appointed President of the Federal Administrative Court and had now returned to Karlsruhe as President of the Second Senate; from 1983 he was also President of the Court. Of the justices who came from the world of politics, Hirsch was probably the one for whom the change of role worked out least satisfactorily. The letters in which he protested against this snub to Willy Brandt and to Friedrich Schäfer, vice-chairman of the SPD parliamentary group, show how justified the decision to overlook him was. 'What has Zeidler ever done for the SPD and its legal politics as a constitutional justice compared with me?', he asks indignantly.[13]

The change of justices is evident in the final decision in the series, the judgment on worker codetermination.[14] The rapporteur in those proceedings was Konrad Hesse, who had not been a member of the Court when the First Senate gave its judgments on higher education and abortion and who was averse to judicial activism. The proceedings were conducted with a huge input of legal expertise from both sides and culminated in full constitutional approval of the statute. Over and above the case at hand, the judgment is significant because the Court readjusted its powers of scrutiny vis-à-vis the legislature. If the constitutionality of a law depends on its future effect on fundamental rights, which makes predictions unavoidable, the judicial review is limited in principle to verifying that the prediction has been arrived at appropriately; the Court does not substitute it with one of its own.[15]

III. Reception by the Public and Historians

So although the balance of the judgments delivered on the legal affairs policy of the Social Democratic–Liberal coalition was not by any means entirely unfavourable, those rulings did considerably alter perceptions of the Court. In the reform phase, which was accompanied by great expectations on the part of a sizeable proportion of the population, it was regarded primarily as a reform brake. Braking, it is true,

[13] Justin Collings unearthed the letters in various archives and cites them in *Democracy's Guardians* (Oxford University Press, 2015) 166.

[14] BVerfGE 50, 290 (1979).

[15] ibid, 332 f.

is the business of the FCC. The brake is there to put a stop to unconstitutional conduct of political organs and to do so regardless of the wishes of the public and politicians. It had also halted Adenauer's attempt to create a pro-government television channel and had been praised for doing so. But for applying the brake to the reformist policy of the Social Democratic-Liberal coalition, the Court was hit by a torrent of criticism.[16]

The criticism of the 1970s differed from the earlier torrents of criticism that the Court had faced over its stance on the Western integration and rearmament of the Federal Republic in two key respects. First, the earlier criticism had been confined to the Federal Government and the governing parties, whereas the media and the public had been very largely on the side of the Court. This time, the media, the public and even the scholarly commentators were very largely on the politicians' side. Second, the main focus of the critics in the 1950s was on the Court having allegedly departed 'from the path of law'. The criticism was now being voiced in the name of democracy. The accusation levelled at the Court was that it was preventing the implementation of the democratically formed will.

Some of the criticism was expressed very vehemently, even by SPD politicians, who were not known for a particular predilection for polemics. Not even offensive language was off-limits. Although in the 1950s Federal Minister of Justice Thomas Dehler had likewise been prone to resort to undiplomatic language, he had paid for that with the loss of his post, whereas the vituperators could now count on acclaim. There was even a direct heated exchange between Federal Chancellor Helmut Schmidt and the President of the Court, Ernst Benda, at a panel discussion held by the Evangelische Akademie in Tutzing. Calls were made for curtailment of the Court's powers. The criticism was not confined to verbal onslaughts either. Demonstrations were organised, particularly in connection with the proceedings on the amendments to the Conscription Act and on section 218 of the Criminal Code, the abortion clause. Following the abortion judgment, an arson attack was carried out at night on the Court building.

What politicians and the general public think of judgments is legally irrelevant. It does not alter their validity. Institutionally, however, it is relevant, because the institution, which cannot use coercive means to enforce its decisions, is dependent on political and public acceptance of those decisions. The greatest danger arises when they are seen as a threat to democracy. The democracy argument may often have been used as a smokescreen, the real focus of the criticism being the outcome of particular cases, although that has seldom been made so manifest as it was by Helmut Ridder, professor of public law at Giessen, who, having accused the Court during the period of CDU rule of not exercising its oppositional function, now wrote that the Court was arrogating an oppositional function to itself.[17]

[16] Comprehensively described in Collings (n 13) 126–81.

[17] Helmut Ridder, 'In Sachen Opposition: Adolf Arndt und das Bundesverfassungsgericht' in *Festschrift für Adolf Arndt* (Europäische Verlagsanstalt, 1969) 323; idem, 'Das Bundesverfassungsgericht. Bemerkungen über Aufstieg und Verfall einer antirevolutionären Einrichtung' in Peter Römer (ed), *Der Kampf um das Grundgesetz* (Syndikat, 1977) 70.

But that does not disarm the argument. The 'countermajoritarian difficulty', as it is frequently termed in the United States, is the Achilles heel of judicial review.

If the political institutions had defied the Karlsruhe judgments at that stage, perhaps after the abortion judgment, they would possibly have received acclaim from part of the population. But what could 'defying a judgment' have meant? If the legislature is bound by the Court to act, it may defy the judgment by remaining passive. If the Federal Government is enjoined from performing a specific action, such as deploying troops to a trouble spot, it may decide to do so anyway. But once a law is declared unconstitutional and void, it ceases to exist. Even if the political organs were to ignore the judgment, the courts would nevertheless cease to apply the annulled law. 'Defying', in that case, can only mean readopting the law without amendment the following day. It is very unlikely, however, that the political organs would have taken such a decision.

There was never a test case, in point of fact. On the contrary, from a longer-term perspective, that extremely controversial judgment on reforms proposed by the Social Democratic–Liberal coalition actually had a pacifying effect. Society was no longer split over the legal rules governing abortion, in complete contrast with the United States, where the issue has never gone away since the Supreme Court decision of 1973.[18] The difference derives from the fact that both sides in the Federal Republic experienced success – the opponents of abortion on the principle, and its advocates in practical terms, because the exemption known as the social indication was interpreted broadly, whereas in the United States one side's victory was the other's defeat. That, too, had its roots in constitutional law, because the US understanding of fundamental rights favours an 'either-or' approach, while the German understanding is conducive to a proportionate balancing exercise.

The historical works give extensive coverage to the reform policy of the Social Democratic-Liberal coalition. They portray the initial reformist euphoria and the fierce resistance which the reform proposals encountered in some sections of society and at least in part among the opposition, the waning elan after the early Bundestag election of 1972 and the ending of the reform era as a result of the oil crisis, by which time Helmut Schmidt already held the chancellorship. The change in the political balance in the Bundestag when members changed parties on account of the FDP's participation in the coalition Government and, later, on account of the *Ostpolitik*, the resulting failed vote of no confidence against Brandt and the early dissolution and fresh election of the Bundestag in 1972 are the subject of detailed portrayals.

The fact that it ultimately depended on the FCC whether all of the concluded reforms could enter into force is indicated in the historical accounts, albeit to vastly differing degrees. Of the decisions taken by the FCC during that period, some of which were landmark decisions, seven related directly to the coalition's reform acts – three concerning treaties connected with the *Ostpolitik* and four devoted

[18] *Roe v Wade*, 410 US 113 (1973).

to internal reform proposals. Since the treaties were not always dealt with separately but occasionally as a package under the collective designation *Ostverträge*, or Eastern treaties, one can refer for convenience to five processes which assumed importance for the fate of the reform programme of the Social Democratic–Liberal era.

None of the histories catalogues all five. Wirsching, in his short book, manages to omit any reference to the decisions. The others mention at least one decision. Four of the five judgments feature in Birke, Conze and Winkler. Of the 11 works containing references to individual judgments, all mention the Treaty on the Basis of Relations between the Federal Republic and the GDR, sometimes together with the other Eastern treaties, and nine refer to the judgment on the time-limit rule for abortions. The judgment on worker codetermination features in four works and the higher education judgment in two. The amendments to the Conscription Act appear only in Birke. The torrent of accusations levelled at the Court, which spawned other judgments that did not concern the reform policy, however, cannot be examined if the subjects of criticism are missing.

Accordingly, there is nothing to be found in the history books about the mighty public furore over the FCC. To the extent that anything at all is said about the relationship between the Court and the political institutions in the five years from 1973 to 1978, quite a patchwork image emerges. In Wehler, the Court appears as one of several 'vetoing actors' (237), while Wolfrum writes of a 'vetoing player' that had co-governed, 'so to speak' (323). For Herbert, in that period the Court was 'increasingly taking on the role of an extraparliamentary mediator' (880, English 716). According to Recker, it set limits on the scope for creativity of the SPD and FDP (64) and erected 'obstacles' to their reform policy (66). Birke describes it as a 'key corrective to the reform policy', adding that it had left a legacy of 'concern about judicial policymaking' (48).

That the Court had descended into a serious legitimacy crisis cannot even be guessed after reading the works. The sole statement which at least alludes to the existence of a conflict is once again to be found in Birke, who says that the Court had come 'under heavy fire' on account of its judgments against the reform policy (48). That wording does not convey any conception of anger within society towards the FCC. In spite of the observations that it became a vetoing body during the reform period, the impression obtained from the works is rather that of a steadily growing appreciation of the Court. Yet at times the reactions threatened a key institution of the constitutional structure. The fact that the Court ultimately recovered from that loss of acceptance does not make the intervening crisis a non-event. It could even have left a disempowered Court in its wake. That worst-case scenario, however, did not occur. Instead, the disappointment soon turned to overwhelming approval when the Court stopped the 1983 census.[19]

[19] See ch 12 below.

Since then, the FCC has only once had to experience similarly fierce onslaughts and loss of popularity, namely in 1994 and 1995. Unlike the protests of the 1970s, these were not about an elected majority being prevented by the Court from realising its political intentions. This time, the fury was ignited by a small number of decisions that did not relate directly to political measures but quashed court judgments for insufficient consideration of fundamental rights. The decisions met with widespread incomprehension and indignation in society, politics and the media, and kept the FCC in the headlines for months on end. Some observers believed that it would never recover from that condemnation.

What began in the spring of 1994 as irritation, when the rules regarding criminal penalties for the possession of cannabis were relaxed,[20] swelled into a storm of protest shortly afterwards following a briefly substantiated chamber order of 25 August 1994 quashing the conviction of a pacifist for having publicly communicated the phrase 'Soldiers are murderers', borrowed from Kurt Tucholsky, on the ground that the criminal courts had failed to distinguish sufficiently between strident or even intemperate statements against militarism and war, which were covered by freedom of expression, and personal defamation of military personnel, which was punishable. Widespread criticism of the Court's alleged bias towards freedom of expression, which had been prevalent for quite some time, now came to a head.[21]

In January 1995, the decision on the criminality of sit-down strikes[22] further fuelled the protest, which reached its climax in May 1995 with the order overturning the requirement to hang a crucifix in primary school classrooms in Bavaria.[23] Protest marches took place, led by the Minister-President and bishops. Some politicians likened the FCC to the Nazi regime, which had also attempted to ban crucifixes from public places. The binding nature of the judgment was repudiated in some quarters. Nonsensical conclusions were drawn – that all crosses would now have to be removed from mountain summits in the Bavarian Alps or that Lessing's *Nathan the Wise* could no longer be staged in state theatres because the Templar's cloak showed a cross.

As in the 1970s, the outrage led to calls for curtailment of the powers of the FCC, for a two-thirds majority requirement for the annulment of acts of state and court judgments or for a higher constitutional instance to oversee the FCC. Several of the historiographical works end before these events. The historians who include the 1990s in their accounts do not address the decisions and the storm of protest they provoked. The observation that society's acceptance of the Court was high from the outset 'and so it has remained down to the present day' (Conze 121) can only be made if one disregards the major crises in which the FCC became embroiled.

[20] BVerfGE 90, 145 (1994); the ruling was delivered in response to a number of court referrals and a constitutional complaint.

[21] By the time the full Senate of the Court confirmed this ruling in October 1995, the storm of protest was already abating; see BVerfGE 93, 226 (1995).

[22] BVerfGE 92, 1 (1995); see also ch 7 above.

[23] BVerfGE 93, 1 (1995). An impression of the situation is conveyed in Dieter Grimm, *Ich bin ein Freund der Verfassung* (Mohr Siebeck, 2017) 145 ff; English *Advocate of the Constitution* (Oxford University Press, 2020) 95 ff.

10

The Taming of the Party State

I. Role of the Political Parties

How a Federal Chancellor tried to enlist the mightily effective medium of television in the service of his party, how all of the parties, in their role as 'socially relevant groups', pressed for seats on the supervisory bodies of the public broadcasters, and how one party, putting aside its core values, championed the commercialisation of television, because it saw the prospect of sympathetic reporting on the part of private providers, are only a few manifestations of a wider strategy pursued by political parties to extend their reach into areas of public activity which, though not subject to the logic of inter-party competition, do involve the management of resources which may play a part in that competition.

This strategy affects the public administration, which, according to continental (not American) conceptions of democracy, must be party-politically neutral, because it is required to execute loyally the programme of government of the ruling majority. It also affects the judiciary, which is bound by the law alone. Then there are the independent operational and supervisory entities within the machinery of state, such as central banks, supreme audit authorities and ombudsman services, then the numerous bodies governed by public law plus fully or partially state-owned business enterprises and, of course, the public broadcasters as well as the bodies assigned to them, the Commission on Funding Requirements of Public-service Broadcasters (KEF) and the Commission on Concentration in the Media (KEK).

All these authorities perform tasks or take decisions that have implications for the political parties, for the attainment of their political objectives, the presentation of their intentions and achievements, their image and their approval ratings. The authority of the political leadership of the state to give instructions, however, applies only to the public administration, and then only within the framework of the law. Otherwise the way in which the governing party, sometimes together with the opposition, can exert influence is through appointments to public posts in which party viewpoints can be brought to bear. The extensive public sector, moreover, offers scope for stalwart party politicians or young hopefuls to be given positions or for defeated rivals to be sidelined into such posts.

From the parties' perspective, that is rational. Parties are founded to serve as a vehicle for their members' and supporters' convictions and interests and to turn them into a programme of action for the state. To do that, they need to win elections. Their conduct is governed by that imperative, and so they will always be exposed to the temptation to grasp every opportunity to enhance their own election prospects and damage those of their rivals and to secure influential positions in case of electoral defeat. From the overriding perspective of the democratic constitution, that is not rational. The constitution is designed precisely to ensure that the logic of the political system is not imposed on the other systems and does not interfere with their functions. Yet the constitution proves to be singularly weak when it comes to reining in political parties.

The weakness has structural causes. It derives from the fact that the constitution is based on a distinction between the state and society, whereas the political parties, which were not a factor at the dawn of constitutionalism, cannot be defined in terms of that distinction.[1] They have their roots in society but grow towards the state and, if they have been successful in inter-party competition, determine the actions of the state. That distinguishes the democratic state from the monarchic state of the nineteenth century. In a democracy, the parties not only present the state with the views and interests of the population but take those views and interests into the state institutions and thereby make it the people's state. Crossing that boundary is therefore essential to the functioning of political parties, but it is also the reason why they are so difficult to pin down constitutionally.

That is well illustrated by the example of public broadcasting. Although it is a state-created service, it enjoys fundamental rights protection against the public authority to enable it to perform its function of imparting information without being influenced by political expectations or pressure but being guided only by the criteria of public communication. Parliament and the Government must not exert any influence on its programming; nor must political parties, it follows, in so far as they are operating within those organs of state. The task of overseeing the broadcasters' performance of their function is therefore taken from the state and entrusted to society, represented by its relevant forces. These include the political parties as social entities. This twofold status gives them room for manoeuvre that other organisations lack.

In the state framework, it is the principle of the separation of powers which is intended to prevent accumulations of power. It is not confined to the division into the legislative, executive and judicial branches but extends to the separation of political from administrative bodies as well as from the devolved public entities, whose respective forms of functional logic it is intended to protect against excessive alien influence. That separation is also in danger, however, of being subverted by the political parties operating within the organs of state; this they can do by means of the personnel selection which is their prerogative as government members or parliamentarians, because every public office requires democratic legitimisation.

[1] See Dieter Grimm, 'Ursprung und Wandel der Verfassung' in idem, *Die Zukunft der Verfassung II* (Suhrkamp, 2012) 11, 47 ff; English 'The Origins and Transformation of the Concept of the Constitution' in idem, *Constitutionalism: Past, Present, and Future* (Oxford University Press, 2016) 3, 27.

Separation of powers does not come into play until the parties have already implemented their recruitment policies.

That does not make the separation of powers pointless. Once civil servants are in post, they are protected from the clutches of the parties. But the protection only helps those who are willing to use it for defence against the expectations or unreasonable demands of a political party. The braking mechanism in Article 33(2) of the Basic Law, which names 'aptitude, qualifications and professional achievements' as the sole criteria for public office, is one of the blunter instruments of constitutional law. That is demonstrated by every survey conducted on civil servants' membership of political parties. The main cause of the weakness is that the selection of criteria for appointment decisions is subject to motives which are not normally visible. Even if party-political motives have swayed a decision, its unconstitutionality is rarely recognisable.[2]

The indispensability of political parties to democracy and the risks they pose to democracy are therefore closely related. Parties are the necessary intermediaries between the uncontrolled diversity of convictions and interests in society and the dictate of unified action in the state. Only by bringing together related views and interests, reconciling them internally, consolidating them into an action programme and selecting a leadership team which is committed to the programme do political parties make it at all possible for the people to exercise the primordial democratic right of election. The competition between parties works as an engine, driving the democratic process and sensitising the parties to voters' concerns.

It is beyond doubt that this competition can only fulfil its democratic function if it is conducted independently of the state. The state is not the subject in elections but their object. The people decide which party, with which objectives and which leadership teams, to entrust with government of the state for a limited time. For that reason, the state must maintain a neutral stance towards the inter-party competition and refrain from exerting any influence for or against any competing party. State partiality would mean distorting competition. It would threaten the parties' equality of opportunity and voters' freedom of decision. The neutrality of the state with regard to the election of people's representatives is a prerequisite for democracy.

The problem is that the state, which is constitutionally bound to neutrality, is itself in the hands of political parties. The abstract term 'state' must not obscure the fact that behind its institutions are those parties which won the last election and have no wish to lose the next one. They are entitled to define the common good on the basis of their party programme, albeit within the bounds of the constitution, and have at their disposal the instruments of state power, particularly legislation and the budget. It is this constellation that is commonly referred to as the 'party state'. The Weimar Republic, which, in institutional terms, had adopted

[2] See Dieter Grimm, 'Nach der Spendenaffäre: Die Aussichten, den Parteienstaat rechtlich einzugrenzen' in idem, *Die Verfassung und die Politik* (CH Beck, 2001) 158.

democracy but still clung mentally to the old ideal of a state transcending political parties, never managed to deal with that problem, which ate into its legitimacy and contributed to its collapse.

In the Federal Republic, the issue of the party state was by no means resolved, but since it was the only option for a post-war democracy, and in view of its growing acceptance, it was no longer of existential importance. Nevertheless, it remained a source of conflict or even scandal and provided the Federal Constitutional Court (FCC) with ample material for judgments with significant implications for the democratic system. The staunchest advocate of the party state in the young Federal Republic was Gerhard Leibholz, who was a justice of the FCC for 20 years and was the rapporteur for political parties legislation. Leibholz, who obtained his *Habilitation* in Berlin in 1928, at the age of 27, had become a professor in Greifswald at 28 and had been appointed to a chair at Göttingen in 1931. As a Jew, albeit a baptised Jew, he had emigrated to England in 1938 but returned to Göttingen in 1947.[3]

Leibholz considers that the institutions of parliamentary democracy have been circumvented through the intervention of political parties, which is connected in turn with the democratisation of the franchise. It is only within political parties that the people acquire the capacity to act. The people therefore cease to feature politically as a separate entity that is distinguishable from political parties. Leibholz thus concludes 'that in this form of democracy, the parties "are" the people'.[4] The members of Parliament presented by and attached to the parties no longer have anything in common with representatives of the entire people elected on the basis of their personal qualities but are 'bound party delegates'.

The conclusion for Parliament is that now 'decisions taken elsewhere are only registered' there. Elections likewise undergo a change of function. The aim of elections is no longer the selection of individuals, but a public vote on the course pursued by the Government. It might therefore be said that,

> just as in direct democracy, the will of the majority of the active citizenry is identified with the will of the people, … in the mass democracy of the party state, the will of the current majority party … is equated with the *volonté générale*.

That majority then becomes, for the time being, the state. Leibholz concludes from this that the system of party rule has transformed itself into a 'rationalised manifestation of plebiscitary democracy or, if one prefers, a surrogate for direct democracy in the modern territorial state', to which he gives the name 'party state'.

[3] See Anna-Bettina Kaiser (ed), *Der Parteienstaat. Zum Staatsverständnis von Gerhard Leibholz* (Nomos, 2013). In the following section, I have drawn on my contribution 'Die politischen Parteien' in Ernst Breda, Werner Maihöfer and Hans-Jochen Vogel (eds), *Handbuch des Verfassungsrechts* (De Gruyter, 1983) 317, 331 ff; in the 2nd edn (De Gruyter, 1994) 599, 613 ff.

[4] Gerhard Leibholz, 'Verfassungsrechtliche Stellung und innere Ordnung der Parteien', presentation to the 38th German Jurists Forum, 1950, in Ständige Deputation des Deutschen Juristentages (ed), *Verhandlungen des 38. Deutschen Juristentages*, (Mohr, 1951) C7. The subsequent quotations are from the same source.

With this twofold identification of people with parties and parties with the state, Leibholz sacrifices the distinction between state and society without explicitly saying so. Through the agency of political parties, state and society become one. A gap could only open, says Leibholz, if party apparatuses broke free of their grass roots and, in that elitist form, took possession of the state. They would then no longer be instruments of democracy but 'dictatorial bodies'. According to Leibholz, the constitutionally prescribed internal democracy of political parties, which guarantees the identity of the people with the political parties, and hence the democratic nature of the state, serves to prevent such a development.

From his identity theory, Leibholz draws conclusions for the position of the political parties. He seeks to break down the traditional restriction of the parties to their sphere of activity within society and accord them a place in the political system which matches their actual function. On the basis of his concepts of identity, that leads to an 'incorporation of the political parties into the apparatus of state rule'.[5] He regards this as having been accomplished by the constitutional recognition of political parties in Article 21 of the Basic Law. That goes far beyond the mere 'recognition' of the parties. Leibholz does not hesitate to put them on the same level as organs of state. They attain for themselves the position of a state organ.

The 'party state' in that sense is no longer the shorthand term describing the fact that, in a representative democracy with universal suffrage, the political parties, by reason of the system, perform an indispensable function and cross the threshold into the state, regardless of whether or not they are constitutionally 'recognised'. Nor is 'party state' the pejoratively loaded term describing the rampant invasiveness of parties into areas outside their proper sphere of activity. On the contrary, it is the normative conclusion drawn from the 'changing shape of democracy in the twentieth century',[6] a conclusion which gives constitutional approval to the parties' appropriation of the state, thereby ironing out the distinction between state and parties, especially governing parties.

There is good reason to doubt that Leibholz thus mirrors the intentions of the authors of the constitution. Identifying the state with the parties operating within its organs was far from their minds. The strongest indication of that comes from the second sentence of Article 38(1) of the Basic Law, which guarantees the free parliamentary mandate, specifying that Members of the Bundestag are 'representatives of the whole people', so clearly not of their respective parties but actually 'not bound by orders or instructions'. With these words, the provision prevents the parties from exercising absolute control over their members who hold parliamentary mandates. The parties do not send members to Parliament; rather, the people

[5] Gerhard Leibholz, 'Volk und Partei im neuen deutschen Verfassungsrecht' in *Deutsches Verwaltungsblatt 1950* (Heymanns, 1950) 196.

[6] 'Gestaltwandel der Demokratie im 20. Jahrhundert', the title of an essay in Gerhard Leibholz, *Das Wesen der Repräsentation und der Gestaltwandel der Demokratie im 20. Jahrhundert*, 2nd edn (De Gruyter, 1960) 211, based on the first edition, which appeared under a different title in 1929.

elect them from a list of candidates selected by the parties. The members' powers of governance stem from their election, not from their nomination by a party.

As a scholar of constitutional law, of course, Leibholz cannot ignore Article 38 of the Basic Law. But he presents it to some extent as an error on the part of the authors of the constitution, who had supposedly lacked awareness of the implications of their choice of system for parliamentary democracy. For Leibholz, Article 38 is a relic of the liberal representation principle which has been superseded by the party state. Yet since it is nevertheless enshrined in the Basic Law, he cannot summarily declare it obsolete either. He has to give it a normative purpose. In Leibholz's interpretation, however, that purpose is confined to 'averting the extreme consequences of the party state'.[7] A residual difference remains between political parties and the state. The Federal Republic is an incomplete party state.

Most of the historical works use the term 'party state' to characterise the political system of the Federal Republic (Conze 594, Görtemaker 109, Rödder 164, Wehler 7, Winkler 371/English 661 f). Leibholz is mentioned by Rödder and Görtemaker. Rödder presents him as the author who 'interprets and legitimises' the party state, though whether he does so conclusively is left unanswered, while Görtemaker accuses Leibholz of having clung, even in the context of the Federal Republic, to the outdated notion of a supposedly 'conceptually essential antithesis between democracy and representation' (112). That, Görtemaker writes, reveals once again how difficult it is to break away from the conventional paradigms of the specifically German political and constitutional tradition.

In most of the works, the term 'party state' is understood to mean the strong or even dominant position of the parties in politics which is assigned to them in the Basic Law. The contrast with the Weimar Constitution, in which no place was allotted to the parties and the only reference to them was in a negative phrase (Article 130: 'Officials are servants of society as a whole, not of a political party'), is emphasised. Görtemaker sees in the Basic Law 'an unequivocal commitment to the party state' (109), which he assesses as a switch from a continental to an Anglo-Saxon understanding. Winkler also sees 'a type of democracy different' from the one that existed in the Weimar Republic (133, English 251). Others speak of a 'load-bearing function' (Conze, 595) or 'constitutionally significant role' (Wolfrum, 59) which the Basic Law had assigned to the parties.

Wehler seems to see even more than that in Article 21 of the Basic Law. The Basic Law, he says, 'explicitly and decidedly' upgraded the role of the political parties. 'Indeed, they were assigned such a decisive function in the political system that the term "party state" emerged' (7). Wehler does not say what function he is referring to, and a perusal of the Basic Law raises doubts about his assumption. The definition of parties' function in Article 21, in fact, has a rather modest ring: 'Political parties shall participate in the formation of the political will of the people'. The people are central, and the parties give them assistance. The underlying *aporia*

[7] Leibholz (n 4) C18.

of party democracy, which gave rise to the concept of the party state in the Weimar Republic, is not reflected, nor is the genesis of the concept in the Weimar discussion, where conservative jurists and intellectuals used it to vilify the system.[8]

Occasionally, however, critical elements combine with the largely functional use of the term 'party state'. One criticism relates to the encroachment of parties into some of those very areas that are shielded against politicisation (Conze 595, Rödder 19 and Winkler 376/English 662). According to Wehler, parties operate with an aspiration to be the '"hegemonic gatekeepers" of key dimensions of the political process' (237). The other criticism relates to 'patronage' (Görtemaker 112 and Winkler 376/English 662) in favour of party members. Wehler, however, sees the 'patronage system of the parties' in the fact that they monopolise the selection of candidates for election to the Bundestag (238). That, however, has nothing to do with patronage. The selection of candidates is one of the most important functions of political parties. They cannot prevent the candidature of unattached individuals. The only snag for the latter is that they rarely succeed at the ballot box.

Overall, the authors are almost unanimous in their favourable assessment of political parties. The stability of the Federal Republic during the reference period is attributed to them. Thanks to the concentration of the party landscape following the second Bundestag election and the emergence of two mass parties, which, from 1953 onwards, consistently won a joint total of more than two-thirds of the vote, even topping 90 per cent in 1972, and thanks to smooth changes of government, the parties feature in the authors' white list. Their contribution can scarcely be prized highly enough, writes Görtemaker, who ascribes the success to the break made with German constitutional tradition by the Basic Law (114). Wolfrum differs only to the extent that he does not regard the 'integrative contribution' as an automatic consequence of Article 21 of the Basic Law (59 f).

The authors possibly find it easy to pass that favourable verdict because they brush over the structural problem of the party state rather than delving into it. Where the works address the problem – and not all of them do – they mostly settle for a few sentences. As players in the political arena, by contrast, the parties are omnipresent. The writers describe the shaping and evolution of the party system. They assign a pre-eminent role to elections, electoral campaigns and election results. They discuss electoral law, which influences the party system and the conversion of votes into parliamentary seats. They descibe government programmes and their implementation in the course of legislative terms. They take account of parliamentary clashes and public discussions. All of these are genuine subjects of historiography.

On the whole, however, the historians are very fixed on events. Structural problems are more likely to flash up if complications arise in connection with events. The complications receive broad coverage. The tone changes when the focus turns to the party donation scandals that rocked the Federal Republic, to the reform

[8] See Christoph Gusy, *Die Lehre vom Parteieenstaat in der Weimarer Republik* (Nomos, 1993).

backlog which was the legacy of a long period of Christian Democratic Union (CDU) predominance or to the political stalemates which are ascribed to party self-interest. Instead of achievements, the emphasis is then placed on failures; instead of acceptance of the system, disenchantment with the parties or with politics comes to the fore. The systemic stability achieved through the parties and their role in undermining trust in the system are abruptly juxtaposed. The historians' neglect of structural issues comes home to roost here.

II. Party Funding

The utmost attention is devoted to the party donation scandals. That brings historiography right into the heartland of constitutional law, because what made these malpractices into scandals was the carefree manner in which the political parties flouted the law and, almost more so, the repeated attempts to obtain impunity for the offenders by means of amnesty acts. The Basic Law, however, only partly regulates the funding of political parties. Article 21 is confined to requiring parties to account publicly for the sources of their funds. Not until a constitutional amendment was adopted in 1983 was the obligation extended to party assets and the use of the funds. The origin of the funds remains an unregulated matter.

The existence of a legal vacuum, however, must not be inferred from the absence of a specific set of rules. On the contrary, in this case conclusions for specific issues must be drawn from general constitutional norms. In the final instance, that is a matter for the FCC, provided that it is seized of the case. But if the Court is asked to adjudicate, its decision will have extensive implications. The more incomplete the norm, the greater the Court's scope for interpretation, and the greater that scope, the wider the margin for preconceptions and background assumptions on the part of justices. Conceptions of the 'party state' such as that of Leibholz may then affect the interpretation of Article 21 of the Basic Law.

The first relevant case was heard as early as 1958. It was brought by the *Land* Government of Hesse and was directed against a revision of the Income Tax Act which had made donations to political parties tax-deductible from 1954.[9] Not only were elections, as a public responsibility, to be funded by the state, the FCC held, but state allocations were also permissible for political parties, without which no elections could take place. In making such allocations, however, the state had to adhere to the principle of equal opportunity. Although that did not require the state to compensate for actual disparities between parties, it did prohibit the state from using allocations to perpetuate or even widen them.

The FCC saw such a widening of disparity, and hence distortion of competition, in the state's tax exemption, which directly benefited the donor and, by serving as a donation incentive, indirectly benefited the parties. The Income Tax Act therefore

[9] BVerfGE 8, 51 (1958).

had to be reviewed in terms of inter-party equality. But did it treat the parties unequally at all? Everyone is allowed to donate, every party can receive donations, every donor can claim a tax exemption for his or her donation, and the tax deduction benefits all parties. With that the case file could have been closed, for the wording of the Act gave no indication of inequality, and if the question had arisen before the enactment of the Basic Law, when the constitution was still interpreted in a more formalistic manner, the file probably would indeed have been closed.

As had already been seen on various occasions, however, the FCC had moved away from the formal interpretation of the constitution dating from the pre-war period and was now proceeding on the basis of a material understanding. In those circumstances, it was not enough to ask whether the Income Tax Act treated parties differently. Rather, consideration also had to be given to its impact on the parties. That, of course, could not be done without reference to the subject matter, that is to say the parties in all their diversity. The question was then whether equal treatment of the parties on a legal level led to instances of unequal treatment in terms of impact.

When it came to answering that question, significance attached to the fact that the parties appealed to different layers of the electorate with different interests and income levels, and those parties which leaned towards the wealthier classes of the electorate and promoted their interests would profit considerably more from the tax regime than those which were closer to the lower social classes. The progressive tax bands would further widen that gap. Those who could donate more would be disproportionately favoured over small donors. On the basis of 'general life experience', the Court found that party donations, unlike donations for charitable or religious purposes, were not driven by idealistic motives but were made in pursuit of a goal. The contested provisions were declared unconstitutional and annulled.

That judgment was not the end of the matter. The issue of donations to political parties occupied the FCC on several more occasions, and few lines of jurisprudence are as wavering as this one. The limitation of the tax exemption to 600 deutschmarks a year which was enacted after the first judgment and approved by the Court[10] was subjected to a further review because of the declining revenue from donations, coupled with the rising cost of party activity; that review, however, only led to a modest increase in the exemption ceiling.[11] The Court did not deviate from the line it had adopted in 1958 until it delivered its ruling on the amendment of the Political Parties Act in the wake of the party donations scandal. In the revised Act, the tax exemption ceiling was greatly increased, but the consequences for less-favoured parties were mitigated by means of an equalisation mechanism in the realm of general party funding.

On the basis of that 'comprehensive arrangement', the Court permitted the deduction of tax in respect of donations of up to 100,000 deutschmarks, contrary to

[10] BVerfGE 24, 300 (1968).
[11] BVerfGE 52, 63 (1979).

the reasoned objection made by Justice Ernst-Wolfgang Böckenförde in a dissenting opinion, to which Justice Ernst-Gottfried Mahrenholz subscribed.[12] Six years later, that dissenting opinion became the majority view. The tax exemption ceiling had to be reduced to a donation amount that any citizen would be able to raise. Donations on the part of legal entities, however, could no longer be exempted at all, because they gave the natural persons behind those donations additional influence potential which was denied to other citizens.[13]

The direct monetary allocations from the state to political parties, however, had a greater impact on conceptions of the party state than indirect state funding through tax exemptions for donations. The parties had viewed the first donations judgment as an encouragement to avail themselves more liberally of the public treasury. That led in 1966 to another action brought by the federal state of Hesse. Leibholz, whose theory of the party state is visible in some of the early rulings of the FCC, was not permitted to participate in these proceedings, because his recusal had been sought on grounds of bias and the Senate had granted the request.[14] The judgment became a turning point, as Leibholz's identification gave way to differentiation. But that jurisprudence was also subject to significant wavering.

In its judgment, the FCC took as the starting point for its assessment the free and open process of formation of the popular will, which was protected by fundamental rights.[15] That process culminates in the election, the crucial act in the formation of the will of the state. A distinction had to be made, however, between the formation of the popular will and that of the will of the state. The democratic principle, the Court ruled, required the will of the organs of state to be formed by the will of the people and not vice versa. Within that bipartite model, the Court assigned the political parties to the sphere of formation of the popular will, a process which must, in principle, be state-free. State funding of political parties, the Court feared, created such an extensive overlap between parties and the state that freedom from the state was no longer guaranteed and the direction of the will-forming process was being reversed.

In a second line of reasoning, the FCC posited the ideal (*Leitbild*) of political parties, which were constitutionally recognised in Article 21 of the Basic Law but not thereby shorn of their individual character as freely competing groups operating autonomously. For that reason too, the Court held, the state should not be funding them. In a formulation that came as a surprise after this reasoning, however, the Court permitted the reimbursement of essential costs arising from a reasonable electoral campaign on the grounds that the parties, by campaigning, were helping to perform a state task which was sufficiently distinguishable from their other activity and therefore avoided the risks inherent in general state funding.

[12] BVerfGE 73, 40 (1986).
[13] BVerfGE 85, 264 (1992).
[14] BVerfGE 20, 1 (1966).
[15] BVerfGE 20, 56 (1966).

The Senate had therefore abandoned the Leibholz variant of the party state, but at the same time it had gone to the other extreme by drawing a sharp line between formation of the popular will and formation of the will of the state and limiting the parties to a function in the formation of the popular will.[16] Yet it is precisely through their activity in the organs of state that the parties achieve their democratic mediation between the people and the state. The people and the state are brought into a relationship with each other with the aid of the political parties. The will-forming process necessarily unfolds in both directions. In these circumstances, the aim cannot be to keep the parties out of the state sphere as far as possible. On the contrary, they must be adequately equipped for their mediatory function. This means that they must indeed be rooted in society. Financial payments from the state, however, do not necessarily sever those roots.

Nor does the judgment explain plausibly why the reasons that prohibit state funding of political parties do not also apply to the reimbursement of electoral campaign costs. Having insisted one-sidedly on the position of the parties within society in the first part of its judgment, in the second part the Court presents them just as one-sidedly as agents of the state. Yet the parties do not undergo metamorphosis around election times. Since electoral success depends far more on developing basic attitudes among the electorate over time than on short-term material expenditure before the election, the parties switched their focus long ago to continuous public relations activity. In the absence of a clear demarcation, however, the reimbursement of campaign expenses then becomes nothing more than general party funding, the amount of which is calculated on the basis of election results.

The FCC addressed this criticism in 1992.[17] In view of the fact that the distinction between general party funding and the reimbursement of electoral campaign costs was not a true reflection of reality and had no constitutional basis either, it abandoned the jurisprudence which had prevailed since 1966 and which prohibited funding for the performance of general tasks but allowed it for electoral campaigning purposes. Instead, proceeding from the principle that financial assistance must be granted in a way which ensured that the political process remained open, that inter-party competition was safeguarded and that the link between each party's leaders and its grass roots was maintained, the Court sought to shape and measure state allocations in such a way that they neither alienated the party from society nor drove it into the arms of powerful donors.

The details of the relevant provisions are not the focus of the present volume. The principles that govern party funding, however, are of such great importance to the democratic reality of a country that they are not merely of interest to legal scholars. If there are no rules on party funding in the constitution, they remain a

[16] I have drawn once again here on my contribution to the *Handbuch des Verfassungsrechts* (n 3) 348 ff (updated in the 2nd edn in response to the new jurisprudence of 1992, in which the Court addressed this criticism (635 ff).

[17] BVerfGE 85, 264 (1992).

matter for the legislature and sometimes only for the budgetary legislators, which ultimately means the parliamentary parties. Regardless of their differences in other areas, their interests with regard to party funding are identical. This is one area where inter-party competition cannot be relied on to curb the pursuit of self-interest. The shared interest of all parties in financial assistance from the state is liable to prove decisive.

The weaker the restraining effects that are generated by competition between parties, the more important compensatory rulings of a constitutional court become. If there are gaps in the constitutional rules, however, it can happen that a norm having the characteristics of a constitutional provision is not adopted by the *pouvoir constituant* but is derived from case law. Just how unsafe that can be is demonstrated by the tortuous jurisprudence from Karslruhe on party funding. In such a scenario, the Constitutional Court becomes the key player. Yet it is only Winkler who at least mentions four of the six leading judgments (376/English 663, 377/English 664 and 413/English 724 f). Birke refers to the judgments of 1958 and 1966 (37). The latter is also mentioned by Rödder (21), while Conze refers to the judgment of 1979. They do not feature in the other authors' works.

III. Keeping Democracy Open

Alongside the series of judgments on party funding runs another strand of rulings on the subject of the party state, which concerned the relationship between the parties in government and the opposition or between the parliamentary parties and the party organisations outside parliament. Here too, the issues included financial or non-monetary contributions from the state to the established parties and the use of government resources for electioneering purposes, but the main focus was on statutes regulating the conditions of competition between political parties to the detriment of either the parliamentary opposition, parties not elected to Parliament or newly created parties.

The list is long. The legislation governing political parties, electoral law and the law relating to parliamentary matters were the battlegrounds. Examples of the measures that were annulled include the increase in the electoral threshold for parliamentary representation from five per cent to 7.5 per cent in Schleswig-Holstein, the need to furnish a large number of signatures for the authorisation of parties with no parliamentary representatives or of non-affiliated election candidates, the exclusion of voter associations from local elections, the restriction of remuneration of electioneering expenses to parties that were successful in the election, curtailments of the opposition's rights of scrutiny, particularly in connection with the appointment of parliamentary committees of inquiry and their information rights, and reduction of the powers of unattached members of parliament.

On the basis of the material understanding of the constitution that characterises the jurisprudence of the FCC, the principle of the equality of political parties was extended far into the run-up to elections, particularly as regards electioneering material. Among the issues in this context were the refusal to permit particular parties to use municipal meeting rooms for electoral events and unfavourable treatment of small parties in the provision of advertising opportunities in an election campaign, for example in the form of billboards. The allocation of free transmission time for party political broadcasts or invitations to candidates to take part in discussion panels on public-service television were particularly frequent subjects of Constitutional Court rulings.

The question of the relationship between political parties and the state becomes even more vexed when the Government enters the scene. Although the Government is an organ of the state which is duty-bound to serve the entire people, it may determine what is good for the people on the basis of its party objectives. That is in conformity with the system and is legitimate. It is the reality of the 'party state'. Naturally, the governing party has an interest in winning another electoral majority, and it can best achieve that goal by campaigning on its successes in government. But can the Government itself also campaign for its own re-election? The judgment of the FCC on that very question is particularly revealing.[18]

In the 1976 election campaign, the Federal Government formed by the Social Democratic Party (SPD) and Free Democratic Party (FDP) had done its own electioneering and had also made advertising material available to the two party organisations, using budgetary funds for that purpose. The CDU regarded that as an infringement of the Basic Law. For Leibholz it would surely have been easy to justify the practice on the basis of his identity theory. But in the field of political parties law, the Senate had long since moved away from the Leibholz doctrine, and Leibholz himself, moreover, had reached the end of his term of office in 1971. But he did have a follower in the Senate in Justice Joachim Rottmann, though not in his former seat. What it means that the Federal Republic is a party state and where the limits of the party state lie was therefore back on the agenda.

The judgment simply postulates the effectiveness of the political parties within the organs of the state and defines them as combinations of citizens 'with the aim of participating in formation of the will of organs of state' but stresses that even the state manned and guided by party politicians is the state of the whole people. According to the Court, the purpose of the state organs was therefore to serve everyone, just as their actions were attributable to everyone. That link to the whole people, the Court held, precluded any identification of the parties with the organs of state and hence any campaigning input from the government for the parties that formed it or indeed for its own re-election.

Justice Rottmann, by contrast, held that the parties' constitutionally legitimised aim was to take the reins of government. Voters, he argued, were likewise focused on the formation of a government when they cast their votes. The election turned the leaders of the victorious party into office holders of the state and its manifesto

[18] BVerfGE 44, 125 (1977).

into the action plan of the state. Such a government, according to Rottmann, was not on a higher plane than the political parties but was one with the majority party of the day. From these premises, which were close to those of Leibholz, Rottmann concluded that, in a party state, the Government was entitled to campaign for the party from which it had been recruited and for its own re-election.

In Rottmann's view, the Government was a constitutionally restricted but otherwise empty shell into which the victorious party slipped, and with which it became one for a time.[19] It is not the Government operating through the majority party, but the majority party operating through the Government. The only limit to full identification of the party with the state lies in the fact that the party cannot make its occupation of the shell permanent, because changes of government must remain possible. In the view of the majority in the Senate, although the organs of state were necessarily manned by party politicians, their party mandate was overridden by their governmental office. The Senate majority presented the organ of state not as a recipient shell but as a catalyst, transforming the majority party. The members of the Government thus undergo a kind of metamorphosis. When they are chosen to serve in government, they leave their party coats in the cloakroom, so to speak, and enter the auditorium as statesmen or stateswomen.

Rottmann's view seems to be borne out by reality. No constitution that engages the parties to participate in the formation of the political will of the people can do anything to alter the fact that the very individuals who belong to party elites, write manifestos, wage election campaigns, etc, now find themselves in offices of state, striving to remain in office beyond the current electoral term, which they can only do through ceaseless commitment to their party. The requirement which the Senate majority makes of government members seems artificial by comparison. It expects them to forget their party-political roots and the contingency of their position when they take office, and to behave differently when acting as party leaders from how they behave as government leaders.

We are basically familiar with such differentiation between roles. Conduct in one area is not imputed to another area, even if the agent is one and the same. What differs between such cases and the present one, however, is that party leaders and government members are not only the selfsame people, but also operate in largely the same fields of action. The requirement to play two roles thus becomes almost unfulfillable. Linguistically, this manifests itself in abnormally frequent use of the term 'as such'. The Government as such must not stand for re-election, but the party which forms it and is led by it can. Government ministers as such must not campaign for election, but as party members they can. The programme of government as such must not be identical with the party manifesto, but in practice extensive correspondence between the two is unavoidable and constitutionally unobjectionable.

[19] What follows relates again to my remarks in the *Handbuch des Verfassungsrechts* (n 3; in the 1st edn 357 ff, in the 2nd edn 640 ff).

On the basis of his position, Rottmann cannot prevent the Government from using the state for the purpose of keeping its own party in power and thereby prejudicing the other parties' equal opportunity to form the Government. If constitutional law is brought into line with political reality in Rottmann's way, its normativity is sacrificed. If it is given a meaning that is hard to reconcile with reality, as it was by the majority in the Senate, its effectiveness is sacrificed. The interpretation of the constitution must lie somewhere between these two poles. The attempt to find that interpretation in the electioneering case was not entirely successful. Although its outcome merited approval, its grounds left the Government in the dark as to what the constitution expected of it.

This second strand of the jurisprudence relating to political parties, a strand that is of considerable importance in terms of ensuring the transparency of the democratic process and restraining the self-interest of political parties, has left no traces at all in the history books. The reason for this is probably to be found in the fact that the sequences of events which gave rise to the relevant rulings did not cross the scandal threshold, whereas party donation practice developed into scandals that piled heavy pressure on the political system of the Federal Republic for some time. The judgments thus came to the historians' attention by way of the scandals, not on account of their significant influence on the structure of the political system, and in fact only a minority of the historians focused on them. Most found them unworthy of mention.

Does this mean that the constitution counted for little? Most of the authors certainly do attach significance to the political parties article of the Basic Law. They are aware that, unlike the Weimar Constitution, the Basic Law recognises the political parties. The parties existed and functioned, of course, regardless of recognition. The democratic system depends on them, whether or not that dependence is expressed in the constitution. But that does not make the first sentence of Article 21(1) superfluous or meaningless. It makes clear that the parties are seen as an integral component of the democracy established by the Basic Law. The democracy enshrined in the Basic Law is a party democracy. The political parties cannot be represented as illegitimate usurpers of the role that actually devolves on the people.

Even their expansive conduct would not have differed in the absence of the first sentence of Article 21(1). It is determined by the imperative of election victory, but the law must keep that imperative within the bounds of compatibility with the system. The contribution of Article 21 of the Basic Law to the achievement of that goal is limited, however, because there are key issues of the function of political parties and inter-party competition which it does not regulate. The provisions set out in the second to fourth sentences of Article 21(1) are responses to Weimar experiences, but do not focus on the real problems pertaining to the party state. Intra-party democracy has so far been confined to the requirement that the grass roots of each party must be involved in the processes of nominating its electoral candidates and compiling its electoral lists for Bundestag elections, in other words that these decisions cannot be made by the party executive. Much has already been said about the patchiness of the rules governing party finances.

Even without Article 21(2) of the Basic Law, it would still have been possible to ban political parties under the general legislation governing associations. Such was already the case under the Weimar Constitution. Article 21(2) of the Basic Law, however, is the main indicator of the fact that, in contrast to the predominant understanding of democracy in the Weimar Republic, democracy in the Basic Law is not synonymous with the majority principle, but subordinates majority decisions to substantive principles, as formulated in the fundamental rights, and is also dedicated to defending those principles against political forces that seek a different basic order. At the same time, Article 21 of the Basic Law makes the prohibition of political parties more difficult, compared with the Weimar situation, for a ban cannot be imposed by the Government, but only by the FCC.

The gaps in the regulatory framework of Article 21 of the Basic Law are reflected in an increase in the importance of jurisprudence. The FCC must fill in the gaps in the event of disputes and has a considerable margin of appreciation to do so. The historians devote no attention to that. There is therefore a need to ask whether history would have unfolded differently if there had not been a FCC or if its jurisprudence had taken a different turn. The first part of the question is easy to answer. There would have been no institutional counterweight against the expansionist tendencies of the parties and against their endeavours to shortcut the democratic process. All of the measures which the FCC found unlawful would thus have taken effect.

Had the FCC adhered to the formalist interpretation of the constitution which had prevailed until the end of the Weimar Republic, judgments such as those on donations to political parties or on government electioneering could probably not have been delivered. The rules and practices which were prohibited in those judgments would have been regarded as constitutionally unobjectionable. The likelihood that the parties' practices would be approved would have been all the greater if the Court had embraced Leibholz's party-state theory. The established parties, and especially those in government, would have been able to pursue their interests more blatantly. A more ossified democracy would have been the likely result. What consequences that would have had remains uncertain.

11

Achieving Gender Equality

I. Unconstitutional Constitutional Law?

The proclamation of equal rights for men and women in Article 3(2) is regarded as a great achievement of the Basic Law. It was a hard-won victory and would not have been secured without the perseverance of Elisabeth Selbert, a member of the Parliamentary Council from Kassel, and the barrage of submissions from the public that she unleashed. Herbert regards equality of women and men as 'one of the most remarkable innovations' of constitution-making (688, English 557). The other works do not mention it in their appraisals of the Basic Law, but some address the subject in other contexts, for example when dealing with family policy, the women's movement or the modernisation of society. There are also works in which, in spite of its innovative content and wide impact, Article 3(2) of the Basic Law does not feature at all.

Article 3(2) of the Basic Law was at odds with current civil law. The German Civil Code, which had entered into force in 1900, was still dedicated to the paternalistic social model. In family law, the male held sway; in property law and the law of contract, a married woman was dependent on her husband, and she could only conclude employment contracts with his consent. It was clear to the authors of the Basic Law that the Civil Code could not be brought into line with Article 3(2) of the Basic Law in a day. From the appointment of the first preliminary commission until the date of adoption, it had taken 15 years to draw up the Civil Code. Accordingly, it was specified in the transitional provisions of the Basic Law, in Article 117(1), that law which was inconsistent with Article 3(2) of the Basic Law was to remain in force, but not beyond 31 March 1953.

That was a tacit call to the legislature to amend the Civil Code and any other laws perpetuating inequality. As the deadline approached, however, the legislature had taken no action. Instead, the Christian Democratic Union (CDU) vainly tried to enlist the support of the Social Democratic Party (SPD) for an extension of the time limit. The legal consequence of the legislative inactivity was spelled out unequivocally in Article 117(1) of the Basic Law: any law that infringed Article 3(2) of the Basic Law was to become null and void at the end of deadline day. Frankfurt Higher Regional Court, however, which had to rule on a petition for divorce, found it inconceivable that great swathes of matrimonial and family law should be annulled *in toto*. What was a judge to do in that case? There was only one option – Article 117(1) of the Basic Law, which permitted such a thing, must be found unconstitutional on the grounds that it breached the overarching principles of legal certainty and separation of powers.

The Higher Regional Court invoked Article 100 of the Basic Law to obtain a decision from the Federal Constitutional Court (FCC) declaring Article 117(1) unconstitutional. There is nothing to preclude the possibility that a provision of the constitution is unconstitutional. Article 79(3) of the Basic Law stipulates that amendments affecting a number of specified constitutional principles are inadmissible. It thus binds the amending legislature. The FCC can review the legislators' compliance with Article 79(3). But can the constitution be infringed by a provision which was part of the original Basic Law and was not introduced by means of an amendment? That, of course, would require the existence of a law which outranked constitutional law. In the absence of any higher-ranking positive law, the only possibility was supra-positive law, in other words natural law.

The FCC did not wish to rule out that possibility categorically. Memories of the National Socialist regime were still vivid. One of the lessons of that particular period, the Court stated, was that lawmakers could also create injustice. It followed that, 'in extreme cases, there must be a possibility … of assigning greater value to the principle of material justice than to that of legal certainty'.[1] That statement is reminiscent not only of the famous post-war formula with which Gustav Radbruch toned down his pre-war positivism.[2] The Court, moreover, cites Radbruch approvingly: 'Those extreme limits of justice' must not be exceeded by constitution-makers either, the Court states. 'Even an original constitution-maker is not necessarily immune from the danger of transcending the extreme limits of justice.'

The FCC, however, goes on to state that 'The possibility of a free democratic constitution-maker exceeding these limits at some point is, indeed, so minute that the theoretical possibility of original "invalid constitutional norms" comes close to a practical impossibility'. That this could have happened in the Parliamentary Council, 'in which representatives of the most varied schools of thought and ideologies cooperated, with the unanimous will to serve in creating a new basic state order of justice', was 'surely difficult to imagine'. Frankfurt Higher Regional Court, which was not alone in holding Article 117 of the Basic Law to be unconstitutional, was thus overruled.

Other civil courts had sought a way out of the dilemma by holding that Article 3(2) of the Basic Law did not possess the character of a legal norm, because no clear legal content could be drawn from it, given the connection with Article 6(1) of the Basic Law, which put marriage and the family under the special protection of the state. The FCC rejected that argument too, pointing out that the Parliamentary Council had regarded Articles 3(2) and 6(1) of the Basic Law as compatible, which indeed they were. The gap in civil law which had resulted from

[1] BVerfGE 3, 225, 232 ff (1953).

[2] Gustav Radbruch, *Rechtsphilosophie*, 4th edn (Koehler, 1950) 353; English *Legal Philosophy* (Harvard University Press, 1950); the passage cited here does not feature in the English version.

the expiry of the time limit, the Court ruled, was to be closed by the courts in the spirit of the constitution. 'Even such creative closure of wide gaps on the basis of a guiding clause is a conventional judicial task which has always been performed', the Court stated.[3]

Although that ruling averted the worst-case scenario, namely inconsequentiality of the hard-won Article 3(2) of the Basic Law, equal rights were not yet established. The Bundestag now set about reshaping the Civil Code in accordance with the requirements of Article 3(2) of the Basic Law. On 18 June 1957, three and a half years after the FCC judgment, the Act on Equality between Men and Women under Civil Law, or Equal Rights Act, entered into force. That was not the end of the story, however, for the Bundestag had not broken entirely with the traditional assignment of roles, in which the man pursued a career and was the breadwinner, while the woman looked after the household and the children. Some male privileges survived the revision.

Needless to say, the FCC was seized of the matter again. The actions centred on the man's final say within the family. Under the new version of section 1627 of the Civil Code, parents had to exercise parental custody jointly and, in the event of differences of opinion, make efforts to reach agreement. If they could not agree, however, section 1628 of the Civil Code gave the father the final say. Under section 1629, the father was likewise entitled to represent the child unless the mother had sole custody. In the proceedings on these provisions, the Federal Ministry of Justice defended them as constitutional. Asked for an opinion, the Federal Court of Justice stated that it had implicitly held the norms to be constitutional. The FCC annulled them as incompatible with Articles 3(2) and 6(1) of the Basic Law.

Men and women have equal rights in marriage and the family too; that had already been stated in principle in the 1953 judgment. Now the FCC reaffirmed that equal rights also applied to parents in their relationship with their children. In reforming the law, the Court found, the legislature had acknowledged the ideal of equal parental rights but in the subsequent provisions had 'obscured' and 'devalued' it. Possible functional or biological differences between the parents, the Court held, could not have any bearing on the parent–child relationship, because the relationship of both parents to their children was 'in essence equal'. In the light of that judgment, the legislature had no option but to leave decisions about children to the judiciary in the event of an unresolvable conflict between parents.

Not until 1991 did the Court declare the unconstitutionality of another residue of male privilege, namely the right to choose a surname. Since the reform of matrimonial law in 1976, it had been established that spouses were permitted to choose their family surname. If they could not agree, however, the wife had to take the husband's name.[4] This default rule, the Court found, already compromised the spouses' equality of opportunity in the process of choosing their married name

[3] BVerfGE 3, 225, 243 (1953).
[4] BVerfGE 84, 9 (1991).

by reducing the husband's willingness to reach an agreement, which was to the detriment of his wife. Other discriminatory rules outside the realm of family law, which were actually intended to protect women but were rooted in a paternalistic mindset, also failed to survive judicial review.[5]

In point of fact, the traditional role models persisted stubbornly for quite some time. Time and again, the FCC had to combat the assumption of a 'natural division of functions' between men and women and recall that the purpose of Article 3(2) of the Basic Law was not to perpetuate the traditional conditions but to change them. The constitutional precept, the Court considered, would lose its purpose of establishing equal rights for women and men for the future if it were reduced to accepting the social status quo.[6] In the order declaring unconstitutional the monthly day's leave for housework which was granted exclusively to women with their own household, a judgment based on the reasoning that working men with their own household also had to do housework, the Court stated succinctly: 'Performing housework is not one of the functional characteristics of women'.[7]

Similarly, the constitutional amendment of 1994 in which a second sentence was added to Article 3(2) of the Basic Law, reading 'The state shall promote the actual implementation of equal rights for women and men and take steps to eliminate existing disadvantages', merely put into constitutional words what the FCC had already been reading into the old version of Article 3(2). In its order on the differentiated treatment of men and women with regard to the pensionable age, the Court had ruled that the legislature was entitled to compensate for pensions insurance arrangements by which women were typically disadvantaged by granting them advantages relating to the pensionable age. That was explicitly designated as an addition to the existing jurisprudence on Article 3(2) of the Basic Law, even before the amendment of that paragraph.[8]

The Court expressed itself even more clearly in its decision on the prohibition of night work: 'The sentence, "Men and women shall have equal rights" is intended not only to invalidate legal norms which are based on the characteristics of either sex but to establish equal rights for women and men for the future'.[9] The normative content of Article 3(2) of the Basic Law, the Court ruled, went beyond a mere *prohibition* of discrimination in so far as it established an *imperative* of equal rights and extended that into social reality. It follows from this interpretation that legal norms which make no distinction between men and women but have typically had a detrimental effect on women – the phenomenon known as indirect discrimination – are also in breach of Article 3(2) of the Basic Law.

The reluctance of politicians and civil courts to discharge their constitutional duty of equal treatment was also illustrated by the treatment of children born outside of marriage. Under Article 6(5) of the Basic Law, children born outside of

[5] BVerfGE 85, 191 (1992).
[6] BVerfGE 57, 335, 345 f (1981).
[7] BVerfGE 52, 369, 376 (1979).
[8] BVerfGE 74, 163, 180 (1987).
[9] BVerfGE 85, 191, 207 (1992).

marriage[10] 'shall be provided by legislation with the same opportunities for physical and mental development and for their position in society as are enjoyed by those born within marriage'. That provision, however, unlike Article 3(2), did not set a time limit for its implementation. Once again, the legislature remained inactive. Back in 1958, the FCC had already left no doubt about the binding nature of the constitutional duty, but in the instant case the Court did not deem it necessary to annul the incompatible law, because the requirement imposed by the Basic Law could be fulfilled by means of interpretation.[11]

New reaffirmations of the duty to act in 1963 and 1964 at least prompted the Federal Ministry of Justice to undertake the task, but its efforts did not culminate in the adoption of a statute by the Bundestag. In 1965, when the Regional Court in Kiel dismissed an action brought by a person who had been born out of marriage with the argument – which was untenable according to the Karlsruhe jurisprudence – that Article 6(5) of the Basic Law was a call to the legislature but was not a valid right, the FCC took serious action on Article 6(5), ruling that, if a duty to legislate were still unfulfilled 20 years after the entry into force of the Basic Law, the Court had no choice but to annul the incompatible statutory provisions in the absence of any further action in the current legislative term.[12] The requisite law was adopted before the year was over.

II. Equality in Marriage

The relationship between the sexes is also covered by matrimonial law, though the latter does not fall directly within the scope of Article 3(2) of the Basic Law. Matrimonial law was the subject of one of the major reform projects of the SPD–Free Democratic Party (FDP) coalition.[13] At the heart of that project was the law governing divorce. The reforms, which were tabled as early as 1967 and enacted in 1976, effected the transition from the fault principle to that of irretrievable breakdown and introduced new rules on the distribution of property after a divorce. The old divorce legislation, it must be said, had already been eroded long before the reforms. The Federal Ministry of Justice estimated that 80 per cent of all divorces were mutual. Nevertheless, allegations of serious matrimonial misconduct had to be made, and the accused spouse had to admit to them. The need to gather evidence of matrimonial misconduct was thereby avoided.

Yet the reforms were highly controversial within society. The divisions between conflicting positions did not run along party lines. The Christian churches did not seek to oppose the principle of irretrievable breakdown either, although the

[10] In all German statutes, the term *unehelich* ('illegitimate') has been replaced by *nicht ehelich* ('not born in wedlock'). In the Basic Law, the term *unehelich* is still used.

[11] BVerfGE 8, 210 (1958).

[12] BVerfGE 25, 167 (1969).

[13] See ch 9 above.

Catholic Church was more hesitant than the Protestant. In these circumstances, the main source of conflict was the hardship clause, which specified the conditions in which a marriage was not to be dissolved, even if it had irretrievably broken down, namely if, in exceptional cases, its preservation appeared necessary in the interests of minor children or divorce would inflict extraordinary hardship on the respondent. After the spouses had been separated for five years, however, these exceptional obstacles would no longer apply.

No actions were brought from the political side against the new divorce legislation. Several individuals did lodge constitutional complaints, however. They regarded the irretrievable breakdown principle as a violation of Article 6(1) of the Basic Law, which protects marriage and the family, because that fundamental right was based on the Christian ideal of marriage, in which the possibility of divorce, or at least of unilateral divorce, which was tantamount to 'repudiation', was ruled out in principle. A local court also shared that view. It held that the reforms were unconstitutional, because the legislature was not empowered to enact divorce law which was clearly contrary to the original values underlying the constitution; it sought a decision from the FCC in accordance with Article 100 of the Basic Law.

These actions were unsuccessful.[14] The new divorce legislation, the Court found, likewise recognised that marriage was intended to be for life. In the real world, however, marriages could fail 'without the laws of the state being able to maintain or restore them'. The Basic Law, the Court stated, did not guarantee lifelong marriage 'abstractly' but in a way that reflected current thinking. Underlying the Basic Law was not the Christian ideal of marriage but rather 'the image of the "secularised" civil marriage'. In that conception too, divorce was supposed to be the exception. It was up to the legislature, however, to determine the conditions in which divorce was permissible. On the same day, the FCC also upheld the provisions on pension rights adjustment between divorced spouses, which had likewise led to referrals from courts and constitutional complaints.[15]

III. Equal Rights in Historiography

Juliane Kokott notes that the decisions of the FCC on the equality clause and the discrimination bans reflect social history.[16] But that is not all: they are actually a key element of that history. The historiography of the Federal Republic gives no indication of this. In spite of Herbert's verdict that equality of women and men was 'one of the most remarkable innovations of the constitution-makers' (688, English 557), the tortuous course of its realisation and the role played in that by

[14] BVerfGE 53, 224 (1980).
[15] BVerfGE 53, 257 (1980).
[16] Juliane Kokott, 'Gleichheitssatz und Diskriminierungsverbote in der Rechtsprechung des Bundesverfassungsgerichts' in Peter Badura and Horst Dreier (eds), *Festschrift 50 Jahre Bundesverfassungsgericht*, vol II (Mohr Siebeck, 2001) 127.

the FCC do not play a significant part in the history books. The changes in gender relations in the areas of family life, careers and education are largely discussed without reference to the law.

While many authors deal with the women's movement, they describe it as part of the wave of new social movements or as an expression of the individualisation of society, not primarily as the response to an equality issue. Some authors address the Equal Rights Act of 1957, but without tracing it back to the fundamental right set out in Article 3(2) of the Basic Law. As it gives concrete expression to the principle of equality between men and women, that Act is more important in practical terms than the fundamental right. But the Act is dependent on the fundamental right and would not have materialised without the intervention of the FCC in 1957. Conze alone, however, mentions that it only came about because the FCC had taken decisive action on the basis of Article 117(1) of the Basic Law and ruled that all provisions of the German Civil Code which were inconsistent with equality had ceased to be in force at the end of 31 March 1953 (189).

Herbert writes that the principle of male and female equality came up against a social reality which was far removed from such a norm. Anyhow, he adds, the FCC rejected the 'most discriminatory of the existing regulations' as unconstitutional. Other male privileges, he writes, were removed by the Equal Rights Act of 1957 (688, English 557). It is unclear which judgment Herbert is alluding to here. His sentence conveys the impression that the judgment in question predates the Equal Rights Act. Only the 1953 judgment fits that description. That judgment, however, did not annul any discriminatory regulations but only confirmed that they had already ceased to be in force at the end of 31 March 1953. That was the only reason why the Equal Rights Act of 1957 entered the statute book. The discriminatory provisions that it still contained were annulled by the FCC in 1959.

The histories do not give any indication as to how many more judgments were needed to establish equal rights, not only in matrimonial and family law but also in labour law, inheritance law and pensions law. It is apparent, however, how inherited perceptions died hard and how much support they still enjoyed in the civil courts. One of the steps towards equal treatment was not taken until the European Court of Justice forced the issue with a judgment in the year 2000, which even resulted in an amendment of the Basic Law, mentioned by Henrich-Franke (183). The rule in Article 12a of the Basic Law which excluded women from armed service in the Bundeswehr was in breach of the EU Equality Framework Directive and was transformed into a rule prohibiting any compulsion for women to render service involving the use of arms.

The fate of Article 3(2) is a particularly striking reminder that it is not enough to enshrine a principle in the constitution. If the opinion of Frankfurt Higher Regional Court and other civil courts had prevailed, the constitutional provision would have remained largely ineffectual. It took the FCC, and its view that the legal consequence of Article 117(1) of the Basic Law was beyond dispute, to give effect to Article 3(2) of the Basic Law and to many other decisions which lent more weight to that provision.[17] Equal rights surely could not have been held back for ever. That can be concluded from the historians' accounts. But without the Court there would have been no progress towards equality in the 1950s, and probably in the 1960s too.

[17] At the time of that judgment, the Federal Constitutional Court comprised 24 members, of whom Justice Erna Scheffler was the only woman. There remained only one female member until 1986, when a second woman joined the Bench. Thereafter, the number of women grew steadily, and parity was achieved in 2000.

12

The Basic Law in the Risk Society

I. 1973 as a Watershed Year

The year 1973 has already featured several times in this volume as a turning point. The historical accounts are in agreement that it marks a caesura in the history of the Federal Republic. For some, it appears to be even more pivotal than reunification (Conze 573). The faith in progress of the preceding quarter-century gave way to a pervasive sense of crisis. Optimism was replaced by fear of the future. What politicians were most expected to deliver now was security. Conze even makes the quest for security the leitmotif of his book. Some of the fundamental problems of the modern age had their origins in that year. General awareness of others only emerged then, although they had been inherent for some considerable time, and the political institutions were forced to respond. New political players and forms of action generated additional pressure.

The triggers – and here, too, the history books are in agreement – were the first report from the Club of Rome and the drastic increase in the oil price imposed by the Arab oil-producing states in response to the Yom Kippur War. The report highlighted the finite nature of the resources from which the Western world derived its prosperity, and it captured particular attention in Germany. The oil price hike was perceived as an 'oil shock' which exposed the vulnerability of the affluent society. The Sunday driving ban that entered into force on 25 November 1973 for the Federal Republic was a particularly tangible and symbolically highly effective manifestation of the threat for the car-besotted population, as people were able to go for walks on motorways.

These events coincided with the aforementioned transition from an industrial to a service society, which was reflected in increased unemployment and left the industrial cities of the Ruhr with large areas of wasteland. Herbert illustrates this transformation with a distressing portrait of the situation in Dortmund (900 f, English 732 f). In 1976, unemployment in the Federal Republic hit a shocking all-time high, That led in turn to severe pressure on the system of social security, which was further increased by demographic trends. In 1972, the birth rate sank below the mortality rate, while life expectancy continued to rise. Technological progress was no longer seen in terms of the blessings it promised but in terms of the risks it entailed. 'Nuclear energy became the focus for criticism of the modern industrial society and the general survival anxiety' (Rödder 67).

Fears for job and pension security, and anxieties regarding nuclear power and data collection were compounded by fear of terrorism, which reared its head in Germany in the form of the Red Army Faction, reaching a peak in 1977, in the period known as the German Autumn. Since East–West tension had resurfaced at the same time, prompting the West to respond with NATO's two-track intermediate-range nuclear forces (INF) decision, fear of a nuclear war grew, because while the aim of the decision was disarmament negotiations with the Soviet Union, it also increased the pressure on the East by providing for new US Pershing II missiles, armed with nuclear warheads, which would mainly be deployed in the Federal Republic.

The 1970s were therefore the period in which people's concerns were no longer channelled into the political process through the political parties alone but were articulated by civic movements and initiatives, which exerted pressure on the political institutions by means of mass protests. The citizens' initiative for environmental protection and the peace movement both emerged at that time. Both of them organised mass gatherings. In 1975, the campaign against nuclear plants began at Wyhl and continued with numerous actions at other locations. In the late 1970s a campaign was waged against the creation of a new western runway at Frankfurt Airport. From 1981, the vast lawn in front of the former Electoral Palace in Bonn was the scene of several mass demonstrations against nuclear rearmament, attended by crowds of up to half a million.

The historians have tried to capture the essence of the watershed from various angles – as the end of the industrial age, as the start of the postmodern age, as a second modern age or as the age of transition to the knowledge-based or information society. A particularly convincing concept, however, is that of the *Risikogesellschaft*, or risk society. Almost all of the historical works highlight the book of that name by sociologist Ulrich Beck, which appeared in 1986.[1] Beck points to the flipside of progress, which was uppermost in people's minds from then on. The result was an increased desire for security – job security, social security, security from the dangers of modern technology, security from internal disorder caused by terrorism and crime, and secure peace.

The politicians' answer was a transition to the preventive state, a term which has general currency in the fields of law and political science but which the historians have not invoked. Prevention took place, of course, in liberal regulatory states as well. The state did not have to wait until a crime had been committed or a building had collapsed before it was permitted to act. It could intervene to prevent the crime or the damage. But its intervention depended on the existence of a clear and present danger. By contrast, the concern of the preventive state is to recognise harmful developments as they emerge and to nip them in the bud. The difference between the regulatory state and the preventive state lies in the distinction between danger and risk. State

[1] Ulrich Beck, *Risikogesellschaft. Auf dem Weg in eine andere Moderne* (Suhrkamp, 1986); English *Risk Society. Towards a New Modernity* (SAGE Publications, 1992).

activity was derestricted. It was extended far into the foreground of any violations of legal interests. The state's information requirement swelled to the same extent.

The transition was achieved at the expense of individual liberty. In a preventive state, individuals could no longer keep the state at arm's length by law-abiding behaviour. The well-founded suspicion which had hitherto legitimised and limited the collection of information no longer applied, since the task of the state was now to identify grounds for suspicion in the first place. If it was a matter of detecting where risks or sources of unrest might develop, the eyes of the state could potentially settle on anyone. Essentially harmless data could provide grounds for suspicion, depending on the context in which it was used. That led in turn to fears of blanket state surveillance. The question of the degree of liberty that people were prepared to sacrifice in exchange for greater security became a major issue and an enduring topic of public debate. It is a genuinely constitutional question.

In the historical works, however, none of this is associated with the constitution. References are certainly made to to one statute or another that was adopted in that context – the Counter-terrorism Act or the Contact Prevention Act (*Kontaktsperregesetz*), for example. The *Radikalenerlass*, the decree banning members of extremist organisations from employment in the public service, is addressed. Some works come at least close to constitutional territory when they make the point, in a kind of résumé of measures, chiefly those with counterterrorist aims, that democracy had stood the test and that the limits of the rule of law had not been transgressed, even in the difficult conditions of those years (Conze, 477 and 485, Geppert 52, Herbert 929/English 755, Recker 76 f, Rödder 58, Winkler 348/English 617, Wolfrum 345 f). But anyone enquiring about the influence of the constitution on events, and hence inevitably about the role of the Federal Constitutional Court (FCC), would be left in the lurch by the historians.

II. Subjects and Forms of Protest

A. Sit-down Protests

The FCC, however, was by no means out of the picture. Given the particularly marked propensity in Germany for turning political problems into constitutional issues, anything else would have been astounding. The landmark decision on the right of assembly – the Brokdorf order – has already been discussed in another context.[2] In that order, the Court had responded to the restrictive practice of the forces of law and order with a democratic interpretation of Article 8 of the Basic Law. Sit-down protests, however, which had rapidly become a common form of demonstration, were proving more difficult for the Court to address. Numerous

[2] BVerfGE 69, 315 (1985). See ch 7 above.

sit-down protesters were fined by criminal courts for coercion under section 240 of the German Criminal Code. That was made possible by an extension of the concept of force to cover the exertion of psychological as well as physical pressure and by the recognition of sit-down protests as reprehensible acts.[3]

In the constitutional complaints against the criminal judgments, the focus was not on the fundamental right of freedom of assembly enshrined in Article 8 of the Basic Law but on the questions whether section 240 of the Criminal Code was consistent with the principle of determinacy inferred from Article 103(2) of the Basic Law and whether the criminal courts' practice of regarding pure sit-down demonstrations as reprehensible use of force was compatible with the Basic Law. In 1986, the justices were unable to reach agreement on those questions. There was a four-to-four split, which meant that the convictions stood.[4] Under the third sentence of section 15(4) of the Federal Constitutional Court Act, a violation of the Basic Law cannot be established on the basis of a tied vote. In other words, a majority in the Court is required to set aside an act of the state for infringement of the constitution.

Nine years later, that majority was obtained. Five justices found that including the exertion of psychological pressure in the definition of force was in breach of Article 103(2) of the Basic Law.[5] The threshold of force, as a constituent element of offences, the Court ruled, was blurred by its extension to sit-down protests in such a way that it was no longer foreseeable what physical actions would be classed as the use of force. The criminal judgments were set aside, and the cases were referred back to the criminal courts. This did not establish impunity for sit-down protests but precluded their classification as reprehensible use of force within the meaning of section 240 of the Criminal Code. Many criminal court judges grumbled, and many convicted persons found themselves rehabilitated, at least in so far as their actions could no longer be branded reprehensible. But like the Brokdorf order, these rulings, too, are disregarded by the historians.

Proceedings before the Constitutional Court, however, concerned not only the protest actions but also the subjects of protest – the nuclear plants for energy generation and storage of radioactive waste, the deployment of Pershing missiles, out-of-area Bundeswehr assignments, electronic processing of personal data, the *Radikalenerlass*, the counterterrorism laws, the increased telecommunication surveillance powers of the intelligence and security services, etc. The Basic Law did not contain clear provisions on these matters. In every case the decision could have gone a different way, with correspondingly different effects in reality. How the decision actually went therefore determined to some extent the course of the events that are treated in the history books.

[3] The relevant provisions read as follows: '(1) Whoever unlawfully, by force or threat of serious harm, compels a person to do, acquiesce to or refrain from an act shall incur a penalty of … (2) The act is unlawful if the use of force or the threat of harm is deemed reprehensible in respect of the desired objective. (3) …'.

[4] BVerfGE 73, 206 (1986).

[5] BVerfGE 92, 1 (1995).

B. The Census

One extremely influential decision was the judgment in which the FCC declared the Census Act 1983 to be unconstitutional.[6] At the start of the grounds is a sentence which states that the data collection prescribed by the Act had 'sparked concern among the general public, even among law-abiding citizens who recognise the power and duty of the state to gather the information necessary for rational and well-planned government action'. It is a striking statement, because comments of this nature are unusual in judgments. Whether the public are concerned, and whether the concern has gripped even 'law-abiding citizens', is not relevant to the adjudication of a case. So there must have been quite a furore, and indeed the unanimously adopted Act had aroused people's worst fears.

Since the purpose of the census was not only to count the population but also to establish its composition in terms of demographic and social characteristics, as well as to obtain information on housing situations, employment and commuting times from home to work or to training establishments and modes of transport used for those journeys, and because the census responses could be compared with civil register records, many people feared that the Act would serve as the basis for the transformation of the Federal Republic into a total surveillance state. The name of George Orwell's dystopian novel *1984* was on everyone's lips. The fact that the FCC called a halt to the census in April 1983 and, in a judgment of 15 December 1983, found some of the fears to be constitutionally justified, brought it unimagined popularity. The low-water mark to which its reputation had sunk only a few years earlier[7] was forgotten.

Censuses were a normal occurrence. They were conducted at certain intervals and had never raised constitutional problems. What was new was the use of electronic data processing. That resource had not been available when the Basic Law was enacted. The judgment is thus a good example of the way in which the FCC managed to keep the constitution abreast of the times. Even before that ruling, it had become established that individual privacy was a legal interest protected by the right to free development of the personality which was guaranteed in Article 2(1) of the Basic Law. Behind that jurisprudence was the principle, which was by no means self-evident but had been developed over the course of time in legal scholarship and judicial rulings, that the protection of fundamental rights must encompass the conditions for the exercise of those rights.

The conclusion drawn for free development of the personality was that such development would be possible only if individuals were not under constant observation and compelled to exercise continuous self-control but had the opportunity to withdraw into a private sphere shielded from public attention. The FCC had already found that the right to privacy included substantively private personal

[6] BVerfGE 65, 1 (1983). See also ch 9 above.
[7] See ch 9 above.

data. Electronic data processing, however, now made it possible to store unlimited volumes of personal data, to retrieve it at any time, to merge it with other data in a matter of seconds and make it usable for purposes other than those for which it was collected. The FCC saw that as a threat to free development of the personality, a threat which necessitated further refinement of the right to privacy.

It is not hard to recognise that this could not have been achieved by means of an interpretation method such as that of legal positivism, which still prevailed in Germany in the Weimar Republic, or that of originalism, as employed today by prominent justices in the United States. Neither method offers scope for adapting the meaning of the constitution to changing conditions by way of interpretation. Besides all other differences, those methods are characterised by a static understanding of the constitution, whereby responses to social change in the sphere of the application of constitutional norms are the preserve of the amending legislature. The FCC opted instead for a dynamic approach to the constitution which permits adjustments to the meaning of constitutional norms even without prior amendment of the text, albeit within the bounds of the interpretations that the text allows.

This approach involves four steps. The starting point is an ascertainment of the current valid understanding of a constitutional norm, especially of a fundamental right. The Court then asks whether changes have occurred in the subject matter covered by the fundamental right and, if so, whether those changes, if unheeded when the right is interpreted, would result in a gap in the protection afforded by the right in question. In that case, the Court must find a new interpretation of the constitutional text which closes the gap. Since the identification of social change and the assessment of its significance are not the task of the legal profession, it follows from this methodological approach that the Court may have to draw on expertise from empirical disciplines in some circumstances in order to determine the normative meaning of the constitution.

In the context of the census, the FCC concluded that restricting Article 2(1) of the Basic Law to data of a private nature was no longer a sufficient means of achieving the purpose of the fundamental right. In electronic data processing, the Court considered that distinctions between private and non-private data and between sensitive and non-sensitive data were untenable. On the contrary, protection had to be extended to all personal data. The result was the 'right to informational self-determination', legally derived from Article 2(1) of the Basic Law but in substance a new fundamental right, with which a social order was incompatible in which 'citizens were no longer able to tell who knows what kind of personal information about them, at what time and on which occasion'. This right therefore dictated more stringent requirements with regard to the collection and storage and, in particular, the combination and use of data.

The census itself was not rendered impossible by that judgment, but the statute had to take account of the stricter requirements that had been formulated in the judgment. The legislature took these into account in the Census Act of 1985. The census was now scheduled for 1987 with a new format, based on the judgment;

calls for a boycott nevertheless continued. Tips on how to sabotage or at least prevent the individualisation of the collected data were disseminated. They elicited a far less receptive response than in 1983. Many agitators were convicted for their actions. Constitutional complaints against criminal penalties occupied the FCC for years to come, but the census based on the judgment was not the subject of a new judicial review.

In terms of implications, the census judgment is hard to beat. Since a great deal of state activity depends on personal data, hundreds of laws had to be amended, and new authorities had to be established to oversee data protection. Every individual feels the effects of the judgment on an almost daily basis, having been given a legal position vis-à-vis the state in matters concerning the collection and use of his or her personal data. Individuals' personal data is no longer protected against the state alone; thanks to the subsequent establishment of a state duty to protect fundamental freedoms, the protection now extends to the treatment of personal data by private individuals and entities. The consent of each individual must now be obtained before his or her personal data can be used. The judgment made Germany the frontrunner in the field of data protection.

In the history books, Conze (664 ff) and Herbert (996 ff, English 809 f) deal briefly with the census and the corresponding judgment, Conze in the section on 'Protest Movements and Alternative Milieux' and Herbert under the heading 'The Political Culture of the Eighties'. Both assess the judgment not only in relation to the specific case but also, albeit in fairly general terms, on account of its long-term effect. For Conze, it laid the 'essential foundation for the judicial and legislative shaping of the information society'. Herbert regards it as 'a new conception'; 'data protection', he writes, 'now quickly became a widely accepted and universally used concept'. The great majority of the works pay no heed to it.

C. Security

After the start of the 1990s, the problems associated with state acquisition of information shifted to the activities of the intelligence, security and prosecution services. The end of the East–West polarisation and the greater permeability of national borders brought considerable increases in organised crime, drug trafficking, arms smuggling and, after 11 September 2001, international terrorism. Human risks were added to technological risks. Security became the main subject of discussion. The state took account of that with a number of laws that extended its right to acquire and process information. That, however, led to growing concerns that too much freedom might be sacrificed to satisfy the need for security.

Authorisation to restrict fundamental rights was considerably widened. Even though an 'abrogation of fundamental freedoms' did not occur anywhere, contrary to Conze's contention (484), the firewall around personal freedoms and privacy certainly became more permeable whenever terrorism or organised crime reared its head. The dividing wall between intelligence services, which only supplied the

Government with information but could not act on it vis-à-vis third parties, and security bodies was threatening to crumble. Accordingly, none of the security laws escaped actions for constitutional review, and virtually none of them emerged from that review without censure. One the other hand, none of them was entirely annulled, but almost every one was criticised for having unduly restricted fundamental freedoms and had to be amended by the legislature.

The series of judgments began with the decision on the extended phone-tapping powers of the Federal Intelligence Service (BND).[8] There followed a long series of other rulings, which has continued to the present day.[9] The issue was always the proportionality of restrictions placed on fundamental rights, primarily those guaranteed by Article 10 (privacy of correspondence, posts and telecommunications) and Article 13 (inviolability of the home) of the Basic Law, and most of the cases focused on the intervention threshold: the greater the danger and the higher the probability of its occurrence, the lower the threshold may be set. Under these rulings, however, not even a very great danger can justify unrestrained intervention. Although the influence of the Court on a particular policy area has seldom been manifested in such a high concentration as in that series of decisions, none of the historical works refers to them.

D. Nuclear Power

Before the census judgment, the far more bitterly controversial use of nuclear power, which, according to Rödder, led to a 'fundamental politicisation of society' (67), had become a constitutional problem. The FCC was confronted with it in connection with proceedings on a nuclear reactor of the new fast breeder type near the town of Kalkar. Court proceedings in such cases are not about a major political or social problem as such in all its dimensions. On the contrary, the subject matter is limited by a particular state decision, the lawfulness of which is at issue, by the norms that are applicable to that decision and by the applicants' motion. The Court does not have to rule on freedom versus security or on the case for or against nuclear power. Its adjudication of the specific case may, of course, have implications for those wider issues.

The approval for the construction and operation of the fast-breeder reactor had been challenged before the administrative courts, and the North Rhine-Westphalian Higher Regional Court in Münster had found the legal basis of the approval, section 7 of the Atomic Energy Act, unconstitutional. Essential

[8] BVerfGE 110, 313 (1999).

[9] BVerfGE 109, 279 – acoustic surveillance of private homes (2004); 112, 304 – global positioning system (2005); 115, 320 – electronic profiling (2006); 118, 168 – account master data (2007); 120, 274 – remote searches (2008); 125, 260 – telecommunications traffic data; 129, 208 – covert investigations (2011); 130, 151 – subscriber data (2012); 133, 277 – counterterrorism database (2013); 141, 220 – Federal Criminal Police Office (2016).

key political decisions, the court had noted, had to be made by Parliament on account of the principles of democracy and the separation of powers. Although the Bundestag had taken the key decision in favour of the use of nuclear energy, the court found that the fast breeder type of reactor put the fundamendal rights to life and health in greater jeopardy. Approval, therefore, should not have been left to the executive but should have required a separate statutory empowerment.

The FCC, however, did not share the concerns of the Higher Regional Court. In the Kalkar order of 1978,[10] it found that the provisions of the Atomic Energy Act also covered reactors of the fast breeder type. The dynamic reference in section 7 of that Act to the current 'state of research and technology', the Court stated, made it possible to establish appropriate safeguards, even for the particular risks posed by the fast breeder. The clause took even more effective account of the need for protection, the Court added, because it eliminated the need for time-consuming legislative amendments in response to every new research finding or every technical innovation. The duty to protect, it ruled, did not require a safeguard 'which precludes with absolute certainty the possibility of fundamental rights being jeopardised'. Absolute certainty was unattainable, said the Court, and setting such a requirement would make the use of technology impossible. A 'residual risk' was 'inescapable and must therefore be borne as a socially acceptable burden by all citizens'. Nothing of this is communicated in the books either.

E. Nuclear Armament (Pershing Missiles)

Similarly, the case of the US Pershing II nuclear missiles deployed in the Federal Republic was not about nuclear weapons as such nor yet about nuclear weapons on German soil. The parliamentary group of The Greens, which had initiated the proceedings, merely doubted that the Federal Government was permitted to agree to the deployment without obtaining an act of parliament. The FCC came out firmly against that view. It regarded The Greens' motion as an attempt to extend the rights of the Bundestag in the realm of foreign relations beyond those granted to it in the first sentence of Article 59(2) of the Basic Law. This, the Court held, 'would encroach on the central decision-making powers of the executive and run counter to the system of distribution of power, responsibility and oversight provided for in the Basic Law'.[11]

In 1994, when the issue of parliamentary involvement arose again, the world, and Germany's role in it, had changed. In the old Federal Republic, Article 87a(2) of the Basic Law, whereby armed forces could only be deployed for purposes other than defence if explicitly authorised by the Basic Law, had always been understood to mean

[10] BVerfGE 49, 89 (1978).

[11] BVerfGE 68, 1 (1984), headnote 1. Several constitutional complaints from individuals had previously been rejected on the ground that the deployment of the missiles had no impact on citizens' fundamental rights; see BVerfGE 66, 39 (1983).

that combat missions of the Bundeswehr in other countries were prohibited unless their purpose was to defend German territory. It was essentially part of the political rationale of the old Federal Republic that the armed forces must never again be led into war for any purpose other than national defence. That served to reassure neighbouring states as well as reflecting the prevailing attitudes of the post-war population.

After the end of the East–West confrontation, however, it was the foreign powers themselves that were pressing Germany to contribute, not only financially but also militarily, after hopes that the new constellation would banish the danger of war had been quickly dashed. The war in Yugoslavia and the civil war in Somalia were the catalysts. The Federal Republic became involved there in the framework of NATO and Western European Union (WEU) operations and United Nations missions. The Kosovo War marked the first combat engagement of German troops since 1945. The Social Democratic Party (SPD) group in the Bundestag, which was then in opposition, brought actions against this and other decisions of the Federal Government. Curiously, the Free Democratic Party (FDP) did likewise, although it was part of the indicted government and had been party to the contested decisions.

The point at issue was whether the deployments were compatible with Article 87a(2) of the Basic Law and, if so, whether they would have required the consent of the Bundestag. The FCC answered the first question in the affirmative, citing Article 24(2) of the Basic Law, which authorises the Federal Republic to enter into collective security systems.[12] That, the Court held, would be pointless if its forces could not be deployed for the purposes of those systems. On the contrary, it followed that participation in peacekeeping missions undertaken by those systems was permissible. Article 87a(2) of the Basic Law, the Court found, related only to the domestic deployment of the Bundeswehr. On the question that had arisen in 1984, namely whether the Bundestag's rights of participation defined in the first sentence of Article 59(2) of the Basic Law had been infringed, the justices could not reach agreement. It was a tied vote, four against four, but the dividing line was not determined by the justices' party-political leanings.

In 1984, the examination of Article 59(2) of the Basic Law had been the end of the matter. But now that the political boundaries for Bundeswehr assignments had shifted, the Court went a long way back to bring the Bundestag into play. The rules of the Basic Law relating to the armed forces, it ruled, had 'always' been designed to ensure that the Bundeswehr was not left to the executive alone as a 'potential source of power' but to integrate it as a 'parliamentary army'[13] into the constitutional system of a democratic state under the rule of law. For that reason, 'the principle of a constitutive requirement of parliamentary decision' was to be derived from the Basic Law. That, the Court observed, had been part of Germany's constitutional history since 1918. What the separation of powers had forbidden in 1984 was thus dictated now by the same principle.

[12] BVerfGE 90, 286 (1994).
[13] The quotation marks are in the original text on p 382.

That judgment is mentioned in all of the larger historical works except Wehler's, and in several of the shorter works. The authors identify the departure from an article of faith of West Germany's post-war society, but not the jurisprudential U-turn, because the decision that made the later ruling historic, namely the *Pershing* judgment, was not assessed in any of the histories, perhaps because the political decision underwent no changes, given the affirmative judgment. The change wrought by the out-of-area case, however, is by no means insignificant. Since then, every Bundeswehr assignment outside Germany has required the consent of the Bundestag. If the Government has an adequate parliamentary majority, consent will not be withheld. But adequate majorities can no longer be taken for granted, and some parties are split on issues concerning the armed forces.

III. Extremism and Terrorism

A. The '*Radikalenerlass*'

Extremism and terrrorism also contributed to the *caesura* of 1973. Extremism was not a new phenomenon. In the wake of the student revolt, however, it assumed new dimensions. Critics of social conditions sought their theoretical reference framework in Marxism. The emergence of the new German Communist Party (DKP) as well as the formation of numerous communist groups (*K-Gruppen*) in the wake of the 1968 revolt provoked a toughening of the state authorities' reaction. The battleground was appointment to public service posts. Because of developments after 1968, the vast majority of state measures were focused on left-wing radicalism. There were differences, however, between Christian Democratic Union (CDU)-led and SPD-led governments. That was the reason for the instrument commonly known as the *Radikalenerlass* (radicals decree) or *Extremistenbeschluss* (extremists order), which the Federation and the *Länder* adopted in February 1972 with a view to standardising appointment practice.

As far as conditions for appointment to posts in the public service were concerned, the decree contained nothing new. In Article 33(2), the Basic Law prescribes that every German 'shall be equally eligible for any public office according to his aptitude, qualifications and professional achievements'. The Civil Service Framework Act (*Beamtenrechtsrahmengesetz*) specified that aptitude included commitment to the free democratic basic order and willingness to uphold it. The radicals decree did not affect the criteria that were already laid down in the Act, but merely established guidelines for the assessment of aptitude. An examination was required in each individual case. Membership of an unconstitutional organisation was not sufficient in itself to disqualify a candidate but was indicative of lack of aptitude. In practice, this rule led to what was known as the *Regelanfrage*, a screening request to the Office for the Protection of the Constitution, for every candidate for public office.

It was that screening request, more than anything else, that now drove the generation of aspiring career entrants into dissociation from or opposition to the state. The very characteristic that was supposed to distinguish the state and make it worth defending – its free democratic basic order – made it contemptible in their eyes. 'FDGO', the German abbreviation of 'free democratic basic order', became a term of derision or an expletive. Their parents' generation, who identified with the free democratic basic order, had forfeited their credibility for the younger generation through their involvement in National Socialism. And even advocates of aptitude screening did not always find it plausible that the same rules which applied to a judge were supposed to apply to a postman. In fact, while the number of those on whom information was obtained from the intelligence services was high, the number of rejected candidates who were hit with exclusion from a public service profession (*Berufsverbot*, or career lockout, as it was dubbed polemically) was very low. But the state was left with a stigma.

In spite of the great irritation potential generated by the *Radikalenerlass* and the large number of people subjected to screening, no constitutional complaints resulted. At that stage, those affected did not expect anything good to come from the FCC. The DKP, whose members were particularly susceptible to rejection, even advised them against lodging constitutional complaints. As a result, only one case reached the Court, and it was referred by an administrative court and related to a matter on the fringes of the general problem, namely whether it was permissible to refuse admission to a legal traineeship (*Referendardienst*) for insufficiently upholding the free democratic basic order. By the time of the decision, however, even that peripheral matter was of purely academic interest, for the person concerned had been admitted in the meantime to a legal traineeship in another federal state. There was nothing more logical for a court to do than abandon the case because there was no need for it to proceed to judgment.

Not the FCC! Although the case offered no grounds at all for further action, the Court was even resolved to establish clarity on the major issue too.[14] It singularly failed to do so. The question from the administrative court was quickly and unanimously answered. Since the legal traineeship and the subsequent second state examination were essential qualifications, not only for legal professionals in the public service but also for those working in the private sector, access to a legal traineeship and to the state examination had to be possible even for persons who did not appear fit for public service, if necessary without their having the status of established civil servants (*Beamte*). Everything else was of no relevance to the adjudication of the case; in judicial terms, therefore, it was only obiter dictum.

Why the Court nevertheless undertook to address the whole problem will perhaps be revealed by a few remarks on the situation. During a legal traineeship, the Court observed, the state had sufficient opportunity to form a picture of the trainee, and for that reason a 'provisional' assessment was enough to warrant

[14] BVerfGE 39, 334 (1975).

admission. What the state intelligence services could add to that were only reports of modes of behaviour 'which occur in a young person's trainee and student days, often spring from emotions connected with militant protest and are part of milieu and group responses' but have little value as assessment elements;

> they also poison the political atmosphere, shake trust in democracy, not only that of the persons concerned, discredit the liberal state, are disproportionate to their 'yield' and pose a risk in so far as their storage can all too easily be abused.

From these observations, which are undoubtedly very sympathetic, the Court, turning again to the legal dimension, concluded that the intelligence services' screening could 'scarcely' be reconciled with the 'proportionality requirement' rooted in the principle of the rule of law. The statement about the consequences of the screening request which discredited the state applies not only to legal trainees, of course, but its legal consequence is expressly limited to legal traineeships. Then follows the examination of the *Radikalenerlass* and its general application in practice. That is where the Court's intention to establish clarity goes awry. The text of the judgment revolves, in ever new twists and turns, around what a person can still do if he or she wants to become a civil servant and what will prevent his or her appointment. This part consequently spawned three dissenting opinions, and after the decision no one was any wiser than before.

In spite of the significant damage done by the decree to the young generation's acceptance of the constitutional order and the fact that it was actually put into practice for seven years by the federal and *Land* authorities and for a further six years thereafter by the CDU-governed *Länder*, the historians give it little consideration. Conze alone mentions the decision of the FCC, but only with the explanation that the Court thereby reaffirmed the principle of militant democracy and public servants' duty of loyalty (482). In terms of impact, however, its importance lies in the fact that the judicial opportunity, which most certainly existed, to reconcile those affected by the decree with the 'FDGO' by emphasising the limits that the free democratic basic order places on the state was never taken.

B. Terrorism

Terrorism was a different story. For over a decade, it held the Federal Republic in its grip and more than once exposed the political institutions to a temptation to transgress their constitutional limits. While a huge expansion of the security forces took place, and the country was effectively living under siege for a short time, legislative responses remained within reasonable bounds. In 1976, criminal law was amended to include a new offence – that of forming terrorist organisations – and following the kidnapping of Hanns Martin Schleyer, president of the Confederation of German Employers' Associations, on 5 September 1977, the Contact Prevention Act (*Kontaktsperregesetz*) was adopted in that same month, after it had emerged that defence counsels of imprisoned terrorists had been providing them with illegal courier services. Both detainees and their lawyers lodged constitutional complaints challenging the Act.

In its decision of 1 August 1978, the FCC left no doubt that the complainants' fundamental rights had been severely restricted by the Act. The Court found, however, that the restrictions were outweighed by a duty of the state to protect the life, limb and freedom of persons threatened by terrorist organisations. In the balancing exercise between these two fundamental rights, the Court came down unanimously in favour of the Act:

> It would be a perversion of the spirit of the Basic Law if anyone sought to prohibit the state from using the necessary constitutional resources to combat terrorist activities the declared aim of which is to destroy the free democratic basic order and to engage in the planned destruction of human lives as a means of achieving that goal.[15]

While the political drama of that autumn of 1977 reached an absolute peak with the hijacking of the Lufthansa airliner *Landshut*, the FCC experienced its most dramatic situation as a result of the ultimatum issued by the kidnappers of Hanns Martin Schleyer. Many acts of terrorism had already occurred in the early 1970s. In February 1975, terrorists abducted Peter Lorenz, chair of the Berlin CDU, in order to obtain the release of imprisoned Red Army Faction members. The state acceded to the terrorists' demands through the mediation of the Rev Heinrich Albertz, a former Governing Mayor of Berlin. The notion that this would bring calm was a miscalculation, however, because the group of RAF leaders arrested back in 1972 remained in prison. In April 1975, the German Embassy in Stockholm was occupied with the aim of forcing the release of the Baader-Mainhof group leaders. Military attaché Andreas von Mirbach was shot and killed during the siege.

The year 1977 saw the assassination of Federal Public Prosecutor General Siegfried Buback in April. Shortly afterwards, the Baader-Meinhof trial began at Stammheim Prison, Stuttgart. On 30 July 1977, Jürgen Ponto, chairman of the board of directors of the Dresdner Bank, was assassinated. Schleyer's abduction and new demands for the terrorists' release followed on 5 September. Federal Chancellor Helmut Schmidt regarded the accommodating approach in the Lorenz case as a serious error and refused to meet the demands. On 13 October 1977 came the aforementioned hijacking of a Lufthansa aircraft by Palestinian terrorists, who sought to lend weight to the demands of the Schleyer kidnappers. Feverish attempts were made to find where Schleyer was being held. Failings in the search operations prevented his discovery.

At 1 pm on 15 October 1977, a Saturday, Schleyer's son applied to the FCC for a preliminary injunction requiring the Federal Government to accept the kidnappers' ultimatum in order to save his father's life. He cited the state's duty to protect which the Court had first recognised two years earlier. The FCC arranged for a hearing to take place that very evening and deliberated on the application

[15] BVerfGE 49, 24, 56 (1978).

during the night of 15–16 October with six out of eight justices. Justice Wiltraut Rupp-von Brünneck had died in August, and her successor had not yet been appointed. Justice Karl Haager was absent. At 5.50 am on 16 October, the President of the Court, Justice Ernst Benda, pronounced the judgment: 'The application for a preliminary injunction is rejected'.[16]

The Court confirmed the duty of the state to protect Schleyer's right to life under Article 2(2) of the Basic Law but did not accept the arguments advanced by his son, who expressed the view that, when a clear and present danger to an individual's life is balanced against the merely abstract danger to others in the event of leniency, the life of the acutely endangered person must take precedence over the lives of many third parties which may only possibly come under threat at some later stage. The Court stated that, since human life was of paramount value, the obligation to protect it must be taken particularly seriously. It added, however, that 'The Basic Law not only gives rise to a duty to protect individuals, but also to protect all citizens as a group'.

If the state were constitutionally bound to meet the abductors' demands, it would mean 'that terrorists would be able to predict the state's response … That would make it impossible for the state to protect its citizens.' Presumably because the state had proceeded differently in the *Lorenz* case, the Court also explained that the equality clause in Article 3(1) of the Basic Law did not prescribe that all abduction cases were to be treated uniformly. 'It is up to the respondent', the Court ruled, 'to decide what measures are to be taken to fulfil the duties of protection incumbent on it.' Shortly afterwards, Schleyer was murdered. The kidnappers announced it. His body was found on 19 October in Mulhouse in Alsace.

In the meantime, the *Landshut* had arrived in Mogadishu, Somalia, after its aerial odyssey. There, with the agreement of the Somali Government, it was stormed by the police tactical unit GSG 9 during the night of 17–18 October. All of the hostages were rescued alive, except for the pilot, Jürgen Schumann, who had previously been murdered, while three of the four abductors were killed. Chancellor Helmut Schmidt announced that he would have resigned if the action had failed. On the morning of 18 October, Andreas Baader, Gudrun Ensslin and Jan-Carl Raspe were found dead in Stammheim Prison, while Irmgard Möller survived. Following the news of the rescue from the Lufthansa airliner, they had committed suicide, as Ulrike Meinhof had done in May 1976.

The fact that Schleyer's life ultimately depended on the FCC, which led to the *Karlsruhe* judgment (*Urteil*) sometimes being referred to as a *Todesurteil* (death sentence),[17] is mentioned only by Winkler (346, English 612). Yet nothing shows more clearly the huge significance that the Basic Law and the FCC had now acquired for the conduct of the supreme political organs. One can only speculate what the Federal Government would have done if it had been enjoined to meet the

[16] BVerfGE 46, 160 (1977).

[17] See the detailed description in Justin Collings, *Democracy's Guardians* (Oxford University Press, 2015) 171 ff.

abductors' demands. That judgment was not without alternatives either, but the legal community as well as the media deemed it correct. The political organs were not dispensed from their responsibility, but were able to exercise it in awareness of the constitutionality of their decision.

In all of the areas catalogued in this chapter under the heading of the 'risk society', constitutional issues arose, that is to say questions as to what the political institutions were permitted to do or what they had to do or refrain from doing, or sometimes merely which organ of state was empowered to act. The political institutions had to answer these questions themselves. But every answer could be reviewed by the FCC if an applicant was there to refer it. The Court, then, had the final say. In no case, however, was the text of the Basic Law so unequivocal that only one possible decision could be made. Interpretation of the constitution therefore takes its place alongside the constitution itself as a relatively autonomous decision-making factor.

What exactly depended on the Court's decisions varied from one subject area to another and from one case to another. In the case of data protection, the answer delivered by constitutional law opened up a whole new field of law which permeates public and private life today. In the Schleyer case, a human life depended on the Court's ruling. In other cases, such as those concerning the new forms of protest or the radicals decree, the judgment given on the case at hand also constituted an implicit decision on the exclusion or integration of sections of the population. In the case of the nuclear power plants, the case was ostensibly focused only on the peripheral problem of where responsibility lay for the Kalkar nuclear reactor, but the far more essential issue was the nature and extent of the risks to which politicians may subject the population. In the cases concerning information rights, the debate centred on the freedom that has to be sacrificed as the price of security.

The thematic areas in which these constitutional questions were raised are treated in almost all of the historiographic works, albeit in varying degrees of detail, depending on the size and purpose of the books. The importance of the subject areas, then, is recognised. The same cannot be said for the significance of the constitution. Overall, a total of only four of the FCC's judgments are discussed, most of the books dealing with only one judgment or at best two judgments. What depended on them over and above the adjudicated issue has not usually been taken into consideration. That would be understandable if those additional implications largely related to secondary matters. It would surely not be easy, however, to demonstrate that convincingly.

13

The Constitution in the East–West Approximation Process

I. Unification Treaty and Election Treaty

At the stroke of midnight between 2 and 3 October 1990, the reunification of the two German states was politically and legally accomplished. The German Democratic Republic (GDR) was absorbed into the Federal Republic. The area of application of the Basic Law was now extended to the territory of the former GDR, the constitution of which had lost its validity with the extinction of the state that it regulated. But the state is something abstract, a subject to which the actions of organs and institutions and those within them who are authorised to exercise public power can be attributed. It is a regulatory context and a tapestry of relationships within which the lives of the population are played out. If the state ceases to exist, its specific components are still there; some, like its armed forces or embassies, no longer possess any powers, while others, like the police and schools, still exercise authority. The state institutions must be dissolved, assimilated or incorporated, and the employment contracts of their officials must be terminated or transferred.

And of course the people who served that state or lived in it are still there, and most of them continue to live in the same place, although that place, for its part, will not stay unchanged. Those people are expected to adapt to the new conditions, to obey new rules, to cast aside the abilities and skills that were useful under the old system and to acquire those which are necessary or customary under the new system, and to develop the ability to act on their own initiative in matters that were the responsibility of the state under the old order. To a considerable extent, that requires a change of mentality, which does not happen overnight. There will be winners and losers, and that is not synonymous with a reversal of the existing hierarchies. Some changes had already occurred with the fall of the Berlin Wall, while others resulted from the Treaty Establishing a Monetary, Economic and Social Union which entered into force on 1 July 1990. But in numerous areas, the process of reunification did not begin until after 3 October 1990.

As far as government and the law were concerned, the Unification Treaty negotiated between the Federal Republic and the GDR regulated the transition. An impressive document, prepared by the departmental administrations working against the clock with unparalleled dedication, it was signed on 31 August 1990 and ratified by the parliaments of the Federal Republic and the GDR on 20 September 1990. There are few historical examples of such a total dissolution of a legal system. It happened in the French Revolution, but took place over a period of 15 years. In the Russian Revolution, the entire body of Czarist law was annulled at a single stroke, leaving a legal vacuum. The German transition differed from both of these, because the new body of law was instantly available. In principle, the law of the Federal Republic was taken over in its entirety, and the Unification Treaty contained exceptions to that rule along with implementing arrangements, adjustments, transition periods, etc.

There are, of course, limits to what can be regulated by law, and in some circumstances proposed rules meet with opposition or are confronted with different de facto conditions in the new part of the country from those that could be taken for granted in the old part. And the mere fact that particular arrangements were agreed by both governments did not ensure that they met with general approval within society. As soon as the implementation of the decisions began and detrimental effects on individuals became evident, disappointments were inevitable. These effects could take many forms, such as job losses, the loss or reduction of assets, the devaluation of people's qualifications, the dissolution of social facilities or the loss of welfare entitlements, termination of housing lets or even punishment for conduct that had been considered lawful in the old state.

The adaptation difficulties are discussed in more or less breadth in the history books, depending on the scope and slant of each work. The Unification Treaty is absent only in Wehler, who ends his account of the reunification process with the accession decision and the consent of the former victorious powers. Not all of those who deal with the Unification Treaty, however, convey an impression of the extent to which the Treaty altered the basic conditions of people's existence. The legal system is the subject of the Unification Treaty, but the law relates in turn to the focal points of people's everyday lives: family, housing, the economy, culture, etc. The law is merely the medium through which the transformation of these focal points is effected. That does not come across very strongly at all.

The Unification Treaty necessitated a number of subsequent decisions and also required adjustments here and there. That task devolved on the first Bundestag elected by the whole of Germany. It was elected on 2 December 1990. The two states had agreed in a treaty of 3 August 1990, ratified by both parliaments, on the law governing the election. On 3 September 1990, after a further amendment, it entered into force. The Treaty prescribed that the Federal Electoral Act was to apply, with some modifications, to the first parliamentary election for the whole of Germany. Among the modifications was that combined lists were permitted, but only if the participating parties and groupings were not standing against each other in any *Land*. The five per cent threshold for parliamentary representation remained in place, but now applied to the enlarged electoral area. The established parties had taken good care of their own interests. They were well practised in that.[1]

[1] See ch 10, 132 ff.

It went without saying that the East German protest groups and civic movements could only stand for election in the territory of the former GDR. The threshold clause, however, applied nationally. A party therefore had to achieve five per cent of the entire national vote to enter Parliament. For those groups that had brought about the revolution in the GDR, but also for the Socialist Unity Party of Germany (SED), which had now changed its name to Party of Democratic Socialism (PDS), this meant that, in the limited area in which they operated, they had to obtain some 25 per cent of the vote in order to surmount the national threshold. The option of combined lists further aggravated the situation. Because of the no-competition clause, the only feasible combinations of electoral lists in practice were those between eastern and western parties. The clause therefore benefited only those East German parties which had allied themselves with one of the major West German parties and were thus able to tap into the allied party's resources.

The Federal Constitutional Court (FCC) saw through the ploy. In its judgment of 29 September 1990,[2] it did not content itself with a formal review, but focused on the conditions governing the forthcoming election. It observed that the election was taking place

> in particular circumstances that will not recur in this form … It differs from other elections in that the political parties and associations must adapt at short notice to an enlarged electoral area and, moreover, in that some of the parties and associations taking part in the election have only been able to organise themselves and become politically active since a few months ago.

This development, the Court noted, left a number of parties 'no adequate opportunity to extend their sphere of activity to the new electoral area and to present themselves there and campaign for votes with any prospect of success'.

Now it is normal that parties' relative power and geographical reach in elections depend on their popularity with the electorate. The state must accept that as an expression of the voters' will, but it must not do anything itself to perpetuate or enhance the standing of any party or parties. That is why the Court went on to state that the specific differences between the parties and associations in the first election for the whole of Germany were not attributable to the parties and associations themselves. 'On the contrary, their cause lies in the changes to the applicable law'. The law was therefore declared unconstitutional for infringing the principles of electoral equality and equal opportunity of the parties. The five per cent threshold clause could only remain in place if it did not apply to the entire national territory but to East and West separately. Accordingly, combinations of lists must also be permitted for purely East German parties or groups.

It is not hard to recognise that, without the intervention of the FCC in the first election for the whole of Germany, those groups which had brought about the demise of the GDR on the one hand and the supporters of the old system

[2] BVerfGE 82, 322 (1990).

on the other would not have been represented in Parliament. Yet the historians show no great interest in the election of December 1990. Half of the authors do not mention it at all. The other half largely confine themselves to communicating that the governing parties in Bonn celebrated a resounding victory. Only Conze (776) and Birke/Wengst (59) consider it worth mentioning that the separate thresholds enabled East German opposition candidates to enter the Bundestag. Of those two, however, only Wengst indicates that the outcome would have been different without the FCC. What the established parties had concocted is described by no one.

II. Transitional Conflicts

What interests the historians most about the implementation of the Unification Treaty after the Bundestag election are the subjects of conflict, but even in those cases their interest is highly selective.

A. Abortion

The question of pregnancy termination attracts wide attention. The GDR had more liberal abortion legislation than the Federal Republic and did not want to lose that at any price. The Federal Republic found its negotiating margin restricted by the 1975 judgment of the FCC. These contrasting positions almost scuppered the Unification Treaty, which could only be saved by outsourcing and deferring the problem. It was delegated to the first unified Bundestag. There too, however, an agreement proved hard to achieve. A compromise was eventually found, which was adopted as a statute in July 1992 but was immediately challenged before the FCC, primarily by the Christian Democratic Union (CDU)/ Christian Social Union (CSU) as well as by the Bavarian State Government; given the controversial nature of the issue, that was only to be expected.

In 1975, the FCC had adopted a very restrictive position on pregnancy termination.[3] The Pregnancy and Family Assistance Act of 1992 then came to grief in Karlsruhe.[4] Unlike the 1975 judgment, however, the later ruling scarcely features in the historical works. Yet that judgment of 1993, which followed lengthy wrangling in the Court, reflected in the length of the judgment and the copious catalogue of requirements for the legislature, is of interest in itself, not only on account of its outcome. It differs from the 1975 decision in that the means of discharging the duty of protection is no longer implicit in the constitution. Under the new judgment, the legislature is no longer constitutionally bound to use the

[3] See ch 9 above.
[4] BVerfGE 88, 203 (1993).

instruments of criminal law, a requirement which had already been criticised in the dissenting opinion and by a host of legal scholars at the time of the first judgment.

B. Land Reform

The second issue on which the GDR was unwilling to compromise in the negotiations on the Unification Treaty was the land reform which had been carried out in the Soviet zone of occupation after 1945. Land owned by war criminals and leading National Socialists as well as entire landed estates with an area exceeding 100 hectares was expropriated; the total area of such land amounted to about a third of all farmland and forestry in the Soviet zone. Some of this land was distributed to farmers and farmworkers as well as to refugees and resettlers from former German areas to the east of the new Polish border, while much of it was retained by the state. Industrial and commercial property was also expropriated. A considerable quantity of plants and their inventory were dismantled and transported to the Soviet Union. Banks, insurance companies and mining and energy enterprises were nationalised. In addition, the assets of the National Socialist German Workers' Party (NSDAP) and its subsidiary organisations were confiscated.

While the principle that restitution took precedence over compensation was to apply to expropriations made after the founding of the GDR, the Unification Treaty ruled out restitution in the case of expropriations made under occupation statutes or pursuant to sovereign decisions of the occupying powers. The reason behind this provision was not only the determination of the GDR not to give way on that point but also the Soviet Union's demand that none of the expropriations effected or ordered by it should be reversed. The Unification Treaty came about as an international agreement between two states, and international agreements cannot be amended unilaterally. With its entry into force, however, one of the parties to the Treaty was absorbed into the other. The Treaty thus became ordinary federal law and, as such, was amendable by the legislature. To exempt the property provisions from that option, they were also perpetuated in the Basic Law, as Article 143(3).

The rules laid down in the Unification Treaty and their protection in the Basic Law disappointed and infuriated many old proprietors, who contested them with constitutional complaints. The proceedings involved great effort and expense, but the actions were ultimately unsuccessful.[5] Since the restitution of land and assets had been ruled out by Article 143(3) of the Basic Law, the only way in which a breach of the constitution could have occurred was if that provision of the constitution were itself unconstitutional. The Court, however, saw no grounds for such a decision. There was no interference with property rights by the Federal Republic, because the complainants had lost their property through the expropriations made by the Soviet Union. The fact that these expropriations would have been

[5] BVerfGE 84, 90 (1991).

inadmissible under the Basic Law was irrelevant, the Court ruled, because the Basic Law was not in force at that time, and even if it had been in force, it would not have bound the Soviet Union. The Federal Republic could not be held accountable for the Soviet acts.

All that remained, therefore, was the problem of unequal treatment of the expropriations that occurred before and after 1949. The FCC saw a justification for that inequality, namely the aim of reunification which was expressed in the preamble to the Basic Law and declared binding in the judgment about the Treaty on the Basis of Relations with the GDR and which would have been jeopardised if restitution had not been ruled out. In the hearing before the First Senate of the Court, the last Premier of the GDR, Lothar de Maizière, testified that the GDR had made retention of the land reform a condition for its consent to reunification and could be sure that the majority of the East German population agreed with that position. State Secretary Dieter Castrup, chief negotiator of the Federal Government at the Two-plus-Four negotiations, testified on the basis of his negotiating records that the Soviet Union had actually imposed that condition.

Those two bones of contention were far from being the only post-reunification problems that were ultimately resolved in Karlsruhe. The FCC had to spend about another 10 years dealing with reunification issues.[6] There is no need to reproduce them all here – and by no means all of them are of historiographic interest – but some did have such a wide impact or played so significant a part in the transition process that they should not go unmentioned. Besides land reform, the main issues with broad impact were pension reform, mass redundancies in the public service (known popularly as the *Warteschleife*, or 'holding stack') and the conversion of GDR government loans into real debts. Foremost among the typical transition problems was the question of criminal liability for past actions of the state.

C. The Holding Stack

The 'holding stack' was the arrangement whereby the employment contracts of members of the East German public service were put on hold if their institutions were not absorbed into the Federation or the *Länder*. These were mostly institutions which had no equivalent in the Federal Republic or were not run as public bodies there. Under the Unification Treaty, the employment relationships of the staff of those institutions were held in abeyance. If the staff were not taken on by other administrative entities within six months, their employment was terminated. In the meantime, they received reduced salaries. The Federal Government sought to nip judicial actions in the bud with the argument that, on the dissolution of the GDR, employment relationships with its institutions had also ceased

[6] English translations of the most important decisions are collated in a volume edited by the Court, entitled *Decisions of the Bundesverfassungsgericht, Vol. 3: Questions of Law Arising from German Unification 1973–2004* (Nomos, 2005).

to exist. The FCC found, however, that they had been taken over by the Federal Republic as the successor in title to the GDR. But it did not regard their suspension and termination as a violation of the fundamental right of occupational freedom enshrined in Article 12 of the Basic Law, as it was an unavoidable consequence of the regime change.[7]

The judgment nevertheless reveals the hardship caused by the arrangement for numerous public servants, particularly for those who had little prospect of new employment, such as older people, people with disabilities and lone parents as well as those whose specialised qualifications had been devalued. The Court identified a need for special assistance for these groups that went beyond offering a range of retraining opportunities. It held, moreover, that not possessing formal proof of qualifications required for certain occupations in the Federal Republic should not of itself be a reason for rejection of any application for continued or new employment. The Court declared the arrangement unconstitutional in so far as it also applied to women who, under maternity protection law, ought not to have had their employment terminated.[8] The Court dealt in a similar way with the special arrangement for staff of the Academy of Sciences of the GDR, who, because of the different way in which the system of research institutes was organised in the socialist states, were far more numerous than their counterparts in the Federal Republic.[9]

D. Old Debts

The problem of old debts particularly affected the collective farms. The FCC deliberated on this as it did on the 'holding stack' in East Germany, and its deliberations elicited keen public interest. It found interference with the fundamental rights of the collective farmers in the fact that they were bound by contracts, the meaning of which had changed in the meantime for reasons beyond their control. They had previously been part of the centrally managed economic system of the GDR, just like the banks. Of the former contingent relationship between borrowing and fulfilling the state plan, including the transfer of profits, all that was left for the collective farms were the outstanding loans. For the banks, conversely, loans were no longer a means of implementing the plan, but a source of profit. The sanction for default was altered accordingly. The collective farms now faced the threat of foreclosure.

In this case too, the FCC did not object to the statutory arrangement, firstly because the legislature had taken account of the likely hardship by providing fiscal relief for the collective farms, and secondly because the banks' claims had been halved as a result of monetary union while their liabilities to depositors had

[7] BVerfGE 84, 133 (1991).
[8] *ibid.*
[9] BVerfGE 85, 360 (1992).

remained unchanged. Any further disadvantages would have to 'be endured on account of the special situation of reunification. In that situation, which was characterised by great imponderability, a more refined set of provisions could not be expected.' However, as the implications were not yet entirely foreseeable at the time of the judicial decision, the legislature was instructed to monitor developments and to make any necessary amendments.[10]

E. Pensions

The assimilation of pensions, which affected some four million pensioners, had already been regulated in principle in the Pensions Assimilation Act of the GDR of 28 June 1990, and parts of that assimilation regime had been amended by the Unification Treaty and statutory provisions before and after unification. Existing pensions were converted into deutschmarks at the rate of 1:1 and brought into line with the level of pensions in the Federal Republic, which considerably increased the value of pensioners' income. One problem was the existence of numerous supplementary pension systems for particular occupational groups as well as the special pension schemes for the *Volksarmee*, the People's Police and the Ministry of State Security, which accounted collectively for about half of all the transferred pensions. Provision was made for pension cuts or for disentitlements in cases where the amount of a pension was based on particular complicity with the system or where the recipients had breached principles of humanity and the rule of law.

The rules were referred to the FCC by the social courts in some cases and in other cases were challenged by pensioners through constitutional complaints. The FCC delivered four landmark judgments, comprising almost 200 pages in total, on that extremely complex material.[11] As it had done in the 'holding stack' cases, it began by disposing of the Federal Government's argument that the dissolution of the GDR had also meant the dissolution of the legal relationships which had been established there. Accordingly, East German pensioners were entitled only to benefits to which their right was re-established on reunification. That had consequences for the subsequent examination. The claims of violations of the fundamental right to property enshrined in Article 14 of the Basic Law would have been unfounded if the pension rights established in the GDR had become invalid. Breaches of the precept of equal treatment derived from Article 3(1) of the Basic Law, however, did not depend on whether property rights existed at the moment of unification.

The FCC raised no objections to the general transfer system, which provided for ceilings and capping for supplementary and special pensions. The Basic Law, it stated, did not provide absolute protection of an existing legal position, particularly

[10] BVerfGE 95, 267 (1994).
[11] BVerfGE 100, 1; 100, 59; 100, 104 and 100, 138 (1999).

'if the legislature is confronted with the task of adapting a system that was integrated in a legal system governed by quite different principles to the legal system of the Federal Republic of Germany'.[12] The Court held various provisions, however, to be incompatible with the Basic Law, partly because they reduced pension entitlements to an unreasonable extent and partly because they had disadvantaged certain occupational groups in relation to other equivalent occupational groups. The particularly extensive imposition of ceilings on special pensions accruing to Ministry of State Security ('*Stasi*') staff was also considered disproportionate, because the ceilings were even lower than the lowest pensions. The judgment tempered much of the indignation felt within the circle of affected pensioners.

F. Criminal Liability

Problems typically arise during transitions between politico-social systems with regard to treatment of political leaders of the subjugated system and their executive staffs. Should they be punished? Should they be permanently excluded from the public service of the new regime? The punishment question arose with regard to the top GDR leaders, the Politburo of the SED, the high command of the *Volksarmee*, spies and Berlin Wall marksmen and indeed was already on the agenda before reunification. Most of the criminal proceedings, however, were not instituted until after reunification. In terms of constitutional law, the criminal prosecutions raised the question of the prohibition of retroactive punishment in Article 103(2) of the Basic Law.[13] It is one of the foundational elements of the rule of law. Accordingly, the criminal law of the Federal Republic could not be applied to offences committed in the GDR, and the criminal law of the GDR had to be interpreted as it was understood there.

For the worst injustices, such as the construction of the Berlin Wall, there could therefore be no question of punishment. For other crimes regarded as serious violations of the law, however, particularly the fatal shootings at the border fortifications of the GDR, the same did not apply. But the criminal courts found themselves caught in a dilemma. On the one hand, a sense of justice demanded, as did large sections of the GDR population in particular, that the crimes must not go unpunished. On the other hand, the Federal Republic had to beware of disavowing supreme principles of its own constitutional order. Where prosecutions were brought, some courts found themselves compelled to deliver acquittals. Others tried to derive criminal liability from the international human rights covenants or the Helsinki accords. Others again relied on Radbruch's formula, according to which suprapositive principles of justice permitted punishment in

[12] BVerfGE 100, 1 <40>.

[13] The provision reads as follows: 'An act may be punished only if it was already defined by law as a criminal offence at the time when it was committed'.

cases of extreme injustice.[14] The Federal Court of Justice, as the supreme criminal court, also adopted that position.[15]

The FCC chose a different way to resolve the problem.[16] It was not prepared to relativise the prohibition of retroactive punishment contained in the Basic Law. That, it held, was absolute and must be stringently applied to the letter. However, it did not wish the crimes to go unpunished either. The gateway to a solution that presented itself to the Court was restriction of the absolute nature of the prohibition to a legal order in which laws were made democratically and lawmakers were bound by fundamental rights. The absolute prohibition of retroactive punishment, the Court reasoned, depended for its existence on the trust in the law that followed from compliance with those conditions.

> Such a special basis of trust is lacking where the repository of state power excludes criminal liability for the most serious category of wrongs by means of justifications for instigating or favouring such injustice, thereby overstepping the written norms, and thus gravely violates human rights generally recognised by the community of nations.[17]

This meant, of course, that those who issued the firing orders bore greater guilt than those who obeyed the orders. Where Berlin Wall marksmen were actually convicted, their sentences were therefore relatively lenient. Even in proceedings against political or military leaders of the GDR which led to convictions, the sentences were not particularly severe. Where convicted persons lodged constitutional complaints, these were not accepted for adjudication by the FCC, and their applications to the European Court of Human Rights were also dismissed.[18] Convictions for treason of intelligence agents and spies who had conducted their activity from the territory of the GDR, on the other hand, were quashed by the FCC on the ground that they had only come under the criminal jurisdiction of the Federal Republic because of the incorporation of their state into the Federal Republic, whose own spies, however, did not face punishment.[19]

[14] Gustav Radbruch, who had been a strict legal positivist in the Weimar Republic, set out his formula as follows after the end of National Socialist rule: 'The conflict between justice and legal certainty may well be resolved in this way: the positive law, secured by pronouncement and power, takes precedence even when its content is unjust and fails in its purpose of benefiting the people, unless the conflict between positive statute and justice reaches such an intolerable degree that the statute, as "flawed law", must yield to justice. … Where there is not even an attempt at justice, where equality, which forms the core of justice, is deliberately betrayed in the laying down of positive law, then the statute is not even merely "flawed law" – rather, it lacks completely the very nature of law.' (*Süddeutsche Juristenzeitung* I (1946) 105 ff), translated into English as 'Statutory Lawlessness and Supra-Statutory Law' (1946), in *Oxford Journal of Legal Studies* (2006) 1. See also ch 11 above.

[15] Criminal Decisions of the Federal Court of Justice (BGHSt) 39, 1 (1992) and 40, 218 (1994).

[16] BVerfGE 95, 96 (1996).

[17] ibid, headnote 3 (for more details, see the grounds on p 130 ff).

[18] Documented in Friedrich Wolff, *Das Politbüro der DDR vor Gericht* (Berliner Wissenschafts-Verlag, 2015).

[19] BVerfGE 92, 277 (1995).

G. Dismissals

Another level was reached when it came to the transfer of members of the public service of the GDR into that of reunified Germany. In this respect, the aim pursued by the Unification Treaty was integration. It did, however, permit termination of employment by notice if a person lacked the required professional qualification or personal aptitude for employment in the public service. In addition, it provided for special grounds for termination, which applied, for example, to *Stasi* staff. Many labour courts tended to rule that individuals did not possess the aptitude for employment in the public service in reunified Germany merely because they had held a prominent position in professional life in the GDR or had been members of the SED or of a state-led social organisation of the GDR. The FCC received constitutional complaints against terminations of the employment of police officers and teachers.

It annulled terminations based solely on these factors as violations of the occupational freedom guaranteed by Article 12 of the Basic Law. Although those factors could probably be regarded as indicative of insufficient aptitude, the Court found that they alone were not enough to warrant termination of employment. The Court based these rulings on the intention of the Unification Treaty to integrate into the public service of united Germany those members of the public service who were not from areas of activity which had been wound up. Since commitment to the communist social system and the requisite and customary loyalty to their own state and to the SED were prerequisites for a career in such a system, the Court held that those characteristics were no basis for assessing a lack of aptitude. Teachers belonging to the school management team or occupying the position of party secretary within the school, or police officers who were members of the SED, were therefore successful in Karlsruhe.[20] The labour courts were henceforth bound by these criteria.

III. The Appraisal – A Desideratum

An appraisal of the impact of constitutional jurisprudence on the reunification process and on the attitude of the GDR population to the system of government in the Federal Republic on which historians could draw has yet to be made. It is not an easy task either. The comprehensive Dresden survey on trust in the FCC makes no distinction between East and West.[21] According to the Allensbach surveys, while people's trust in the FCC is lower in the East, it has risen steadily

[20] BVerfGE 92, 140 (1995) and 96, 152 (1997); see also the differentiating decision in BVerfGE 93, 213 (1995).

[21] Hans Vorländer and André Brodocz, 'Das Vertrauen in das Bundesverfassungsgericht', in Hans Vorländer (ed), *Die Deutungsmacht der Verfassungsgerichtsbarkeit* (Verlag für Sozialwissenschaften, 2006) 259–295.

and is higher than their trust in all other institutions.[22] Given the subjects of the Court's decisions and their consequences for considerable sections of the population, however, its influence can scarcely be denied. At least the experience that individuals in the new state can make things happen by invoking the constitution, even against the supreme political organs, must have made an impression on the people of the GDR.

If the Court's jurisprudence, other than its judgments on land reform and, in individual works, its rulings on abortion, received no particular historiographic consideration, the reason may be that the FCC did not question the key decisions that underlay the Unification Treaty. And indeed, given the scale and singularity of the task, which the FCC repeatedly emphasised, any other approach would have been misguided. At the next lower level of significance, however, as the foregoing summary of the main thematic areas has shown, numerous corrections or modifications were made to provisions of the Unification Treaty, and numerous court judgments applying those provisions were set aside. Almost all of them mitigated hardships arising from the Treaty, facilitated the transition to the new order and, in particular, helped to ensure that individuals could not be legally disadvantaged on account of those behavioural modifications that had been necessary for survival in a state like the GDR.

[22] See Oliver Lembcke, *Über das Ansehen des Bundesverfassungsgerichts* (Berliner Wissenschafts-Verlag, 2006) 12 f.

14

The Federal Republic as a Member State of the European Union

I. A Different Form of Statehood

Every history of the Federal Republic is also a history of its state as a political manifestation of society. Nothing has changed the statehood of the Federal Republic more radically, however, than the process of European integration. The change, it is true, likewise affected the other five founding states of the various European Communities and the subsequent accession states. To a lesser extent, it affected almost all other states, because it represented a change in statehood itself, a change that began after the Second World War with the founding of the United Nations (UN). Nowhere, however, has it advanced so far as in Europe. In terms of the range of its powers and the depth of its organisation, the European Union (EU) far outstrips all other supranational entities.

What distinguished the UN from the older partnerships and alliances between states, as well as from the League of Nations which had been founded after the First World War, was the possession of certain sovereign rights, which its Member States had conferred on it and which it could henceforth exercise with effects on states if they threatened world peace. That was a politically desired but legally effected and only legally effectable process that fundamentally changed states and relations between them. The identity of public authority with state authority, which had existed for 300 years, was thus ended. There was now a public authority above the states, although it was scarcely ever brought into play after the Korean War, thanks to the outbreak of the East–West confrontation and the power of veto granted to the Permanent Members of the UN Security Council.

The Federal Republic was not immediately affected by the conferral of sovereign rights on the UN. Initially, West Germany was not sovereign and therefore had no rights to confer; after the gradual restoration of sovereignty, the country was still far from being a member of the UN. It took the successful implementation of the *Ostpolitik* to clear the way for the acceptance of both German states into the UN in 1973. By that time, however, the Federal Republic had already been a member of the European Communities for 15 years, and that membership came with considerably greater curtailments of sovereignty than membership of the UN. Entire areas of policy which the Member States had originally been able to regulate in the framework of their own constitutions became Community matters, and for the Member States the public authority of the European Economic Community (EEC), unlike that of the UN, did not remain latent but was continuously exercised.

Such a fundamental change in a country's statehood cannot fail to impact on its constitution.[1] Every transfer of competence takes a particular policy area out of the hands of national policymakers and therefore puts it out of reach of the national constitution. Although the national constitution regulates the procedural and sometimes also the substantive aspects of the transfer of sovereign powers, it no longer has any influence on the exercise of the transferred rights. The ways in which the European Community makes use of its powers is not governed by the Member States' constitutions, but by the European Treaties. Accordingly, with every conferral of competence for a particular policy area, the significance of the state constitution is diminished. It can no longer lay claim to full regulation of the public authority that is exercised in its area of application.

The Basic Law, in point of fact, was open to such change from the outset. The conferral of powers was not effected by derogation from the constitution but on the basis of a prior authorisation. The preamble to the Basic Law stated that the German people were 'inspired by the determination to promote world peace as an equal partner in a united Europe'. That was an ambitious aim, because in 1949 no one was willing yet to regard Germany as an 'equal partner'. The authority to transfer sovereign powers was contained in Article 24 of the Basic Law. It related to 'international organisations' (*zwischenstaatliche Einrichtungen*) and systems of 'mutual collective security'. Provisions relating specifically to the EU were not added to the Basic Law until Germany was reunited, when they were inserted into the space vacated by the repeal of Article 23, which had contained the accession provisions.

None of the history books fails to mention the European integration process. The larger works show how a viable structure was able to emerge, even though its creation was driven by completely divergent motives. While the French policy objectives were to keep Germany down, to exercise oversight over Germany's heavy industry, which was superior to that of France, and to establish French dominance in Europe, Adenauer saw in European integration the key to achieving the goal of equal partnership proclaimed in the preamble to the Basic Law, to consolidating Germany's integration into the Western world and to expanding market access for German business. The enthusiasm for Europe which prevailed among the West German population in the post-war era, driven by the urge to return to the community of civilised peoples, provided a broad basis of common political ground.

[1] See Dieter Grimm, 'Die Verfassung im Prozess der Entstaatlichung' in idem, *Die Zukunft der Verfassung II* (Suhrkamp, 2012) 67; idem, 'Die Bedeutung nationaler Verfassungen in einem vereinten Europa', ibid 92; English 'The Constitution in the Process of De-nationalization' in *Constitutionalism: Past, Present, and Future* (Oxford University Press, 2015) 315, and 'The Role of National Constitutions in a United Europe', ibid 271.

The history books portray the beginnings, with the creation of the European Coal and Steel Community (ECSC), whose structure already prefigured that of the EEC, then the abortive French project for a European Defence Community (EDC), which was rejected in France itself; its downfall, however, cleared the way for West Germany to join NATO, which was a more important objective for Bonn, though it was only achieved after the United States had exerted immense pressure on France. Lastly, they deal with the conclusion in 1957 of the Treaties of Rome establishing the EEC and Euratom. The objectives, structures and powers of the EU are mostly presented briefly and selectively by the historians. In almost all of their accounts, the European Court of Justice (ECJ) is disregarded. The basic question concerning integration – the choice between the intergovernmental and the supranational route – is highlighted but is never considered in connection with its legal basis.

This is a foretaste of the absence of a legal dimension from the historiographic accounts of the European integration process, which is particularly evident in the treatment of the stagnation that followed the euphoric beginnings. Responsibility for that stagnation lay with the President of the French Republic, Charles de Gaulle, for whom France's pre-eminent role was imperative. He had come to power in the founding year of the EEC and had given France a presidential constitution tailored to his own person. De Gaulle opposed every advance towards integration, insisted on a Europe of Nations and blocked the transition envisaged in the Treaties of Rome from the consensus principle to majority decision-making in the Council. This he did by leaving the French seat empty in the European bodies from 1965 and not reoccupying it until after the Luxembourg Compromise of 1966, which reaffirmed the consensus principle.

Yet it was in that phase, which is described in the history books solely as a period of stagnation, in which decisive progress was made towards the main integrative aim, the creation of the Common Market. In that very phase, in which the historians see only standstill, the EU became that unique and unprecedented structure, somewhere between a confederation of states and a federal state, but closer to the latter, which it has been ever since and which distinguishes it from all other supranational entities. That progress emanated from the very institution that the historians have neglected, namely the ECJ, whose task is to ensure that the Member States and the European institutions themselves comply with Community law and whose decisions do not depend on a political *placet*.

For the performance of this task, the ECJ essentially has three powers at its disposal: on the motion of the Commission, it may decide whether Member States are in breach of the Treaties; on the motion of Member States it may determine whether Community institutions have breached the Treaties; on receipt of requests from national courts, which are also required to apply European law, it may determine how provisions of that law are to be understood. Particularly with the aid of that preliminary ruling procedure, the ECJ equipped itself with a means of bypassing political logjams and so becoming the decisive engine of integration. Needless to say, that would not have been possible without the willingness of national courts – which also requires explanation – to refer questions on the meaning of Community law.[2]

Only Conze conveys a faint notion of the role of the ECJ when he states that the Court of Justice, 'on which there devolved to an increasing extent the task of monitoring compliance with Community law in and by the Member States and in their legislation', had become ever more important. It had thereby acquired a very considerable European effect 'that extends far into the individual states and societies' (102). In this way, however, he only half describes the task, because the Court of Justice was also called to monitor the European institutions' compliance with the Treaties. Nevertheless, he accurately portrays the activity of the ECJ, because the Court of Justice tended to evade the second part of its task. Rulings against the European institutions were a rarity.

Wehler also speaks of 'countless provisions, rules, instructions' which had to be transposed into national law and which made deep inroads into the 'German regulatory framework'. However, he does not ascribe them to the Court of Justice but rather to the Commission and later to the European Parliament too, noting that, 'strictly speaking, they remained immune to autonomous deliberation by the Bundestag' (71 and 239). Only it was not primarily the Commission which made deep inroads into national law, but the ECJ, and the main cause was not a surfeit of European legislation, but the eradication of national law which the Court of Justice found to be incompatible with Community law. Besides, the task did not devolve on the ECJ, as Conze asserts; rather, the Court of Justice took it upon itself.

That happened as a result of two judgments that were delivered in cases of minor import but major impact in 1963 and 1964, at the precise time when political integration was making no headway. In the first judgment, in the case of *Van Gend & Loos*, the ECJ ruled that Community law was directly applicable in the Member States; in the second case, *Costa v ENEL*, it ruled that Community law took precedence over national law, even – as was expressly reaffirmed later in response to Italian dissent – over the constitutional law of Member States.[3] That was unexpected, for no such statement is to be found in the text of the Treaties. The Member States which made observations in the proceedings denied having agreed on anything like that in the Treaties of Rome. The Advocate-General of the ECJ, who has the task of proposing a decision to the Court of Justice, shared the position of the Member States.[4]

It was certainly established that European law applies directly in the Member States and does not first have to be transformed into national law, as is customary

[2] See Karen Alter, *Establishing the Supremacy of European Law* (Oxford University Press, 2009).

[3] ECJ, *Van Gend & Loos*, EU:C:1963:1; *Costa v ENEL*, EU:C:1964:66; *Internationale Handelsgesellschaft*, EU:C:1970:114; *Simmenthal*, EU:C:1978:49.

[4] See Morten Rasmussen, 'The Origins of a Legal Revolution – The Early History of the European Court of Justice' (2008) 14 *Journal of European Integration History* 77; idem, 'From International Law to a Constitutional Dream' in Ignacio de la Rasilla and Jorge Vinuales (eds), *Experiments in International Adjudication* (Cambridge University Press, 2019) 287.

in the case of international law. Had that been the only point at issue, the ECJ would simply have repeated the text of the Treaty. But the ECJ had a wider aim. It had the pillars of the Common Market in mind – the four fundamental economic freedoms: free movement of goods, services, capital and labour. These freedoms and their more detailed elaboration in the Treaties required states to shape their legal systems in a way that was compatible with the Treaties, which meant abolishing customs duties and import quotas, eliminating obstacles to market access for products from other Member States, not privileging their own industries by means of subsidies, etc. In the view of the Court of Justice, they should also license economic operators.

Through the *Van Gend & Loos* judgment, the ECJ thus transformed objective obligations of the Member States into subjective rights of economic operators. Consequently, the latter did not need to wait until the Member States had fulfilled their obligations or had been sued by the Commission. On the contrary, if they considered that national regulations interfered with their fundamental economic rights, they could claim before the national courts that those regulations were in breach of European law, and in case of doubt the national courts had to refer the matter to the ECJ, which then delivered a binding decision. That, of course, could only have the desired effect if Community law, besides being directly applicable, also took precedence.

What was already implicit in the content of the *Van Gend & Loos* judgment but had not been made explicit there was expressed in *Costa*, along with the legal consequence that national law which infringes Community law loses its applicability.[5] The ECJ explained its view by stating that there would be no Common Market if every Member State were allowed to decide whether or not to apply European law. That was certainly true, but it did not necessarily justify the power of the Court of Justice to render national law inapplicable. What matters here, however, is not the juridical solidity of the two judgments. On the contrary: the diverse legal positions are mentioned in order to make it clear that there was no absence of alternatives to the judgments. What matters to historians is not the legal argumentation behind judgments, but their practical effect.

II. The Unique Nature of the EU

The effects, however, were profound. The immediate consequence of the judgments was that the Member States were no longer needed for the realisation of the Common Market. The ECJ was able to take that into its own hands by declaring

[5] It did not have to be made explicit in *Van Gend & Loos*, because that case was about the law of the Netherlands, where the national constitution contains a blanket provision according precedence to international law over domestic law. *Costa* was a case from Italy, where there is no equivalent to the Dutch provision.

national laws incompatible with European law if it regarded the national provisions as an obstacle to the market and so take them out of circulation. Everything depended now on how it used that power. It did so with missionary zeal. Substantial parts of national law ceased to be applicable, regardless of whether they were protectionist or pursued other objectives, such as consumer protection. It extended the ban on subsidies for national business undertakings to include public enterprises, which meant that the Member States were no longer free to decide which economic sectors they intended to leave to the market and which sectors they wanted to manage directly.

But why did the Member States not act when they found that the case law of the ECJ was diverging from the aims they had formulated when concluding the Treaties or was having damaging consequences? American observers were the first to answer that question.[6] Their answer was 'constitutionalisation of the Treaties'. 'Constitutionalisation' did not mean that the international treaties had now been converted into a constitution modelled on that of a state. Only the Member States could have done that. What it did mean was that the Treaties now functioned like a constitution. Constitutions lay down the conditions for political rule. The prerequisite for that is their precedence. What is regulated in the constitution is withdrawn from political decision-making. It is no longer a subject of policymaking but one of its premises. Elections are inconsequential as far as such material is concerned. In the realm of constitutionalised law, power shifts from the the political institutions to the judiciary.

On account of the associated effect of diminishing democracy however, state constitutions are confined to the formal and substantive regulation of the democratic decision-making process, leaving the decisions themselves to politicians, who take them in accordance with the preferences expressed in the election. The European Treaties, however, which were not intended to be a constitution, make a large share of these decisions themselves. They are full of provisions on matters which, in any Member State, would be regulated by means of legislation adopted by a majority decision which could subsequently be amended by a majority. In Europe, however, the precedence of the Treaty provisions covers all such matters. The essence of constitutionalism, namely the distinction between constitutional law and statute law, is ironed out to a great extent in the EU. Europe is not just constitutionalised, but overconstitutionalised.[7]

If Member States are not in agreement with the interpretation given to the Treaties by the ECJ, their only remedy is therefore a Treaty amendment. That, however, is much harder to achieve in the EU than constitutional amendments in

[6] Eric Stein, 'Judges and the Making of a Transnational Constitution' (1981) 75 *American Journal of International Law* 1; and Joseph HH Weiler, 'The Constitution of Europe' (1991) 100 *Yale Law Journal* 2405.

[7] See Dieter Grimm, 'Die demokratischen Kosten der Konstitutionalisierung – Der Fall Europa' in idem, *Europa ja – aber welches?* (Suhrkamp, 2016) 95; English 'The Democratic Costs of Constitutionalization – The European Case' in *The Constitution of European Democracy* (Oxford University Press, 2017) 81.

the Member States. There are more players involved, and the unanimous approval of all Member States is required. For a comparatively insignificant matter such as the correction of a line of case law, a Treaty amendment is practically unattainable. Through constitutionalisation, then, the ECJ not only empowered itself but immunised itself at the same time against any alteration of its case law by means of legislation. That is the source of its unassailable position. It is freer than any national supreme court.

The case law of the ECJ thus strikes at one of the cornerstones of the European edifice, the principle of conferral. According to that principle, the European Community possesses only those powers which the Member States transfer to it contractually. It cannot take from them the powers that it would like to possess. Competence to assign competence lies with the Member States. The ECJ, too, is bound by that principle. It cannot remove any powers from the Member States. But it can interpret transferred powers so broadly that its rulings are tantamount to establishing competence. The conferral principle is then threatened with erosion.

However, that principle, which is fundamental to European integration, is not mentioned in any of the historical works. Since they do not devote any attention to the ECJ as a key European actor either, they fail to notice the creeping power shift from the Member States to the Community which came about as a result of the extraordinarily extensive interpretation of the Treaties by the ECJ. Since the shift was initiated by that very organ which was supposed to oversee adherence to the boundaries of the European Community drawn by the Treaties, even the Member States' right of action is of no help to them. Since those two cataclysmic judgments, the Member States' hands have been tied. They see many parts of their law judicially quashed. That is the source of the deep intrusions into national legal systems to which Conze and Wehler refer, but only Henrich-Franke mentions the judgments (182).

The ECJ, however, can only quash national law. It cannot use European law to patch the holes torn in the states' legal fabric. That requires an initiative from the Commission and a Council decision, which, until 1986, required consensus and is now taken by graduated forms of majority voting and is subject to the consent of the European Parliament. While a mere stroke of the pen in the ECJ is enough to quash national law, European lawmaking is a painstaking process which many players can veto. That explains the asymmetry between negative integration by means of deregulation on the national level and positive integration by means of re-regulation on the European level.[8] The historians, where they address the matter at all, take note only of European overregulation but overlook the more significant problem of underregulation.

The asymmetry is responsible in turn for the liberalising trait that characterises European case law. The fact that European integration has fostered economic liberalisation is mentioned in some works but is not ascribed to the asymmetry

[8] First uncovered by Fritz Scharpf, *Governing in Europe: Effective and Democratic?* (Oxford University Press, 1999) 43 ff.

deriving from that case law. If national deregulation is not matched by European re-regulation, the result is increased freedom of action for economic operators. The European pressure for competition, which has led to the privatisation of many hitherto public services and amenities in the Member States, further reinforces that tendency. The EU as a whole is more liberal economically than the great majority of its Member States wish to be or than their constitutions permit them to be.

European integration is mostly presented as a success story, which the historians ultimately do too, even though the ones who devote more space to the process are not unaware of the constant alternation of standstill and progress. As far as economic integration and growing prosperity are concerned, it undoubtedly was a success story. The success, however, had a downside too. It was only able to materialise because the integration process bypassed politics for a long time and therefore took place below the threshold of public attention. It lacked democratic legitimisation. The historians refer to that point too. They fail to observe, however, that the conditions for that lack of legitimacy were created to a considerable extent by the ECJ, which made it possible for decisions of the utmost political importance to be taken in a non-political manner.

The historians, in fact, seem to seek the reason for the democracy deficit in the weak position of the European Parliament. They do not ask whether the reason really has its roots in the institutional structure or whether it might not lie in underdeveloped conditions within society for genuine democracy. These conditions include Europeanised intermediary institutions and an EU-wide public debate which keep the Parliament in touch with its social basis. These are lacking in Europe. In addition, because of the institutional arrangement, the European Parliament suffers from a low level of representativeness. European elections are contested by national parties which canvass for votes with national manifestos. In the European Parliament, however, the national parties – which have numbered more than 200 since the 2019 election – do not play a part as such. The business of Parliament is conducted by the European parliamentary groups, which neither stand for election nor are rooted in society.

The Single European Act of 1986 is generally regarded as a breakthrough following a long period of 'eurosclerosis'. It set a time limit for the completion of the Internal Market and strengthened the European Parliament. Its most important contribution, however, was that it gave up the consensus principle for Council decisions and brought in the majority principle. Eight of the 12 authors deal with the Single European Act, but only three mention the majority principle. But even there, it receives no more than a mention. Yet it is 'a huge shift, if one considers the Monnet method and the spirit of expertocracy which had long chracterised the integration process'.[9] For the first time in the history of European integration, it became possible to require Member States to obey legislation to which they had not consented and which they did not want.

[9] Ulrich Haltern, *Europarecht*, vol I, 3rd edn (Mohr Siebeck, 2017) 74.

This takes the integration process into a new problem area, for it exacerbates the legitimacy issue. Why should any nation obey legislation that is not its own but has been forced on it by foreign states? Whether the majority principle is perceived as a new threat or a long-overdue blessing depends on one's perspective, as Ulrich Haltern remarks:

> If 'we' are Europeans first and foremost, the intra-European distinctions between us and them and between ours and theirs will have crumbled, and acceptance of the majority principle will be no more than an everyday exercise in democracy. If 'we', on the other hand, are first and foremost Brits, French, Danes, Poles or Germans, the legitimacy questions will remain on the table and will require an answer which is plausible with regard to both democratic processes and internal justification.[10]

It was hoped that the Single European Act would resolve the problem by expanding the powers of Parliament, but no consideration was given to the fact that the legitimacy generated through the European Parliament cannot compensate for the loss of the legitimacy derived from the Member States. The problem, in fact, lay deeper. It raised identity questions, which the Member States tried to answer six years later with the Maastricht Treaty. With that Treaty, the European Community was to be developed into 'an ever closer union among the peoples of Europe'. It was renamed 'European Union', and a citizenship of the Union was introduced, which flowed from citizenship of a Member State. In addition, monetary union was established, and decisions were taken to integrate other policy areas, albeit on an intergovernmental basis. The status of the European Parliament was also further enhanced.

Herbert calls the Maastricht Treaty 'the most important and momentous agreement' since the founding of the EEC (1182, English 960). He regarded the establishment of monetary union as the most significant innovation. For Görtemaker, the Treaty was 'one more step towards the creation of European statehood' (786), whereas Herbert notes that no agreement had been reached on a federal European state. However, Maastricht was, as Conze states, a turning point in a quite different respect. The discussion about the Treaty suddenly exposed how far integration had already advanced on tiptoe without the peoples of the Member States having had the opportunity to express their views. With Maastricht, the European integration process lost some of its public acceptance. It was 'no longer on auto-pilot from then on' (864).

III. The Role of the Federal Constitutional Court

For the historians, Maastricht marks the first appearance of the Federal Constitutional Court (FCC) on the European stage. Three of the 12 authors do

[10] ibid 73 f.

mention that the entry into force of the Maastricht Treaty depended on a *placet* from Karlsruhe. It was by no means the first time, however, that the FCC had had to deal with Europe. Ten decisions in European matters had gone before, including the extremely influential *Solange* order of 1974.[11] In that order, the FCC ruled that, as long as (*solange*) Community legal acts did not guarantee fundamental rights which were equivalent to those protected in Germany, it would assess such acts on the basis of the German fundamental rights. The protection of human rights, it ruled, was of such overriding importance in legitimising political rule and safeguarding the identity of the German constitutional order that a fundamental rights vacuum could not be tolerated.

The Commission instituted Treaty infringement proceedings against the Federal Republic, and the ECJ ruled that Community law took precedence over national constitutional law without exception and that the reservation of a national constitutional court was irrelevant. Nevertheless, it set about developing its jurisprudence on the protection of human rights without a textual foundation in the Treaties but based on the European Human Rights Convention and the body of fundamental rights that were common to all the Member States, so that the FCC was able to declare 12 years later that, with an adequate European system of human rights protection now in place, it would stop exercising its review jurisdiction – which still existed – over derived Community law.[12] Later, the ECJ, in a case concerning the relationship between the international legal order under the United Nations and the legal order of the EU, availed itself of the same *solange* reservation that it had sought to prevent the Federal Republic from exercising.[13]

Almost all of the history books mention the Maastricht Treaty, but not all of them add that its entry into force depended on the Federal Constitutonal Court, for constitutional complaints were lodged against the Act by which the Bundestag had ratified the Treaty and hence indirectly against the Treaty itself. These were ultimately unsuccessful.[14] There is more to such judgments than their outcome, however. On the contrary, the grounds also reveal the conditions on which approval depends and hence also indicators of the integration limits that the Basic Law draws. By delivering a retrospective verdict on an adopted political decision, judgments also make prospective statements about the legal conditions for future measures of political integration. But it takes a reading of the grounds to bring those conditions to light.

A pivotal choice already had to be made on the question whether the actions against the Treaty were even admissible, for they had been brought not by organs of state but by citizens lodging constitutional complaints. A constitutional complaint can only be used to assert violations of fundamental rights, and the question was whether the ratification of an international agreement can violate the fundamental

[11] BVerfGE 37, 271 (1974).
[12] BVerfGE 73, 339 (1986).
[13] ECJ, EU:C:2013:518 – *Kadi*.
[14] BVerfGE 89, 155 (1993).

rights of indiviuduals. The answer given by the FCC was not self-evident and is still controversial today. Although there was no interference with the fundamental rights enshrined in Articles 1 to 19 of the Basic Law, the Court held that there was an effect on the right of citizens to elect Members of the Bundestag, enshrined in Article 38 of the Basic Law and equivalent to a fundamental right. So what did the Maastricht Treaty have to do with people's right to take part in the election of the Bundestag?

The truth was that electors remained at liberty to cast their votes. According to the FCC, however, the franchise was not confined to the act of casting votes. It also included a requirement that the elected body – in this case the Bundestag – must possess sufficient power to translate the electoral decision of the people into political measures. The election of a body with no political weight would 'eviscerate' the franchise. That interpretation of Article 38 of the Basic Law was new, but the question was also new, and the Court's answer followed the line of interpretation with which it had replaced the formal interpretation practice that still prevailed in the Weimar Republic. The franchise was thus no longer confined to the formal right to put a cross on the ballot paper but was understood substantively. The voting decision had to be democratically effective.

The answer to the admissibility question had important substantive implications. On the one hand, it was now established that limits to the transfer of sovereign rights to the EU could be inferred from Article 38 of the Basic Law. The Bundestag had to retain sufficient political substance to translate the will of the electorate into practical policymaking. The limits did not relate to particular areas of legislation for which competence could not be transferred but to the ratio of conferred to reserved powers. The FCC, moreover, had established that it could review shifts in the balance of competence on the basis of citizens' actions, which was important at that time, because, given the consensus on European matters among the parties represented in the Bundestag, the organs of state with rights of action could not be expected to refer any such issues to the Court.

The door to review of the Maastricht Treaty was thus opened. The FCC noted that the EU was created by states which remained sovereign. Its existence and development lie in the hands of the Member States. It is not a self-sustaining entity. The Member States have transferred certain sovereign rights to the EU, but not sovereignty. The scope for action of the EU rests on the principle of conferral. The Member States determine what the EU is allowed to do. The competence to assign competence lies with them. The validity of European law in Germany derives entirely from the application order issued by the Bundestag. European legal acts for which there is no such empowerment do not acquire validity in Germany. Whether the EU has overstepped the limits of the powers assigned to it is reviewed by the FCC, whose decision has legal force in Germany.

These last findings diverge from the view of the ECJ. While the ECJ does not deny that the Member States are 'masters of the Treaties', which means that they also determine the powers of the EU, it assumes that EU law has emancipated itself from the will of the Member States and is valid in its own right. For that reason, no national court may determine whether legal acts of the Union have overstepped the limits of the Treaties; only the ECJ may make that determination. The FCC, by contrast, does not rule out the possibility that even the ECJ itself may overstep the limits of EU powers. The fundamental divergence between the two courts, therefore, has conflict potential, and it was only a question of time before the conflict broke out. That did not come to pass, however, until after the end of the period that the historians chose to cover in their works.[15]

The FCC did not see any infringement of Article 38 of the Basic Law in the Maastricht Treaty. It found that the Bundestag still possessed sufficient political substance, even after the shift of 1992 in the balance of competence. Similarly, the Court held that monetary union did not amount to an erosion of the budgetary powers of the Bundestag. For that reason, the question of the EU assuming the attributes of statehood was not raised. There was therefore no need for the Court to determine whether the Basic Law would permit German membership of a European Union which had become a state.[16] The role of the Bundestag was strengthened. It bears responsibility for Germany's integration into Europe and must see to it that transfers of competence are specific and limited. This assignment of responsibility to the Bundestag enabled the FCC to overcome its reservations against new integrative steps in subsequent cases too.

Appreciation of the key role of the FCC in matters of European integration, however, depends on familiarity with the historical background. Since the Parliament and Government of the Federal Republic are powerless to prevent the EU from gaining ground at the expense of the national constitution and national democracy through the driving force of the ECJ, the national constitutional courts are the sole remaining effective counterweight to the creeping erosion of powers. Competence and identity reviews are the levers which are available to the national constitutional courts for that purpose. That should not be misunderstood, as it often is, as an anachronistic clinging to national statehood but be seen as a defence of democracy in the Member States, from which the EU also draws life.[17]

[15] BVerfGE 154, 17 (2020). The infringement proceedings against the Federal Republic were abandoned, as had been the case after the *Solange* decision (n 244). The conflict potential remains.

[16] Even after the signing of the Treaty of Lisbon in 2007, that question did not arise. Nevertheless, the Federal Constitutional Court answered it in that context, ruling that the conversion of the EU into a state, in other words the transfer of sovereignty to the EU, is incompatible with the Basic Law. Not even amendment of the constitution can surmount that obstacle. The surrender of sovereignty can only be effected by the German people themselves, not their representatives; see BVerfGE 123, 267, 343 ff (2009).

[17] See Dieter Grimm, 'Zur Rolle der nationalen Verfassungsgerichte in der europäischen Demokratie' in Claudio Franzius et al (eds), *Grenzen der europäischen Integration* (Nomos, 2014) 27; also in Grimm, *Die Zukunft der Verfassung II* (Suhrkamp, 2012) 128; English 'The Role of National Courts in European Democracy' in *The Constitution of European Democracy* (Oxford University Press, 2017) 181.

15

The Underestimated Constitutionalisation of Politics

I. Increasing Importance of the Constitution

One of the characteristics of German law in the second half of the twentieth century is defined in legal scholarship as the 'constitutionalisation of the legal order'.[1] This means that the constitution was upgraded from one branch of the law *among* others – private law, criminal law, administrative law, etc – to the branch of the law that is *above* all others, with the result that the whole of ordinary law must be interpreted and applied in accordance with the constitution. The constitution, it is true, always ranked higher in the sense that it regulated the creation of ordinary law. Only provisions which were enacted constitutionally had a claim to validity. For a long time, that was as far as the precedence of the constitution went. There was no talk of the *application* of constitutional statutes having to be subjected to a further constitutionality test.

That effect, in fact, only materialised as a result of the jurisprudence of the Federal Constitutional Court (FCC). It derived from the move towards a substantive understanding of the constitution and particularly from the interpretation of fundamental rights as a legal expression of supreme values, which dates from the inestimably important *Lüth* judgment.[2] In the metaphorical terminology of that judgment, they radiate onto ordinary law wherever its application touches on fundamental rights. On the basis of that doctrine, the legal order underwent considerable change. Numerous laws were affected, not least the great codifications dating from pre-democratic times. Some of their provisions had to be reinterpreted in the light of the fundamental rights or, where that was not possible, annulled as unconstitutional. Even norms from more recent chapters in the development of the legal framework were vulnerable to reinterpretation.

[1] See Gunnar Folke Schuppert and Christian Bumke, *Die Konstitutionalisierung der Rechtsordnung* (Nomos, 2000); Rainer Wahl, *Herausforderungen und Antworten: Das Öffentliche Recht der letzten fünf Jahrzente* (De Gruyter, 2006) 98; on the three main trends in the development of the law in the 20th century – socialisation, constitutionalisation and internationalisation – see also Dieter Grimm, 'Entwicklungen des Rechts zwischen 1895 und 2015' in Bettina Limperg and Klaus Rennert (eds), *Symposion 120 Jahre Reichsgerichtsgebäude* (CH Beck, 2016) 13.

[2] See ch 7 above.

The fact that, since the *Lüth* judgment, the interpretation and application of ordinary law have been subject to compatibility with the constitution as interpreted by the FCC has meant a loss of autonomy for the branches of the law which predated the constitution and for the jurisdictions which had existed before the introduction of constitutional review, and they have not always found it easy to accept. At times there was even resistance in the form of delaying action, which the FCC, however, was ultimately able to overcome. Today, the constitutionalisation of the legal order has been successfully achieved and is now accepted. That is of the utmost interest in the fields of legal history and of constitutional history, as a component of legal history. As far as general history is concerned, however, the development is only significant to the extent that it helps to explain the importance that the Basic Law and constitutional adjudication have acquired in the Federal Republic.

Of direct importance to historians, on the other hand, is the fact that the impact of constitutionalisation does not stop at the boundaries of the legal system. Since legislation is the main instrument for the achievement of political goals in a state based on the rule of law, the constitutionalisation of the legal order also spills over into politics. Subjecting politics to the law is, of course, the primordial purpose of a constitution. But for a long time constitutions were confined to prescribing the organisational structures, forms of action and procedures to which political institutions had to adhere. These were free, on the other hand, to determine the substance of their political action. That choice was made on the basis of political criteria. This is still true today, but the political criteria are always accompanied now by those of constitutional law, which apply at every stage of political decision-making from the perception of the problem to the implementation of the solution.

Then there is another source of constitutionalisation of politics, which emanates not from constitutional jurisprudence but from the political institutions themselves, namely through constitutional amendments.[3] This means, first of all, the practice of loading the constitution with substantive objectives and intervention requirements, which, in turn, enables the FCC to exert additional influence on the political institutions if they do not live up to these constitutional expectations. Secondly, it relates to the tendency to include in the constitution not only the principles governing political action but also details of their application. The first practice is a consequence of changes in what is expected of constitutions, and the second stems from the temptation for political parties to enshrine as much as possible of their policy programmes in constitutional law as insurance against shifting majorities.

These trends can be criticised by reference to both the function of a constitution and the democracy principle. There are sufficient examples of such criticism in literature from the fields of law and political science. As far as the historiography of the Federal Republic is concerned, however, the main requirement is to identify

[3] See ch 4 above.

these trends as a fact which further reinforces the need to consider the constitution as a factor in the observation and explanation of political processes and events. The constant prerequisite, of course, is that the constitution is actually relevant to the political and social conditions in a country. That is made more likely, though not guaranteed, by the existence of constitutional adjudication. What ultimately counts is the attitude of political organs to the constitution and constitutional jurisprudence and the public support that they enjoy.

With regard to the first requirement, the constitutionalisation of politics encounters greater difficulties than that of the legal order. The latter is an internal process within the legal system. The essential activation code within that system is the distinction between lawful and unlawful. From time immemorial, it has been common knowledge that opinions can differ on questions of lawfulness. They are typically resolved through hierarchical structures. Against court judgments there are appeals. The decision of the court at the top of the hierarchy is right, in the sense that no further judicial remedy is available. Since 1951, that top court has been the FCC.[4] If judgments of the final instance are considered unsatisfactory, the next move lies with the political organs, which must consider whether to reprogramme the judiciary for the future by amending the law.

When politics is constitutionalised, by contrast, systemic boundaries are transgressed. In a constitutional state, political institutions are required to review their political intentions and measures on the basis of a systemically alien criterion, namely constitutionality, and, if necessary, correct them. It may then happen that an action which appears desirable or even necessary in the light of political criteria must not be carried out or that an action deemed to be politically undesirable or even harmful must be carried out for constitutional reasons. Constitutional courts are the agents of binding force, which they activate against political organs in cases of doubt or dispute. For that reason, greater resistance is likely at the interface between the political and legal systems than in the case of conflicts between players within the legal system.

One of the characteristic features of the Federal Republic, however, is that the claim to validity of the constitution as interpreted by the FCC has never been fundamentally called into question by a political organ.[5] As the preceding chapters have shown, relations between the FCC and the political institutions have been anything but stress-free. The conflicts, however, have never degenerated into disregard of Constitutional Court rulings by political organs or curtailment of the powers of the Court. Nor, conversely, have they led, for example, to subservience on the part of the FCC to political expectations, which would certainly have been conceivable too. On the contrary, the constitutionalisation of politics is a

[4] On the relationship between the Federal Constitutional Court and European courts, see ch 14 above.

[5] See Helmuth Schulze-Fielitz, 'Wirkung und Befolgung verfassungsgerichtlicher Entscheidungen' in Peter Badura and HorstDreier (eds), *Festschrift 50 Jahre Bundesverfassungsgericht*, vol I (Mohr Siebeck, 2001) 385.

reality in the Federal Republic which cannot be ignored by political observers and chroniclers.

Whether their attitude to the Karlsruhe court is on the affirmative or the critical side, observers agree on the high level of impact and compliance. Helmuth Schulze-Fielitz speaks of an 'extraordinarily large and broad social and legal impact of Constitutional Court decisions', adding in his conclusion that 'The ultimate generally uncontested compliance with its decisions to date is a seismograph for the well-ordered constitutional condition of the Federal Republic of Germany.'[6] Matthias Jestaedt writes:

> No German constitution before … the Basic Law was of such significance in terms of legal practice, in other words of juridical significance in the narrower sense, on the one hand and of such prime importance to the underlying political mood of the German people on the other.[7]

The Basic Law is omnipresent in the public discourse.

It takes a comparison with other constitutional states, however, to reveal that Germany holds a unique position in this respect. Neither the degree of compliance with judgments nor the doctrinal processing and judicial refinement that take place in Germany are matched in any other country.[8] Major innovations developed by the FCC, particularly in the realm of fundamental rights, have been adopted by foreign and international courts. Nevertheless, as far as the degree of constitutionalisation of politics and the willingness of the political organs to comply are concerned, those countries and international organisations still lag behind the Federal Republic. That even applies to the United States, where, in symbolic terms, the constitution possesses at least as much importance as the Basic Law but where legal doctrine in the German sense does not exist and constitutional review is exposed to far fiercer criticism than in Germany.[9]

Comparative constitutionalists from other countries see the German Constitutional Court in a leading role among the constitutional courts of the world, often to the astonishment of US researchers, who like to see their Supreme Court in that role. Oxford-based political scientist David Robertson, who examined eight constitutional courts or supreme courts and their constitutional jurisprudence, writes: 'The court's record is so huge, all-encompassing, and important that one can find examples of almost any aspect of constitutional review in it. Many other, younger constitutional courts openly admit the influence it has on them.' Further

[6] ibid 386 and 420.

[7] Matthias Jestaedt, 'Phänomen Bundesverfassungsgericht. Was das Gericht zu dem macht, was es ist' in idem, Oliver Lepsius, Christoph Möllers and Christoph Schönberger, *Das entgrenzte Gericht. Eine kritische Bilanz nach sechzig Jahren Bundesverfassungsgericht* (Suhrkamp, 2011) 85 f.

[8] The first voices warning against an excessively doctrinal approach to the Basic Law are becoming audible; see, for example, Uwe Volkmann, 'Die Dogmatisierung des Verfassungsrechts' (2020) 75 *Juristenzeitung* 965.

[9] See Dieter Grimm, 'Neue Radikalkritik an der Verfassungsgerichtsbarkeit' (2020) 59 *Der Staat* 321; also in idem, *Verfassungsgerichtsbarkeit* (Suhrkamp, 2021) 357; English 'New Radical Criticism of Constitutional Adjudication' in *Constitutional Courts and Judicial Review* (Hart, 2025) 257.

on in the book, he states: 'So important is this court that any synoptic discussion [of constitutional jurisprudence – DG] will depend on frequent mentions of the German approach.'[10] In the *Oxford Handbook*, Alec Stone Sweet says of the FCC that it is 'arguably the most powerful and influential CC in the world'.[11]

If that is true, it raises the question as to how this increase in the importance of the constitution and constitutional adjudication could have come about in the Federal Republic in particular. Law as an academic discipline has no adequate answer. It can only ever refer to the law itself and emphasise the quality of the Basic Law and of constitutional jurisprudence, and the productivity of constitutional doctrine. While all of that counts, it does not suffice as an explanation. The discipline most likely to provide an answer – political science – had for a long time lost sight of the law, and particularly of constitutional law and constitutional jurisprudence. That, however, has now changed. For a good 20 years, constitutional adjudication has become a respectable area of research in the field of political science.

The key question in that discipline is where constitutional adjudication, and the FCC in particular, obtain the power and authority[12] to which the historians also testify, though without shedding any further light on them. The question chiefly derives its importance from the fact that constitutional courts have no coercive instruments to enforce their decisions. Those instruments are actually in the hands of the political organs of state, to which the courts' judgments are addressed. The constitutional courts are therefore dependent on the goodwill of the political organs. If the latter are unwilling to comply, constitutional adjudication loses out. The court must then wait for the next case and reaffirm its view. In such stand-offs, however, whether repetiton of the ruling would make the political organs more compliant is highly questionable.

The answer must therefore be sought on a different plane from that of coercive instruments. That is where the symbolic dimension comes in. That means focusing less on the juridical quality of the constitution and of constitutional adjudication than on how they are perceived within society. On that plane, the main prerequisite for the authority of the Constitutional Court is that the constitution serves as a 'symbolic expression of the perceptions of order that underlie the community'.[13] In this case, although the public will not necessarily be familiar with the legal provisions of the constitution in the narrower sense, they nevertheless find that their

[10] David Robertson, *The Judge as Political Theorist: Contemporary Constitutional Review* (Princeton University Press, 2010) 40 and 79.

[11] Alec Stone Sweet, 'Constitutional Courts' in Michael Rosenfeld and András Sajó (eds), *The Oxford Handbook of Contemporary Constitutional Law* (Oxford University Press, 2012) 823.

[12] See, eg, Hans Vorländer (ed), *Die Deutungsmacht der Verfassungsgerichtsbarkeit* (Verlag für Sozialwissenschaften, 2006); Oliver W Lembcke, *Hüter der Verfassung. Eine institutionentheoretische Studie zur Autorität des Bundesverfassungsgerichts* (Mohr Siebeck, 2007).

[13] See André Brodocz, 'Die souveränen Deuter. Symbolische Voraussetzungen – instrumentelle Rahmenbedingungen – praktische Auswirkungen', in Vorländer (n 12) 97; see also Hans Vorländer, 'Deutungsmacht – Die Macht der Verfassungsgerichtsbarkeit' in Vorländer (n 12) 9.

perceptions of a just political and social order are reflected in the constitution and look to the constitution for answers to essential questions, answers which, in an increasingly pluralist society, can no longer be expected from other institutions that used to have an orientating effect.

In addition, however, the Constitutional Court, which develops the meaning of constitutional norms and brings it to bear in the specific case, must be trusted to do that on the basis of fidelity to the constitution, putting its own preferences to one side. Its legitimacy then stems from its being credited with a superior insight into the constitution, an insight that is not distorted by political interests, when it points the way or defines limits for the democratic process, in other words when it does precisely what the Basic Law 'intended', as courts like to say. It is understandable, therefore, that constitutional courts insist so adamantly that they do not engage in politics but only help ensure that the law is observed. If they succeed, that is a source of their authority which must also be acknowledged by the political organs, because disregard for the Court could compromise their own legitimacy.

Therein also lies the answer to the question concerning the second requirement, namely public support. The constitution and the Constitutional Court reinforce each other. The constitution only attains the fullness of public esteem when it is enforced by the Constitutional Court, even against those in political power, and can thus be experienced daily by the public as relevant to the political process and to the life of society. This is all the more valid if individuals also have the right to initiate a constitutional review, which they can do in Germany by means of a constitutional complaint, a remedy that is by no means available in every constitutional state. The Constitutional Court, for its part, owes its reputation to the fact that it shows itself to be bound solely by the constitution and is able to demonstrate satisfactorily that its decisions are derived from the constitution. Where that is achieved, one can truly speak of integration by constitution.[14]

The foregoing are key factors which may explain the power and authority of constitutional adjudication, and which exist in the Federal Republic. Appreciation of the Basic Law and, in particular, the public esteem enjoyed by the FCC can be gauged on the basis of the confidence ratings for various public institutions which have been recorded over many years. They consistently show the Constitutional Court in a leading position, its confidence level dipping briefly only in the conflict-ridden period of the Social Democratic–Liberal reforms between 1973 and 1978 as well as in and around the crisis years of 1994 and 1995.[15] That is not sufficient, however, to explain why such extraordinary success was achieved in consolidating

[14] See Hans Vorländer (ed), *Integration durch Verfassung* (Verlag für Sozialwissenschaften, 2002); Dieter Grimm, 'Integration durch Verfassung?' (2004) 32 *Leviathan* 448; also in idem, *Die Zukunft der Verfassung* II (Suhrkamp, 2012) 241; English 'Integration by Constitution' in *Constitutionalism: Past, Present, and Future* (Oxford University Press, 2015) 143.

[15] See Oliver W Lembcke, *Über das Ansehen des Bundesverfassungsgerichts. Ansichten und Meinungen in der Öffentlichkeit 1951–2001* (Berliner Wissenschaftsverlag, 2006); Hans Vorländer and André Brodocz, 'Das Vertrauen in das Bundesverfassungsgericht. Ergebnisse einer repräsentativen Bevölkerungsumfrage', in Vorländer (n 12) 259.

the constitutional state specifically in the Federal Republic in the very period of its history that is covered by the historians' works.[16]

Two factors come into the equation here, factors that may be regarded as specifically German. The first is that, of the two main pillars of the constitutional state – the rule of law and democracy, whose relationship is marked by both interdependence and tension[17] – the rule of law tends to enjoy precedence in Germany. That tendency can also be confirmed by reference to constitutional doctrine, whose exponents have, for long periods, been more comfortable dealing with the principle of the rule of law than with the democracy principle. The difference is noticeable when tensions arise between the two structural principles. The preference for the judicial institution over the political institutions then comes to the fore. The opposite is true in the United States, which may explain the fiercer criticism of judicial review from across the Atlantic.

The second factor has to do with the special situation of the Federal Republic in the aftermath of National Socialist rule and the Second World War.[18] The natural basis, as it were, for the identity and integration of a society, such as a *Volk* or nation, or a common history or culture, was not available in Germany before reunification. The nation was divided; the concept of a *Volk* could not be used in an emphatic sense, given its associations with the supremacist ideology of National Socialism. History was weighed down by the Holocaust, to which all roads now seemed to lead. The West could not claim the whole of German culture for itself. On the contrary, culture was the only bond that still linked the two part-states. The Basic Law managed to fill that gap. In time, it became a symbol for the resurgence of the Federal Republic and its entry into the circle of civilised peoples and for its supremacy over the German Democratic Republic (GDR).

That, it must be said, is inextricably linked with two developments which were not in any way inevitable. One was the economic upsurge, which, though its fruits were unevenly distributed, benefited everyone and made it easier to redistribute wealth in the interests of social equity. The other was the creation of a stable democratic order that withstood even bitter conflicts between the country's political forces. By the time the first difficulties arose, both were already so well established that neither was shaken. In this case, too, the effect was mutual reinforcement. Democracy profited from political rule being exercised constitutionally, while the constitution benefited from the readiness of the democratic political organs

[16] This is evidently easier to discern from a non-German perspective, as is shown by the great depictions penned by Justin Collings, in *Democracy's Guardians. A History of the German Federal Constitutional Court, 1951–2001* (Oxford University Press, 2015), and by Aurore Gaillet in *La cour constitutionnelle fédérale allemande. Reconstruire une démocratie par la loi 1945–1961* (la mémoire du droit, 2001).

[17] See Dieter Grimm, 'Rule of Law and Democracy',in Giuliano Amato et al (eds), *Rule of Law vs Majoritarian Democracy* (Hart, 2001) 107.

[18] See Dieter Grimm, 'Verfassungspatriotismus nach der Wiedervereinigung' in idem, *Die Verfassung und die Politik* (CH Beck, 2001) 107.

to comply with constitutional requirements and judgments, even if that severely disrupted the pursuit of their objectives.

II. Historiographic Perception

What has been written here, by analogy with the common jurisprudential concept of 'constitutionalisation of the legal order', on the constitutionalisation of politics is scarcely perceptible in the historiographic works. The development of the Federal Republic is certainly presented throughout as a success story. Only Geppert, whose book was written at a time when democracy was already coming under threat and long-standing certainties were being eroded, seeks to distance himself from that view (6). The Basic Law also comes in for almost unstinting praise, but readers are left in the dark regarding the actual role that it played in the felicitous development of the Federal Republic. Similarly, the FCC is also adjudged to be a gain for the Federal Republic in brief assessments that mostly remain in the realm of abstraction, even if a transgression of the boundary between law and politics is registered here or there.[19]

The works, however, do not communicate to readers that the rulings of the FCC led to an extraordinary increase in the significance of the Basic Law. Constitutional rulings feature here and there, but always individually, which means that no impression can be conveyed of the scale of the changes that they wrought with regard to the legal and social order, the institutional architecture of the political system and social conditions. The contribution of constitutional jurisprudence, which, though based on the Basic Law, was not entirely determined by it and, to that extent, was truly a separate contribution, escapes the historians' attention. That the specifically Federal German constitutionalism has an 'eminently political effect', as political scientist Verena Frick observes,[20] is not apparent from the history books.

How is that explained? Is it a conscious, theoretically driven decision made within the discipline? In that case, one ought to expect an explanation to that effect in the prefaces or introductions, for those are the places where authors normally provide information about the temporal and thematic scope of their subject matter, the perspectives from which it is to be examined and the methods to be applied. Most of the works analysed here fulfil that expectation. Only three have opted against that approach. Winkler's 'main focus' – though not his exclusive focus – is on politics and political culture (IX, English 20), and Morsey likewise announces a general intention to put politics in the foreground (XI). Most of the authors define their subject matter as politics, economics, society and culture (Birke V, Henrich-Franke 13, Herbert 20/English xxi, Rödder XIII and Wolfrum 18),

[19] See ch 9 above.

[20] See Verena Frick, 'Das Stabilitätsversprechen der Verfassung. Der Aufstieg des Grundgesetzes in der Bonner Republik' (2020) 48 *Leviathan* 90.

dealing with the last three at least where they deem them politically relevant. On the law and constitution they are silent.

Some of the authors name other areas or aspects that are to be addressed in addition to the four major fields, such as religion, the churches, lifestyles and mentalities (Birke V) or political constellations, social tensions, economic challenges, intellectual currents and mental dispositions (Geppert 6). Henrich-Franke announces the aim of laying special emphasis on the 'question of the statehood of the Federal Republic and its gradual embedding in international and European relationships'. Even in those subsidiary areas of the four major fields, however, readers will seek in vain for the law and the constitution. Recker alone has thought of the constitution; her intention is to focus her short history on 'government and politics in the wider sense', which, for her, also encompasses the 'constitutional order' (9).

There are two special cases. One is Wehler, who, in volume V of his social history, continues to focus on the four 'axes', namely the economy, social inequality, political rule and culture, with the aid of which he seeks to paint an overall picture of historical reality. Political history, he states, plays a subsidiary role in his account. Unlike the other authors, however, he cites among the 'other noteworthy areas' the constitution, only to dispense himself instantly from treating it, because 'constitutional history of a high standard can be consulted in the works of some outstanding poltical scientists and legal historians' (XVI). Situations of interdependence, however, cannot be depicted by means of references. Wehler, in fact, is undeterred by the fact that his account, which emphasises the structural side of history, has to make do without the structuring force of the law.[21]

The second special case is Birke (and the later Wengst edition, where the passage in question is identically worded). The constitution already features in the subtitle of his book – *Verfassung, Parlament und Parteien* ('Constitution, Parliament and Parties'). According to his preface, they are 'a key area of the internal development of our countrty'. The modern history of the constitution, he writes, must not be treated in isolation or reduced to the perspective of legal history (IX). In the text, Birke specifies that the 'essence, function and development of the constitution' must 'not be inferred from its normative basis alone', but must be considered 'in the complex processes of constitutional reality', for which, however, the normative framework offers 'indispensable guidance' (54 and 65 f). That statement can be endorsed. But the book does not recognisably outdo the other authors' accounts in its treatment of the constitution and constitutional jurisprudence.

As for the authors who make no comment on the role of the constitution in their prefaces or introductions, there is nothing to suggest a conscious decision not to consider it. On the contrary, it must be assumed that the constitution did not enter their minds when they came to enumerate the key factors. Awareness is

[21] For more on this point, see my disputation with Wehler, which is reproduced in the appendix.

lacking of its relevance to the sequences of historical events which are treated in their works. Nowhere is the significance for a country of the constitution and its application reflected. Accordingly, the constitution has no systematically established place in the historical accounts. There are only a smaller or larger number of spots where articles of the consitution or Constitutional Court judgments feature. Why they feature there but not in other places where they likewise play a part is not explained. Consideration of the Basic Law and of constitutional jurisprudence thus has something of a random character

If awareness is lacking of the relevance of the constitution and its application, however, attentiveness to its effects can never develop. That is made clear by the historians' treatment of constitutional jurisprudence. In quantitative terms, references to FCC judgments range from zero (Wirsching) to 22 (Conze). The most frequently cited judgment is the abortion decision of 1975, but the second abortion ruling of 1993 is scarcely mentioned. Next in order of mentions come the prohibitions of two political parties – the Socialist Reich Party (SRP) and the Communitst Party of Germany (KPD) – and the judgment concerning the Treaty on the Basis of Relations between the Federal Republic and the GDR. It is striking that, apart from the abortion ruling of 1973, only one other judgment on fundamental rights has captured somewhat wider attention, namely the television judgment of 1961. That is consistent with a general disinterest in the fundamental rights which was already apparent in the descriptions of the Basic Law and was confirmed in connection with the liberalisation measures.[22]

This focuses attention on the motives for the selection of constitutional rulings, in so far as the historians' accounts allow any conclusions to be drawn in that respect. The four most-cited judgments related to highly political disputes with extensive media coverage. In the abortion judgment, the Court ruled on a controversial issue that had profoundly split society. At the same time, the authors see in that judgment an obstruction of the Social Democratic–Liberal reforms by the FCC, although the coalition's fiercest attacks on the Court did not follow that decision but the judgment on the revised Conscription Act, a decision which is scarcely mentioned. The two prohibitions of political parties are used to exemplify the basic anti-totalitarian consensus, which, in the view of many authors, permeates the Basic Law. The order approving the Treaty on the Basis of Relations is featured because at that time Willy Brandt's *Ostpolitik*, which receives plentiful attention in all of the works, was hanging by a thread.

The treatment of the television judgment of 1961 is especially revealing. It is mentioned only as the source of Konrad Adenauer's first painful defeat. So the focus of historical interest is not on constitutional provisions and judicial considerations but only on the impact of the judgment on Adenauer's chancellorship. That is entirely legitimate in a historical analysis of the Adenauer era and its closing stages. But the political significance of the judgment goes beyond Adenauer's

[22] See ch 2, sections II and III, and ch 7, section III.

defeat. As shown above,[23] it had a momentous impact on the future development of the communication system in the Federal Republic. Political influence on the new flagship medium was prevented, and the judgment put broadcasting policy on the path to a system based on freedom of broadcasting which was not driven by political or economic interests.

The narrowed perspective that is in evidence here, however, is no exception. Where Constitutional Court decisions are taken into account, the main focus of interest is almost always their immediate effect on the matter at issue. Judgments are perceived as events, the significance of which is limited to their outcome – victory for one party, defeat for the other. Their long-term consequences and structural effects are not explored. Decisions which do not manifestly have a direct effect on a political dispute addressed by the historians therefore stand little chance of consideration in works of modern history from the outset, however profoundly they impact on matters transcending the case at hand. The *Lüth* judgment is the prime example, though not the only one.[24]

These effects, it is true, are not seen in the operative part of the judgment, which only pronounces on whether the state action or omission under review was constitutional or unconstitutional and, in the event of an unconstitutional act, what the consequences are. The act will normally be annulled. Everything else is ascertainable from the grounds of the judgment, in which the implications of the relevant norms for the case at hand are determined. Where the grounds nevertheless receive such scant consideration, it seems reasonable to infer insufficient historiological awareness of the importance of constitutional interpretation as such, which follows from the limited determinative power of constitutional norms. If the grounds of judgments are not expected to yield findings that may have lasting political or social relevance, such findings will not be discovered.

Since the FCC has adopted the practice of setting out in detail the criteria applied to the specific case and how those criteria are derived from the provisions of the Basic Law before characterising the case in terms of those concretised provisions, it is precisely that part of the grounds, with its moderate level of abstraction, known as the *Maßstabsteil*, or 'criteria part',[25] from which the ramifications of the decision and the connection points for future case constellations follow. That is also the part which promises to shed light on the justices' understanding of the constitution, the options facing them, the judicial choice they made and the consequences they considered and weighed in the balance. It is therefore a potential treasure trove for historians if they wish to explore the longer-term effects of constitutional jurisprudence beyond the limits of the historical event itself.

[23] See ch 7, section III, and ch 8.

[24] See again Rainer Wahl, 'Die praktische Wirksamkeit von Verfassungen' in *Festschrift für Klaus Stern* (Duncker & Humblot, 2012) 248 with fn 48.

[25] For a critical appraisal, see Oliver Lepsius, 'Die maßstabsetzende Gewalt' in Matthias Jestaedt et al, *Das entgrenzte Gericht. Eine kritische Bilanz nach sechzig Jahren Bundesverfassungsgericht* (Suhrkamp, 2011) 159.

It cannot be denied, of course, that court decisions are not always easily understood by readers with no legal training. Yet they are not incomprehensible either. The difficulties relate to the juridical derivation chain, legal doctrine, which is therefore the main focus of legal scholars' study of constitutional history. The difficulties do not relate to the effects of judgments in the real world or to society's reactions to Constitutional Court judgments. It goes without saying that those judgments would have to be read. It is striking that scarcely any of the history books cites Constitutional Court decisions by indicating their *Official Digest* reference, if they are given any reference at all. These decisions, then, are – to quote Rainer Wahl – 'a yet-unused source';[26] one could even speak of a buried treasure.

III. What is now Needed?

The starting point for any attempt to sum up must be the fact that the constitution and constitutional jurisprudence are omnipresent in German politics and have acquired such great relevance that historians cannot bypass them. Numerous circumstances, developments and events to which historians attach importance find their explanation in the constitution and in its interpretation and application by the FCC or are at least heavily influenced by them. The extent to which politics is influenced by constitutional law distinguishes the Federal Republic from former German states and from the great majority of other constitutional states.

Constitutional jurisprudence makes its own contribution to the relevance of the constitution. It does not merely amount to pronouncing, in a specific case, what the Basic Law has already laid down in general terms. The determinative power of numerous constitutional norms is so limited that their practical usefulness in resolving conflicts depends on their judicial interpretation, to which there is rarely an absence of alternatives. Moreover, social change in all its manifestations constantly confronts justices with the task of inferring a meaning from the Basic Law to answer questions which were not yet even foreseeable when it was enacted. It is therefore impossible to speak of the influence of the constitution without including constitutional jurisprudence.

Since none of the general histories of the Federal Republic do justice to the significance of the constitution and of constitutional jurisprudence, it must be assumed that the problem does not lie with individual historians but with the discipline of modern history. The historiographers credit the Basic Law with having created a new order. What is truly new in relation to previous epochs of German history in which constitutions also existed, however, is that in none of those previous eras did the constitution exert an influence on politics which was remotely comparable to that of the Basic Law as interpreted and applied by the FCC.

[26] Wahl (n 24) 141.

After the various turns of past years, historiographers of the Federal Republic should take account of this influence by adding a juridical or constitutional turn. The difficulties involved in dealing with the law do not dispense exponents of the discipline from doing so. Since there are certainly examples in the specialised literature of modern history of successful integration of the constitution and constitutional jurisprudence into historical accounts, it may be assumed that comprehension difficulties are not the decisive obstacle to the consideration of legal phenomena. The problem is one of perception. Modern historians must become more aware of the relevance of the constitution and constitutional jurisprudence to the subject matter of their own discipline.

Constitutional history is the place where legal and historical scholarship meet.[27] These two disciplines have different cognitive interests, and each therefore encompasses the subject matter incompletely. This suggests a need to widen their horizons. To that end, legal scholars who study constitutional history would have to understand it to a greater extent as history of the impact of constitutions. The constitutional history studied by historians must first be established as a recognised branch of modern history, just as research into constitutions and constitutional courts has now become established as a branch of political science.

[27] See Christoph Gusy, 'Juristische Zeitgeschichte. Eine verfassungshistorische Perspektive' (2013) 7 *Journal der juristischen Zeitgeschichte* 47; and Ewald Grothe, *Zwischen Geschichte und Recht. Deutsche Verfassungsgeschichtsschreibung 1900–1970* (Oldenbourg, 2005) 28 ff.

Appendix

The Significance of Law in the History of Society: A Query

I.

Hans-Ulrich Wehler's *Gesellschaftsgeschichte* ('history of society') is intended to be a history of 'an entire society'.[1] His aim, then, is not to contribute to a particular field of history that stands alongside others, such as political history, economic history, art history, etc. Instead, he seeks to create a 'synthesis' integrating those historiographic fields,[2] rejecting any thematic boundaries and recognising only geographical and temporal limits: it is a history of the whole of German society in the modern era, beginning around 1700.

Even within those geographical and temporal bounds, however, his venture faces all of the problems associated with a sweeping academic survey of the totality of social conditions. It would therefore have been doomed to failure from the outset if the author did not possess a transepochal theory of the constitution of society that enables him to reduce the complexity of his subject matter to such an extent that he can expect to encapsulate and present it in comparatively few determinants with the result that the inevitable omissions do not diminish the validity of the overall picture.

Wehler develops such a theory in the introduction to the first volume of his work. The following reflections relate only to that theory, according to which society is constituted by what Wehler calls three dimensions – political rule, the economy and culture.[3] These do not exist in isolation from each other but move within a relationship of mutual conditioning and influence, in which one or the other may be predominant, but none can be derived from the others. Political rule, the economy and culture appear in the introduction in turn as main dimensions, fundamental dimensions, basic dimensions, constituent dimensions, central dimensions or else axes.[4] Wehler posits that they make society sufficiently describable and explicable.

[1] Hans-Ulrich Wehler, *Deutsche Gesellschaftsgeschichte* I (CH Beck, 1987) 6.
[2] *ibid*, 9.
[3] *ibid*, 6 f.
[4] *ibid*, 7–9.

Besides these three, however, there are supposed to be other important dimensions or axes. The only one addressed, however is the 'system of social inequality'.[5] Wehler even describes it as one of the central or main axes. Nevertheless, he does not ascribe the same significance to it as he does to the three dimensions referred to above. That, for Wehler, is due to social inequality being a result of the interaction of the other three dimensions. It can thus be derived from them, whereas the dimensions themselves are not derivative and are therefore systemically superordinate to social inequality.

The subject matter of his history of society is then the 'social structure' determined by these dimensions, a term understood as standing 'for the entire internal structure of society'.[6] That clearly does not apply exclusively, however. The reason seems to lie in the fact that history consists, on the one hand, of supra-individual structures and processes but also of individually attributable actions and decisions. If Wehler nevertheless puts the social structure in the foreground, the reason is probably that he regards actions and decisions as being largely structurally determined, which means that they can be explained by reference to the social structure.

In the following pages, the aim is not to call into question the theory of society that underlies Wehler's work and legitimises its conception but rather to examine where the law fits into this theory and, consequently, what significance attaches to it in a Wehler-style history of society.

II.

1. The role of the law is not defined in the theoretical introduction to the *Gesellschaftsgeschichte*. It is sought in vain among the key categories that make a society decipherable and portrayable, but it is encountered in passing at various points. The first references appear in connection with the dimensions. Political rule is described as 'organised and regulated (*normierte*) power', the economy as an 'institutionalised regulatory system (*Regelsystem*)'.[7] Both definitions, then, allude to legal elements, which are, however, absent from the third dimension, culture.

Law also features in the section devoted to 'some epistemological interests' for researchers into the history of society, where it is mentioned in connection with social inequality. Wehler subscribes there to the view that equality rights should be realised more widely and that inequalities must be subjected to 'the most stringent legitimacy test'.[8] He does concede, however, that an insurmountably and profoundly strained relationship exists between democratic equality rights and liberal freedoms which makes certain inequalities unavoidable and justifiable.

[5] *ibid*, 11.
[6] *ibid*, 9.
[7] *ibid*, 10.
[8] *ibid*, 16.

Lastly, the law is mentioned in the section on 'further intentions'. Wehler deals there with the modernisation process and remarks that great significance attaches, in his eyes, to codifications of the law and judicial administrations for their impact on the social order as it was regulated, for example, in the Prussian General State Laws or for the legally enshrined 'rational prior calculability of legal certainty, economic conduct and functions of the state apparatus.'[9] Particularly for the period after the Second World War, he noted, there was a need to enquire into the foundations of the democratic social state based on the rule of law.

These passing references to legal phenomena reveal that the history of society does have something to do with law. It is even described once in the notes as one of the great forces ordering the life of society.[10] What is not recognisable, on the other hand, is the systematic connection with the constituent dimensions of society. One explanation could lie in the abundance of material with which Wehler saddles himself through his concept of a history of society. The author himself recognises a deficit in his knowledge regarding the cultural dimension of society and uses that to excuse his omission of fields such as the history of philosophy, architecture and music.[11] He basically assumes, however, that the essentials of the history of society can still be imparted without venturing into those fields.

The question is how the law fits in. There are various levels at which it could find its place within Wehler's model. It could be one of the numerous societal areas of activity like philosophy, architecture or music. It could also be at home on the level of the important dimensions or axes of which Wehler says there are several, though he names only social inequality. Lastly, it could belong to the basic dimensions, but that would run counter to Wehler's own proposition, which limits their number to three.

2. If one accepts Wehler's assumption that the history of society is largely a history of the social structure, it cannot be ignored that the social structure, for its part, is determined to a considerable extent by the law. That applies to its fundamentals as well as to numerous particulars. Feudal society was defined and consolidated by legal norms just as the modern civic society is. The transition between them has been effected by changing the legal order. It was precisely in law that bourgeois society constituted itself, and even its endeavour to preserve actual inequalities within an order based on legal equality was accomplished by means of the law.[12]

The same applies to Wehler's 'dimensions'. Political rule and the economy have always been subject to legal regulation, as Wehler himself indicates in his definitions. Culture is no different.[13] The education system makes that quite clear, but even the structures of the arts and sciences are likewise shaped by the law, regardless of whether they are instrumentalised for particular extraneous purposes or

[9] *ibid*, 22.
[10] *ibid*, 554, n 5.
[11] *ibid*, 11 f.
[12] See Dieter Grimm, *Recht und Staat der bürgerlichen Gesellschaft* (Suhrkamp, 1987) 19 ff.
[13] *ibid*, 104 ff.

have been explicitly exempted from such instrumentalisation. The object, content and depth of detail of such regulation may vary, as can be seen, but the fact of their legal regulation as such does not.

Law, finally, has its place in the interaction of the three dimensions which Wehler puts in the forefront of his endeavours. That applies to each of the conceivable relationships: between political rule and the economy, between the economy and culture and between culture and political rule. Both political micromanagement of the economy and, at the opposite pole, its detachment from the political system are effected by means of the law. In the relationship between the economy and culture, the question of the extent to which the education system satisfies the needs of the economy is settled by the law, as is the question as to who is entitled to commercialise artistic products. In the relationship between culture and political rule, the law determines whether the state may vet cultural output for acceptability or with what objectives and in what forms education may be delivered.

In these cases, of course, it is never a question of total regulation by law. On the other hand, a situation that is not influenced by the law at all will never be encountered either. On the contrary, a society's basic preferences are likely to be symbolically enshrined in law, converted into regulatory arrangements and equipped with organised sanctions in case of contravention. For that reason, the legal order may also be seen as the self-portrait of a society in which its values and power balances are expressed and acquire potency.

Conversely, it is equally undeniable that the valid law, for its part, depends on the social structure, likewise in its fundamentals as in its particulars. The transition from feudal corporative law to bourgeois liberal law was not the evolution of a concept of law but the fruit of a combination of ideas, catalyst groups within society, propitious social conditions and situational opportunities. Whether success was achieved in abolishing child labour or banning the formation of trade unions was no less dependent on the balance of social forces than was, for example, the status of women in family law, and particularly their property rights.

That dependence exists not only with regard to the statutory introduction or abolition of particular norms or institutions. It extends to the effectiveness of applicable law. When extraneous law is received into a legal system, it has repeatedly been observable that, in a new social context, the received law remains ineffective or has different effects from those envisaged for it.[14] This indicates that there are extralegal conditions for the realisation of law. But even when established law

[14] For extraneous law imported into Germany, see Elisabeth Fehrenbach, *Traditionelle Gesellschaft und revolutionäres Recht* (Vandenhoeck & Ruprecht, 1978); Dieter Grimm, 'Historische Erfahrungen mit Rechtsvereinheitlichung – das frühe 19. Jahrhundert in Deutschland', in *Rabels Zeitschrift* 50 (1986), 61; for the export of the German Civil Code, eg to Japan, see Wilhelm Röhl, *Fremde Einflüsse im modernen japanischen Recht* (Alfred Metzner, 1959); particularly instructive are Andreas B. Schwarz, *Das Schweizerische Zivilgesetzbuch in der ausländischen Rechtsentwicklung* (Schulthess, 1950), and *idem*, 'Rezeption und Assimilation ausländischer Rechte', in *idem*, *Rechtsgeschichte und Gegenwart* (CF Müller, 1960) 149 ff.

is applied in its original social context, social structural factors can influence its interpretation and application and may even hinder its implementation.

3. The key question thus seems to be what rules what – does the law rule the social structure, or does the social structure rule the law? If the law is only a product of social conditions, then it *may* be included in the examination of the history of society and used as a medium within which the author's subject matter is identified. By the same token, however, it may also be replaced by other media. If, on the other hand, the social structure is at least partly a product of the law, then it *must* be included in the examination, because otherwise the author would not merely be neglecting one of several sources of knowledge but inadequately covering his or her subject matter.

The question being asked here is about the autonomy of the law,[15] which cannot simply be taken for granted. There are numerous examples, both historical and current, of non-autonomy of the law. In such cases, the law functions only as an appendage to another social system – politics or religion, for example – serving that system as an instrument for the enforcement of its imperatives. That is evident not only in the enactment of general norms but also in their application in concrete cases. If a conflict arises between the general rule and the expectations of the dominant system, the latter tends to win out if the law lacks autonomy.

Conversely, however, the law cannot be assumed to lack independence. On the contrary, there are sufficient examples of autonomous existence of the law. It is even a characteristic of the modern age in the Western world that dependence of the law on other systems has been either dissolved or broken. That happens, for example, when legal norms that bind society are created within the legal system itself. Not only in Britain has 'judge-made law' long been the predominant source of norms; the *ius commune* which applied subsidiarily in Germany until the codifications was likewise jurists' law. On the application level, there were even numerous judicial restrictions of absolutist rule. For bourgeois societies, the independence of the judiciary, which brooks no binding ties but those of the law, is a core programmatic principle.

Constant vigilance is, of course, of the essence. It could be that case law is merely a particularly effective attempt to conceal continuing dependence. The theory has indeed been proposed. Karl Marx regarded the bourgeois legal order, emancipated from religion and politics, as nothing more than a veil concealing its dependence on economic forces. According to that theory, the privileging or disfavouring of complete sections of the population, defined by their collective interests (class

[15] This key question, remarkably, is seldom asked by legal scholars, particularly in the field of legal history; see Joachim Rückert, *Autonomie des Rechts in rechtshistorischer Perspektive* (Juristische Studiengesellschaft Hannover 1988); also Niklas Luhmann, *Ausdifferenzierung des Rechts* (Suhrkamp, 1981); idem, *Das Recht der Gesellschaft* (Suhrkamp, 1993) esp 62 ff and 76 ff; Engl *Law as a Social System* (Oxford University Press, 2004) esp 95 ff and 105 ff; Gunther Teubner, Recht als autopoietisches System (Suhrkamp, 1989) 42 ff and 87 ff; Engl *Law as an Autopoietic System* (Wiley-Blackwell, 1993) 30 ff and 70 ff; Richard Lempert, 'The Autonomy of Law', in G Teubner (ed), *Autopoietic Law* (De Gruyter, 1988) 152 ff.

law), is an indicator of such veiled dependence, as is the discriminatory or non-existent enforcement of the law in particular areas or against particular groups.

Even then, the law could only be said to lack significance in its own right if it were entirely devoid of autonomy. In Wehler's model, that would be the case if the law were either absorbed into one of the three basic dimensions or, like the system of social inequality, were merely a result of the interaction of all three. In that case, anyone having recognised the dimensions would also have recognised the law. Since the law did not, or did not alone, constitute the subject matter of the history of society but merely an illustrative element, it would not have merited explanation as a separate factor.

For Marx, the law represented a dependent economic variable. In the state monopoly capitalism theories of the 1970s, that view experienced a brief renaissance, while it became increasingly questionable to socialist legal theorists. Interdependence between the law and the economy no longer appeared unthinkable.[16] It is, of course, more logical to assign the law to the dimension of political rule. The political genesis of law, which has become increasingly common in the modern era, and its enforcement through the state coercion apparatus are strong arguments in favour of such a link.

It is equally possible, however, to see the law as a cultural phenomenon. To do that, one need not invoke those systems in which the law features only as a subsidiary appendage of religion. In fact, the law of a society is formally and substantively shaped and sustained by values and cultural models. That applies particularly to the foundations of legal systems such as the principle of the rule of law or of subjective right, which are not creations of the law itself but cultural phenomena. For this reason they cannot be altered in the short term by sovereign acts. On the contrary, lawmaking and law enforcement by political rulers are carried out within a culturally defined framework that is seldom consciously perceived and often emerges only through the comparison of legal systems.

4. In the following paragraphs, I shall confine myself to the most obvious possibility, namely the classification of the law within the system of political rule. What makes it the most obvious is that the great majority of laws today are created by political institutions and serve those institutions as instruments of power. This is not to say that other systems, such as the economy, cannot exert influence on lawmaking in order to create a legal situation that furthers their own interests. They cannot do that in a straightforward way, however, but must take the circuitous route via the political system, because only norms created by that system can lay claim to general binding force. On that route through the political system, however, it is also essential to take account of the inherent rules of that system, which, in functionally differentiated societies, normally prevent any one-sided dependency.

[16] See, eg, *Marxistische-leninistische allgemeine Theorie des Staates und des Rechts*, vol 1 (Staatsverlag der Deutschen Demokratischen Republik, 1974) 305 ff.

It may help to clarify the relationship between political rule and law if we ask the question why rulers rule by means of the law and not simply by means of power or money. The answer must lie in the characteristics of law which are lacking in the other means of political rule. It then becomes evident that one specific capability of legal norms is that of rendering the political dispositions contained in them independent of persons and situations and thereby generalising and perpetuating those dispositions. Together with the pledge that the norms will be enforced even in the event of refusal to comply with them, that capability thus creates the degree of foreseeability and behavioural certainty which is found to a lesser extent in modern societies than in traditional ones and so must first be established as a product of the political system.

That, however, is not the whole story. Law, moreover, functions as a source of the legitimacy of political rule. It adds something which is not inherent in political rule, namely recognition of it as lawful. In that way, use of force, a limited resource, can be minimised and kept in reserve. If it were necessary to enforce the law entirely, or even for the most part, by means of coercive state power, public order would break down, simply because of the shortage of that resource. Precisely because of its legitimising function, however, there is more to the law than political utility. It remains open to discussion in terms of fairness and invites criticism of the exercise of political rule on the basis of a criterion which is accepted by the rulers themselves.

The picture becomes even more variegated if a distinction is made between two basic facets of the law, namely lawmaking and application.[17] As regards lawmaking, the situation seems straightforward – lawmaking depends on the exercise of political rule. What the law is to be is politically determined. The law is a product of political decisions. The law does not create its own content independently of politics. One of the significant achievements of the modern era, however, is that political rulers, in the act of lawmaking, are themselves bound in turn by the law. Although law is made in the political sphere, it can only be made within the framework and pathways defined by the law itself.

That is a consequence of the division of the legal order into two hierarchical levels, namely constitutional law, which constitutes political rule and regulates the acquisition of sovereign functions as well as the manner of their performance, and statute law, which is created on the basis of constitutional law and binds society.[18] Constitution-making, it is true, is also a sovereign act and constitutional law a product of political decision-making. Its purpose, however, lies precisely in the fact that it regulates future sovereign acts and removes particular content and procedures from the reach of the political institutions. The question of effectiveness also arises here. But there are enough examples showing that, in conflicts between political rule and the law, politics does not always win the day.

[17] On what follows, see Dieter Grimm, 'Politik und Recht', in Eckart Klein (ed), *Grundrechte, Sozialordnung und Verfassungsgerichtsbarkeit. Festschrift für Ernst Benda* (CF Müller, 1995) 91.

[18] See Dieter Grimm, *Die Zukunft der Verfassung*, 2nd edn (Suhrkamp, 1994) 14 f and 407 ff; Engl *Constitutionalism: Past, Present, and Future* (Oxford University Press, 2016) 11 f and 237 ff.

It should not be overlooked, on the other hand, that political decisions must be converted into legal forms which present themselves to the political organs and which are not at the latter's disposal. They are partly rooted in cultures and partly stem from the specific rationality of the legal form and are mostly perceived as the only option for as long as changes in the conditions for the realisation of law do not render them manifestly inadequate. One example is conditional programming, which for a long time was virtually identified with lawmaking and only now, in the light of changes in state tasks, is being eclipsed by a different type of programming, namely purposive programming.[19]

In the realm of application of the law, the autonomy question cannot be answered once and for all. There have been and still are systems in which the application of the law is not an autonomous process. Whether and how the law is applied in those systems is determined by the political organs through chains of command or personal dependence. That, however, need not be the case. Another characteristic of the modern era is that, while the law as a general norm is created in the system of political rule, its application in any specific case is uncoupled from political influence. The only remaining link is then the personnel policy for the judiciary. Otherwise the only way to reprogramme the bodies applying the law is by means of legislative amendments, which only programme them for the future, not for the case at hand.

Autonomy in this area, however, must not be confused with having a free rein. Applying the law means ascertaining the meaning of general and abstract norms as they relate to a particular concrete case. Autonomy means that this process can be carried out in accordance with legal criteria, not that the binding nature of norms can be shrugged off. For that reason, the normative requirements must not be underestimated and the results of the application of the law summarily ascribed, regardless of the norm programme, to the religious, class or political affiliation of those who apply the law.

Conversely, the norms to be applied generally allow so much room for interpretation and so many decision options that it would be a misconception to regard those who apply them as dependent agents of the legislature.[20] Moreover, given the dynamics of social development on the one hand and the limited lawmaking capacity of the political system on the other, pressure is generated in the course of application of the law to adapt or develop its provisions, and such pressure makes for a porous boundary with lawmaking yet can scarcely be influenced from the political rule dimension. When it comes to using the available latitude, greater significance attaches to professional standards and socialisation processes than to any political affiliations of the legal apparatus.

The significance of the law as a factor in the history of society is therefore inadequately represented if its examination is confined to its norms. The question as to

[19] See Niklas Luhmann, *Zweckbegriff und Systemrationalität* (Suhrkamp, 1973) 257 ff; Dieter Grimm, *Zukunft der Verfassung*, 166.

[20] See, eg, Regina Ogorok, *Richterkönig oder Subsumtionsautomat?* (Vittorio Klostermann, 1986), and Dieter Simon, *Die Unabhängigkeit des Richters* (Wissenschaftliche Buchgesellschaft, 1975).

how the law shapes the social structure or is shaped by it can only be answered if the scope of the examination includes the application aspect.[21] In historiography, in so far as it addresses the law at all, the importance of that point is often underestimated. This may be one reason why historians are all too ready to incorporate the law into the political rule dimension.

III.

The foregoing reflections lead to the conclusion that the law has a formative effect on the social structure and may also lay claim to a considerable measure of autonomy. For functionally differentiated societies, indeed, such autonomy is usual. There is then no one-sided dependence of the law on the social structure but mutual dependence between the two. The question regarding the place of the law in Wehler's model of the history of society is consequently legitimate.

The first possibility is that the law is to be sought on the level which Wehler defines by reference to categories such as music history or architectural history, these being cited as a *pars pro toto*. Music certainly does not lack autonomy either. It can likewise provide information about a society. But it surely has less of a formative effect than law on the social structure, the revelation of which is the purpose of Wehler's history of society.

The second possible location is the level that Wehler assigns to the system of social inequality, which he understands as a product of the basic dimensions of political rule, the economy and culture. Although the system has a social impact, that is due entirely to its situational character. It is not an action system. By contrast, the law – at least in the society examined by Wehler – cannot be regarded as a mere product of the basic dimensions. The law itself is organised as an action system and possesses relative autonomy in that function. It actively influences the social structure.

That leaves the level of the basic dimensions. The law might then be a forgotten basic dimension. It is also conceivable, however, that the law is a fourth type of entity, on which Wehler has not been any more explicit. Since the present treatment has been based on Wehler's model without criticising it, let alone proposing its own alternative, the answer to the initial question cannot be given here. These reflections remain a query addressed to the author.

(The text of this chapter first appeared in Paul Nolte et al (eds), *Perspektiven der Gesellschaftsgeschichte* (CH Beck, 2000) 47-57.)

[21] See, eg, Dieter Grimm, *Das Reichsgericht in Wendezeiten* (Leipziger Universitätsverlag, 1997).

INDEX